Chicken Soup for the Soul®

O Canada The Wonders of Winter

Chicken Soup for the Soul: O Canada The Wonders of Winter
101 Stories about Bad Weather, Good Times, and Great Sports
Jack Canfield, Mark Victor Hansen, Amy Newmark, Janet Matthews
Published by Chicken Soup for the Soul Publishing, LLC www.chickensoup.com

Front cover photo courtesy of iStockPhoto.com/craftvision (© Oktay Ortakcioglu).
Back cover and interior photo courtesy of iStockPhoto.com/wojciech_gajda
(© wojciech_gajda).

Cover and Interior Design & Layout by Brian Taylor, Pneuma Books, LLC

Distributed to the booktrade by Simon & Schuster. SAN: 200-2442

Publisher's Cataloging-in-Publication Data
(Prepared by The Donohue Group)

Chicken soup for the soul : O Canada, the wonders of winter : 101 stories
about bad weather, good times, and great sports / [compiled by] Jack
Canfield ... [et al.].

p. ; cm.

ISBN: 978-1-61159-931-2

1. Winter--Canada--Literary collections. 2. Winter--Canada--Anecdotes. 3. Canada--Social life and customs--Literary collections. 4. Canada--Social life and customs--Anecdotes. 5. Canadians--Literary collections. 6. Canadians--Anecdotes. 7. Anecdotes.
I. Canfield, Jack, 1944- II. Title: O Canada, the wonders of winter : 101 stories about bad weather, good times, and great sports

PN6071.C26 C456 2013
810.8/02/0811   2013937416

PRINTED IN THE UNITED STATES OF AMERICA
on acid∞free paper

22 21 20 19 18 17 16 15 14 13   01 02 03 04 05 06 07 08 09 10

Chicken Soup for the Soul

O Canada The Wonders of Winter

101 Stories about Bad Weather, Good Times, and Great Sports

Jack Canfield, Mark Victor Hansen, Amy Newmark and Janet Matthews

CSS

Chicken Soup for the Soul Publishing, LLC
Cos Cob, CT

www.chickensoup.com

Contents

❶
~Oh So Canadian! ~

❷
~More than Just Neighbours~

❸

~The Great Outdoors~

❹

~Childhood Memories~

❺

~On the Ice~

❻

~Love in the Snow~

❼

~That Famous Canadian Kindness~

❽

~Lessons Learned~

❾

~Traditions and Celebrations~

⑩

~A Holiday to Remember~

Introduction

I have vaulted over an immense land which is both forbidding and beautiful and it took my breath away. There are no people more fortunate than we Canadians. We have received far more than our share.
~Marc Garneau, Astronaut

As Canadians, we love our winter. Oh we also hate it to be sure; we moan and groan about it—especially in February and March—but somehow we know Canada would not be quite the same without it. Certainly our lives would not be the same. The shocking extremes in temperature, from a steamy hot summer day to those frigid winter days, really help define who we are as a people. (Unless you live in Vancouver...) We're tough. We're flexible. We're creative. We're prepared. We have snow tires and Arctic parkas and hand warmers and warm fleece-lined snow boots. And of course, everyone has at least one toque. We ski, we skate, we toboggan, we curl, and we play hockey. We have central heating. And we LOVE to talk about the weather.

"Cold enough for you?" "Hot enough for you?" "Snowed enough yet for you?" are all standard greetings in any part of the country. We have a sense of humour about it all. For many Canadians, it's a surprise to learn that people from other countries don't talk about the weather with the same passionate obsession we do. Well, we have a lot of weather to talk about! And, of course, so often the kind of experience we're going to have on any given day is directly dictated by the season and the weather.

All this weather, especially our winter weather, creates stories. As Canadians, we have amazing stories to tell—and frequently they are actually about the weather, or at least caused by it, like many of the wonderful stories in this book. When Canadians are confronted with extreme winter weather it usually brings out the best in us. We get creative. We get tough. We improvise. We help each other.

Consider Tanya Ambrose and her family, whose home in rural Eastern Ontario was in the centre of the Great Ice Storm of 1998. All the power lines came down, leaving them without heat or power for more than a week. In her story, "Surviving the Ice Storm," Tanya takes us through her experience. First there were the challenges of simply keeping warm, making meals, and melting icicles to make water for drinking, cooking and "flushing"—which turned out to be a big part of their experience. But then it evolved into something else. People came together from all around to help each other. One man made the old well on his country property available to all his neighbours. With regular life at a standstill, community meals were planned and shared around fireplaces and mismatched candles and lots of laughter. People slowed down, read books, played games, went for walks under the stars... and talked to each other. When it was over, they were actually sad—and everyone was changed. I really love this story.

Difficult winter weather frequently brings out our sense of humour. After all, you can't stop it—so you might as well laugh about it. In "The Harrowing of Hell," Jon Peirce of Dartmouth, Nova Scotia had me laughing so hard I could barely see the words when I read his hysterical story about being disturbed in the middle of the night by a snowplow repeatedly scraping the pavement of a plaza across the road from his home. I cheered when the plow driver finally took off in terror of our incensed writer—and his imaginary Rottweiler Fritz. You'll just have to read it....

Then there is Ian Charter of North Gower, Ontario—who, in the grand tradition of those Crazy Canuks decided along with two buddies to go barefoot water skiing on the partially frozen Rideau River—on Christmas Eve! Oh yes, they were wearing wetsuits of course. And a Santa Hat! Those guys weren't about to let a little cold water spoil their fun!

I think the biggest thing we know about the cold and the snow in Canada is—life doesn't stop. It goes on regardless, and we've learned how to go along with it. Babies are born, teenagers learn to drive, and weddings go off as scheduled. When I first read the story, "The Winter Wonderland Wedding," by Lisa Molinaro of Oshawa, Ontario my heart just opened right up. When a huge blizzard struck on the day of her wedding, the bride managed to tap into a deeper part of herself and resolve that nothing would dampen her day or her spirits. Not only did the wedding come off as planned, most of the guests made it and the story she tells us of love in the snow on her wedding day is simply delightful—and really touched my heart.

And then there's hockey. What would winter in Canada be without hockey? According to one of our writers, Canada IS Hockey, and there are few here who would dispute that. So we have some GREAT hockey stories for you. From street hockey, to backyard rink hockey, to a small boy's hockey dream, to "My NHL Dream" by Vinnie Lecavalier, who shares his experience of what it feels like to win a Stanley Cup—we have hockey!

Of course, an integral part of the winter months in Canada is Christmas—a season that brings out emotions and feelings that usually remain buried or in the background the rest of the year. We found some lovely Christmas stories, and then just as we were ready to finalize the manuscript, Gail Sellers of Aurora, Ontario sent us her story, "The Ultimate Gift." It seems that several years ago, as Christmas was approaching, Gail learned she had an older brother she'd never known about—a full sibling—and she was able to meet him and his family for the first time. In this moving story about love and reunion, a family comes together at Christmas for the first time; it was a life-changing event that brought healing to everyone.

This book has been a lot of fun to create. The one thing I learned when I did Chicken Soup for the Canadian Soul was that from one coast to the other Canadians love Canada. I found the same thing again this time. Even in the depth of winter, we love this country, and we love the land. We love our Canadian experience, and that includes and embraces our frequently challenging weather. We hope these stories inspire you, touch your heart, make you laugh, and remind you how lucky we all are—to be Canadian.

~Janet Matthews

Chapter 1

O Canada
The Wonders of
Winter

Oh So Canadian!

*For many outsiders, Canada appears to be a kind of gullible
Gulliver of the North, an irrelevant hunk of geography on the fringes
of civilization. But for those of us lucky enough to be Canadian,
we know that this is a country blessed with the mandate of heaven,
a land to build dreams on.*

~Peter C. Newman

A Canadian Scrapbook Moment

Somewhere in our souls is a spiritual Canada. Most probably, its bedrock is snow and ice, winter and the land. And if we were to penetrate it a little deeper, chances are we would find a game.

~Ken Dryden

Recently I happened to pass a game of parking lot hockey and I stopped for a moment. It was a scene from the Canadian Scrapbook. It was also a scene out of my past.

The parking lot was fairly big and empty, so the players were making full use of the space. Two well-worn hockey nets were stationed at opposite ends of the "rink." The play remained in one end, with all ten or twelve young boys madly chasing after the ball. It was difficult to determine how the teams were divided, if they were at all.

At the other end of the rink stood a lonely goaltender. He was wearing a set of goalie pads, a mask, and a baseball glove. It was this goalie's intensity that held my attention, that made me pause for so long. He stood in the net, in the goalie's crouch, with his stick on the pavement, glove hand extended, eyes fixed directly on the play at the opposite end. He stood there as if the play was in his end of the rink. He was ready. If someone happened to send a shot blistering out of the other end in his direction he would be there. He wouldn't let his team down. I chuckled a little at the innocence of his over-zealous attitude.

Rolling down the window a little I got the sounds and the smells of the game. My mind filled with memories of these games in my childhood.

•••

These games meant nothing, but they were everything. Good friends liked to play together, on the same line. At the age of ten we understood that chemistry, friendship, and attitude were more important than talent. We played with heart. And when a big pass resulted in a big goal, it was as if we were playing before a crowd of thousands. I don't remember winning or losing. Just playing. I know we kept score, but the next day, when the new game began, yesterday's score was forgotten. Just as it should be.

•••

The play was still in the other end, but my friend in net remained ready. It was as if someone was standing ten feet in front of him ready to shoot. In two minutes I don't think he had moved at all except for perhaps the odd shuffle from left to right as the play shifted at the other end of the parking lot.

•••

I recalled the winter that my dad put an ice surface on our property. Ice meant skates. Real hockey. After school our yard was the centre of the universe. One neighbourhood took on another neighbourhood in a challenge of pride. We played until dinner or darkness made us stop, and the next day we talked hockey all day at school in anticipation of the re-match that afternoon.

•••

I sat and watched those kids, mesmerized. Like a fire, the scene seemed to be ever changing, and yet always the same. I scanned the youthful faces, looking for my own. The scene looked so familiar. I wasn't there, yet I knew I had been. More than once. The goalie still stood there, ready. Waiting.

Suddenly the ball drifted out towards the other end of the parking lot. A boy in a dark blue hockey jacket broke out of the pack chasing after it. My friend in net took a couple of steps forward and froze in position. The boy in the hockey jacket caught up to the ball and with one hand on the stick pushing the ball ahead of him, he raced confidently towards the net. The breakaway. Shooter versus goaltender. One-on-one hockey. My heart raced!

At about eight feet out, the shooter drew back his stick and with as much strength as he could he fired the ball towards the net, hoping to shoot past the outstretched gloved hand of my young friend, and into the upper right hand corner of the net. The goalie's eyes alertly followed the shot. He slid out his left leg to extend his reach, and reaching up with his gloved hand, he watched as the ball smacked sharply into his baseball mitt.

Alone in my car, I cheered. Then smiling, I put the car in gear, and drove quietly back into the present.

~William Bell
Newmarket, Ontario

A Snowstorm
to Remember

*Why don't we embrace them (snow days) for exactly what they are;
a rite of passage, a part of being Canadian. The snow day —
it should be put on a stamp.*

~Rick Mercer

It began as a typical January day. The grey skies were heavy with snow and a brisk northerly wind played havoc with the drifts in front of Valleyview School. I was in my first year of teaching and had no idea that this approaching snowstorm would change my life forever.

When gentle snow began falling the principal kept a careful eye on the brewing storm. It soon took on qualities of something more vicious. By mid-day he called the school buses back so the three hundred kids could get home safely before it was too late.

My students gathered their belongings. They were excited to be going home early. "Snow days" are not uncommon in the snowbelt region of southwestern Ontario. It's "the lake effect" from Lake Huron, we're told, which delivers more than our fair share of winter storms.

The buses arrived but the storm suddenly escalated before the waiting kids could board and it was quickly clear no one was going anywhere any time soon.

Snow fell relentlessly, whirling and whipping itself into

treacherous whiteout conditions. Gusts of wind blasted the school windows with such a fury we feared they would shatter. Menacing snowdrifts wafted in silently under the doors.

By now the bus drivers and a couple of snowplow operators who'd been forced off the road were discussing the situation. There were over three hundred children, staff, bus and snowplow drivers barricaded inside the school.

As night approached and the storm showed no signs of abating, we realized we were prisoners until Mother Nature decided to release us from her grasp. None of us guessed it would be three days before the storm relented enough for us to finally go home.

We faced some basic questions. What would we feed several hundred children for dinner? Where would they sleep?

Earl, our school janitor, began working non-stop to keep the old groaning furnace running, but what if it quit? Concerned about the old pipes freezing, he wrapped them with whatever material he could find. With our hydro lines swaying under the increasing weight of ice and snow in heavy winds, what would we do if we lost power? A plan was definitely needed.

After every parent was called to reassure them their children were safe, a few silent prayers were said, and then people who lived close enough to brave the elements were called and asked if they could help. Soon, a handful of people had managed to wade through the heavy drifts and blinding snow bringing bags of sandwiches, tinned juices, blankets and a couple of board games.

One woman, who lived right on the edge of the school property, bundled herself up and trudged through the blinding snow with a huge kettle and enough ingredients to make tomato soup for at least half of the school. Those who didn't get soup feasted on peanut butter and jam sandwiches delivered by someone else. There wasn't a lot of food, but everything was shared, no one went hungry, and no one complained.

When night fell we worked out sleeping arrangements for the kids. Exhausted by the tensions of the day, most of them slept relatively well on the carpeted floors, drifting off to sleep under coats and donated blankets. I watched with a warm heart as three little first grade girls snuggled up under my own large, furry coat.

Some of the older girls acted like it was a huge pajama party, snuggling, giggling and telling stories as if nothing unusual was happening. Finally, they too gave in to sleep. It became an adventure; no one seemed homesick or even upset about having to stay at school overnight.

The next morning the treks down the long, cold hallway to the washrooms began early. On hall duty, I watched as two little boys in grade one walked down the corridor hand in hand. Jason turned to Jamie and said, "I wonder what we're having for breakfast?" Jamie, in wide-eyed innocence replied, "Eggs and bacon, of course. That's what I always have!"

Well, it wasn't eggs and bacon, but instead a piece of soft toast broiled in the school oven with half a cup of lukewarm cocoa. The bread had been retrieved from a stranded bread truck and delivered to the school by several young men on snowmobiles who were eager to help out however they could. With their parkas and helmets and all those hungry children to attend to, I didn't notice, but one of them noticed me as he trudged back and forth loaded with donations. My life was about to change.

Meanwhile, although the storm continued to bluster, it gradually began to diminish. As it did, some fathers began arriving on snowmobiles to collect their children. One man, well bundled against the elements, arrived on an open tractor pulling a small covered trailer to carry home his kids as well as every other kid that lived along his concession.

As the day progressed our numbers slowly dwindled. We kept those who remained busy playing basketball and volleyball in the gym, watching films or reading in the library.

On the morning of the third day we awoke to the sun shining in a clear blue sky. With the roads now plowed, the last of our students were soon safely on their way home, and all the staff breathed a sigh of relief. We had survived three days of the worst storm on record for our region in the past century. But what might have been a disaster had instead resulted in a strengthening of bonds—first between the community and our school, but especially between the teachers and students.

When the principal finally gave the teachers the "go ahead" to return home, I headed out to my car and went to start it. That's when I was approached by one of the snowmobilers who had delivered bread from the stranded bread truck.

He opened my passenger door, introduced himself as Bob, and asked me if I was planning to go somewhere.

"Home of course," I responded with a laugh.

"Well," he said, "after three days of sitting in a raging blizzard, your car is not likely going to start." Then he continued, saying that as he had been going in and out of our school bringing supplies, he had noticed me. He also admitted that by speaking with some of my co-workers he had learned I was "unattached."

I had to admit that because I had been so busy with my young charges I hadn't paid much attention. "Besides" I laughed, "most of the time your faces were totally covered with toques and helmets."

Undeterred by my initial indifference he asked me if I would go on a date with him sometime. Whether I was too exhausted to say no to his boldness, or whether there was a certain twinkle in his deep blue eyes, I really don't know. I accepted his offer, but it was June before we managed to go on that first date. When we finally did, we got along so well and shared so many common interests it seemed as if we'd known each other forever. Romance blossomed quickly. Soon we were engaged, and in November, less than five months later, we were married.

Throughout the years we have weathered many storms together, but that first storm was the one we both remember. Who could have guessed that the storm of a lifetime would have brought me the love of my life!

~Ardy Barclay
Sarnia, Ontario

My NHL Dream

The Field of our Dreams is flooded and frozen, and has a net at either end.
~Joey Slinger

"Look Vincent!" said my fourteen-year-old brother Philippe, pointing at the photo. "That's me playing with the Notre Dame Hounds. Look at that cool jersey! In this one you can see all the other kids in the stands cheering, and there's our coach. Just think, in a few more years you can do this too!" I was nine years old, and from that moment on, I knew that when I was older I'd be going away to school in Saskatchewan to play hockey.

Growing up in Ile Bizard in Montreal, Quebec, I started skating when I was two-and-a-half, and my mom says that at eighteen months I was stick-handling with mini sticks in front of the TV. It was really then that I started falling in love with hockey. By age four I was playing hockey in a league.

My dad had played junior hockey until he was nineteen and was my coach as I went through the levels of minor hockey. Like every other boy, I dreamt of playing in the NHL, but for me it was really just a dream.

Once or twice a year my dad would take us to a hockey game at the Forum to watch the Montreal Canadiens. I was a huge Steve Yzerman fan so I loved it when Detroit was in town and I could watch him play. I was probably the only person in the stands wearing a Detroit Redwings jersey! As Captain he led the Wings to three Stanley

Cup Championships, and he was really the one who inspired me when I was younger.

At some point my dad met a guy who was recruiting for Athol Murray College of Notre Dame in Saskatchewan. He learned all about the school, and Philippe decided to go there. While my dad may have dreamed of us making it into the NHL, his real goal was for us to get an excellent education first, and when I was fourteen, just like my brother, I left home for grade nine. This was tough for my parents—a real sacrifice because we are a very, very close family. But they wanted what was best for us and they felt strongly this was it.

When I arrived the very first person I met was Brad Richards who had the bunk right next to me. We were the same age, and became best friends. We were hanging out every day, and we were very, very close right from the get-go.

The Notre Dame school motto is "Struggle and Emerge" and I was really moved by it because, really, that's what life is. When it came to hockey there were kids from all over Canada who were really good players. During that first month I was a bit afraid of not making the Bantam AAA team, which was coached by former Olympic Hockey player, Terry O'Malley. But Brad and I ended up being the only two first-year players to make it.

That year we won at the Bantam AAA level in the Edmonton/St. Albert tournament. There were a lot of big strong guys, and we were playing the best teams.

When I finished grade ten I was more confident and more disciplined, but I still didn't know if I would go to college or play Junior hockey. After numerous discussions with my parents we decided that I would play Junior with Rimouski Oceanic, and finish high school there. I left Saskatchewan after grade ten while Brad Richards opted to stay.

Playing Junior Hockey is a very demanding life; you play seventy-two games—all by bus. You're on the road all the time, and it's very hard to keep your grades up. It's more travelling than done in the NHL, and much harder. It was a tough year at age sixteen, but when the scaling lists came out in December I was startled to discover

I was on top! It was then I realized I actually had potential. My dream was born—to make it to the NHL.

At the beginning of my second year in Rimouski Brad Richards joined me and it was great having him back as my teammate. In 1998 when I was only eighteen, I got drafted first overall by Tampa Bay. Back then only one or two guys were making the teams at eighteen so I had no idea if I could make it. Being rated number one I definitely felt that pressure, so that summer I really worked hard, and in September I made the Tampa Bay Lightning!

Realizing I had made it to the NHL was the best feeling in the world. Two years later Brad Richards also made it to Tampa Bay. Once again we were teammates and best friends, sharing the experience.

Over the years I've been proud to play with Team Canada, and in 2004 Brad and I played in the World Cup in Toronto and we won. What an incredible experience. In 2006, I went to the Olympics in Torino, again with Brad, and although we came home without a medal, it was a great experience.

In 2004 Tampa Bay won the Stanley Cup, and I can honestly say that *nothing* beats winning a Stanley Cup. It's not just a two-week tournament, it's a whole year and it starts at training camp. You build a team, then you've got your ups and downs during the season, and that's almost the easy part, because after that you've got the play-offs, which is really a roller coaster ride. You're winning a game, losing a game; losing game 5 you're down 3-2, but then you come back and win game 6 and tie it up.

When you win a Stanley Cup there are so many emotions you're just exhausted. When they started the countdown of ten seconds left I was on the bench and I just wanted to jump onto the ice. There was so much emotion. Watching the clock I couldn't wait until it went to zero, because you just never know what will happen.

For me, winning the Stanley Cup was the ultimate realization of a lifetime dream. That night Brad Richards and I had a big Notre Dame "Struggle and Emerge" right above our lockers. It's something we've taken with us wherever we go; when you've been to Notre Dame, it's something that's just always in you.

Today I'm living in Tampa with my wife Caroline and our three kids. Family is very important to me, and I'm still very close with my mom and dad and my brother and sister. So for me naturally, with my kids, family is everything, and nothing tops that—not even a Stanley Cup!

~Vincent Lecavalier
Canadian living in Tampa, FL, USA

Editors Note: In 2010, through the Vinny Lecavalier Foundation, Vincent pledged $3 million to a children's hospital in St. Petersburg, Florida, which was named The Vincent Lecavalier Pediatric Cancer and Blood Disorders Center in his honour. For more information and how you can help, visit: www.vinny4.org.

Barefooting on the Rideau

Life is a great big canvas, and you should throw
all the paint you can on it.
~Danny Kaye

It rarely happens. We had never seen it, but there it was—open water on December 24th on the Rideau River in the Manotick-Osgoode area near Ottawa. Not only that, it was open on a stretch where we often barefoot waterski.

We started to plan the adventure.

It was mid-morning when I got the call, the usually calm dentist-cum-barefoot water skier was asking the impossible-to-ignore question, "Ya wanna ski today?"

A joke I was sure, but he went on to explain: "The river is open, I'll put my boat in the water, but we need a third." To waterski legally you need a driver, a spotter and (in December) a fool to get in the water. In Marcel's mind I immediately qualified for a third of that equation!

Marcel has the boat, we all have dry suits, everyone has an axe, and we all live minutes from the river. We couldn't find any reasons not to go. Of course my wife could, but I wasn't going to be the one that missed this and then have to listen to the glory stories later.

Dropping whatever I was doing, I ran around the house pulling packed away ski gear and my dry suit out of the basement.

"Hon, can you pack something to eat? Have ya seen my ski rope? Can you pack some latex gloves? Wanna come?" Three yeses and a "NO" followed.

An hour later we all arrived at the Manotick boat launch grinning from ear to ear. "Here's the plan," began Ross, the engineer.

First we had to get the boat in the water, but in front of the boat launch the river was frozen out thirty to forty feet, and three to six inches thick.

Donning dry suits and neoprene gloves we cautiously tested the ice and sure enough we could walk on it. Axes in hand we began chopping slots down each side of the path needed to get the boat to open water. With a pry bar we were able to break the ice into large sections and slowly start them moving out to the open river. With a cheer we watched each one turn with the current and disappear downstream.

With the last piece gone and a clear path to open water, I heard Marcel laughing and looked up to see him holding our long ski rope encased in a solid block of ice, the result of having left it in the boat's dry well—half full of water!

By this point several curious "Manotickians" had wandered by asking what was up, which led to curious stares, laughs of incredibility and guffaws, but we pressed on.

It was cold, and somewhat sunny; air temperatures were -4 to -6, and the water was 0.6 degrees Celsius. But we were riding on excitement. We'd skied here late into the fall, and again in early spring, but never in the winter.

With the boat in the water, engine humming and the gear stowed, we surveyed the half-mile stretch of water we would use for floating debris and ice chunks, and to make a final consideration as to if this should really be done. What? Did I say that? Of course it should be done!

What did we wear? Diving in extremely cold water is fairly common, and as an active scuba diver I knew that layering and staying dry would allow us to stay in the water safely. And of course, if you are truly skiing, not much time should be spent actually "in the water." The technology of a dry suit is based on layers of trapped air, and most importantly—to keep the water out!

We pulled on thin wool gloves, then surgical rubber gloves provided by my wife, a nurse, to keep our hands dry but allow some feel for the ski rope and grip. We wore thin neoprene boots to maintain some feeling in our feet and protect them against any floating ice bits, but believe me they kept them neither dry nor warm.

At the center of the boat an aluminum "boom" pole extended out from the side. With great care we shinnied out on that pole with the boat at speed, and were thus able to start a ski run without having to do a "deep water start" (where your entire body and head are submerged.)

My first pass was like nothing I'd ever experienced! The sensations of skiing with the ice lined banks blurring by, the cold air watering my eyes, the crisp, dark water beneath my feet and my breath producing clouds of white, all joined to create a new, exciting, and unique ski. My hair hardened as it froze in the forty-mile-an-hour wind, and I executed tumble turns, one foot, the other foot, wake crosses and so on. It all leant itself to some new and unique hair molding!

A half-mile downriver I felt the water soften under my feet, the tug reduced in my hands, my shoulders relaxed. I knew it was coming. I inhaled to puff up my lungs, let the rope go and spread my hands and body as wide as I could in an effort to stay afloat. It was fruitless I knew, but still I tried—as I've tried before—to avoid my head submerging. Eyes closed, WHAM—it's the feeling you get when you "over-slurp" a Slush Puppy—only from the outside in!

Bobbing to the surface, I scrambled into the boat laughing and grinning. My head was cold but the rest wasn't too bad. The gloves held, no leaks in the suit; my feet were a little numb but okay, and a cup of hot tea from the thermos was being offered up.

We made pass after pass that afternoon, taking turns between the three of us, the noise of the boat and our shrieks of laughter bringing people to the ends of their docks to watch, waving, laughing, and of course shaking their heads in disbelief.

For several passes I wore a Santa hat, waving to the onlookers and laughing. As we paused between runs we were offered hot chocolate and asked questions. Even a Christmas duck came out and paddled around while we sipped on warm drinks and snacks.

Was it cold? Well, whatever stayed dry was warm, but the end of each run is the same, you always end up in the water, and no matter what we tried we could not find a way to stop our heads from submerging. That was cold, really cold, as we say in Canada "Brain Freeze Cold,"—and it hurt. We jumped into the boat, dried the hair as fast as possible, and got a hat on the cranium before trying to speak. Otherwise, our speech was likely going to be slurred. Nevertheless, we enjoyed ourselves for several hours before packing it in when the light began to fade.

I had fun telling friends and colleagues about our day and got some strange looks, a few laughs and some genuine disbelievers. About a week later, I stopped to grab a drink at a local corner store. The man across the counter looked at me, then looked again, and then burst out, "It's you!"

I, of course, had no idea what he was talking about, and wondered if something from my chequered past was about to re-surface!

"It's you in the paper," he continued excitedly. "Look!"

He handed me a copy of the *Manotick Messenger*, the local weekly paper. To my surprise, there I was on the front page, gliding along the river on one foot wearing my Santa hat and a big grin, under the heading, "Frozen in time."

Those were my fifteen minutes of fame!

All this to say, cold doesn't stop us in Canada. It's just part of the equation when planning how to get the job done. Who said you need a hill and skis to ski in Canada in December? In fact we went back out January 1st, a week later, and did it again. Although I have checked every year since the Rideau River has never again remained open in the middle. As usual it becomes a ski doo super highway, littered with ice shacks and pickup trucks.

Many may not believe my story, but I have a copy of the newspaper to prove it!

~Ian Charter
North Gower, Ontario

Canadian Winter Commandments

Whether it's cold, or whether it's hot, we'll have weather,
whether we like it or not.
~Percy Saltzman, CBC's first on-air Weatherman

I can't believe how many people have no clue how to act during winter, especially since it comes around every year and seems to last for eight months in this country. As soon as you get a few flakes on the ground, people seem to lose their minds.

For their benefit, I've assembled the following Commandments of Winter:

Thou shalt wear boots, hat and gloves. Running shoes in winter are an abomination, and are wont to slideth thyself under a passing car. A hat will cover thy frozen head. Yes, it messeth thy hair and looketh goofy, but it will keep thee from having to explain why thine ears art missing.

Thou shalt not spin thy wheels if stuck in thy car. Thou polisheth only the ice and getteth no traction. Thou shalt rock thy car gently or use sand or litter from thy kitty to escape a rut or snow bank. Otherwise thou art an idiot in my sight and going no place fast.

He who does not brush off his car shall be cast into the deepest pit, for it is a great offence to drive with only a small hole on the windshield out of which to look. Thou shalt clean thy entire windshield, and yea, even thy back window, for it is as important to see where you have been as where you are going.

A man who shovels snow with a broom shall be marked as a fool when snow shovels can be had for less than ten shekels at Canadian Tire.

When thou shovelest thy snow, do not shovel it into the road for it is a sin and a traffic hazard. Pile it on the side or your lawn, for by the snow thrown in the road shall ye know who is virtuous and who is a jerk.

Driveth not thy car on ice faster than thou can think. Thy neighbour's rear bumper is sacred in my sight and needeth not to be hit by you as thou canst not stop on a dime in winter. Patience is a virtue, and 'tis better to be late than dead lest ye discover too soon that there is no ice in hell.

Honour thy mother and father, and heed their advice to use the facilities before zipping up your snowsuit.

The man who throwest his snow unto his neighbour's property is an ass, and if caught shall be buried in the white stuff until the birds of Spring cheepeth, and all shall know him as a wicked man.

Salt and sand may be a gift from heaven, but not when there is more of it than there is snow upon the ground. Too much salt rottest thy shoes and pant cuffs and eats holes in thy car. Too much sand will be tracked into your abode and will vex your hardwood floors.

Listen not to those who sayest "Cold enough for you?" for they art fools and are in need of a good anointing with snowballs.

Runnest thou not thy snow blower before eight in the morning on Saturday, for even though it is not the Sabbath, it is a day of rest for those who have partied the night before.

Blessed is he who shovels his neighbour's walk. He shall surely not have to shovel in front of the Pearly Gates.

Whine not about the cold and snow, for 'tis Canada and wintertime. What didst thou expectest?

~Stephen Lautens
Toronto, Ontario

Disaster Strikes Vancouver

When it snows on the West Coast, ignore it. Maybe it will go away. No matter
how many years in a row it snows, no matter how deep the snow is, remem-
ber, it does not snow on the West Coast.
~Miro Cernetig, The Vancouver Sun

My city, Vancouver, British Columbia, is completely shut down by a natural disaster as I write this. No, we haven't had an earthquake or a hurricane. Tornadoes are not dropping out of the sky onto unsuspecting trailer parks. On the radio this morning, the disc jockey is doing his show by telephone from home, as is the lady who normally flies over the city looking for traffic jams. She has little to report because few people have ventured out of their homes. Many of those who did never made it to their destination.

We have 20 centimetres of snow on the ground.

Seriously, it's very bad. Some Starbucks outlets haven't been able to open. And one of my sons has been hit with a cruel irony. His school ski trip was cancelled due to the snow.

I live in Canada, don't I? Snow shouldn't be a problem, right? I should just go out and build myself a new igloo; hook up my faithful dog to the sled and head off into the storm. The trouble is, I don't know how to build an igloo and my dog, a cross between a Cocker Spaniel and an Airhead, is still trying to figure out how to... well, you know... in the snow.

In Vancouver it snows once or twice a year or not at all. A five-centimetre snowfall causes major problems. Twenty centimetres is a disaster. We are more prepared to deal with an earthquake or a tidal wave than a couple of inches of snow. A white Christmas occurs maybe six or seven times each century.

So, on this day, major streets have not been plowed during the night. The City Engineer for Vancouver was on the radio announcing with some sense of pride that they had plows on the road by 4:00 a.m. (Twelve hours after the snowfall started). And just how many plows did the third largest city in Canada get out on the roads? Fourteen! The actual preferred method of snow removal here is to sit drinking double double latte cappuccino espressos and wait until it rains.

After living in this mild climate for thirty-one years, driving in snowstorms is now a thing to be feared. I once watched a driver's panic-stricken face as he skidded out of control down a steep hill toward a busy intersection. He was driving the truck that was supposed to be putting sand and salt down on the road.

This latest snowstorm has brought another concern. I hope that people in more wintry climes will have pity on me. After all, this latest snow covered my tulips and crocuses.

~Gordon Kirkland
Pitt Meadows, British Columbia

From Darkness to Light

Through it all, I knew I would continue to think of the vast, lonely spaces that reached up above me, and I would wish that I could pucker up my lips and whistle down the northern lights for all of us to see.
~Peter Gzowski

Crunch, crunch, crunch. My bicycle tires sounded like they were running over fortune cookies. The snow was extra crunchy, and the temperature was eighty degrees below zero with the wind chill.

After cycling down the frozen Mackenzie River from Inuvik, which was as far north as roads go in Canada, I was now riding directly on the frozen Arctic Ocean. High in the Canadian Arctic, it was January, and the sun doesn't come up during the day like it does in my hometown of Hamilton, Canada. There were no streetlights, nor even ambient light from a nearby city. The pitch-black darkness during the day was darker than any night I'd ever seen.

I was on the home stretch of the first journey in history under one's own power, from the bottom of mainland Canada, 6,520 kilometres to the top of Canada. My journey was called the TO THE TOP CANADA Expedition, and while en route I had done media appearances and rallies all across the country, asking Canadians to answer just one important question: "What will you do to make Canada a better country than when you found it?" I felt strongly that if all Canadians were working towards making a better Canada with a personal project of their choice, the synergy would take Canada "to the top" of its potential. Now, it was time for me to walk-my-talk, or "cycle-my-talk," through the toughest conditions I'd ever faced in my life!

Riding on the frozen ocean I was totally focused on watching for holes or cracks in the ice. I had to remain vigilantly conscious of changing tides every twelve hours that would break it up. If I went into that water even once my life would be over. The freezing temperature of salt water is about -21 degrees Celsius, far below that of fresh water, making this the coldest water on the planet. Suddenly I noticed something that caused me to instantly stop my bike. Directly crossing my path was a fresh set of polar bear tracks, and the size of those paw prints was enormous! I was wearing large Arctic boots on my size twelve feet, and when I placed one of them into a bear paw print it was not as long as the polar bear's paw was wide! The thought of the huge paws on that dangerous animal made me shiver. Wanting to quickly put as much distance between myself and the polar bear, I remounted my bike and began cycling harder and faster than I'd ever cycled in my life!

My tires had metal studs that grabbed the ice like the teeth of the bear I was trying to avoid. I was covered from head to toe like an astronaut to keep warm. Inside all that protective gear my body was sweating as I kept up the relentless pace. A balaclava covered my entire head including my bike helmet and toque, with the exception of my eyes, which were covered with ski goggles. Unfortunately my goggles had iced up and I couldn't see, so I had to remove them. In only a few moments I could feel frostbite "like a bad sunburn" around my eyes and cheeks. But then I remembered my old football mantra, "no pain—no gain," and I pressed on. This was the point where the rubber hit the road—or in this case the ice—and I was determined to finish and not give up on Canada. Making a nation better is not easy, and I wanted Canadians to know they will always face obstacles, obstacles that can break your heart and slam you down, or obstacles that will freeze your face off! We have a choice; we can give up or we can get up, we can press on and try again. Persistence and perseverance make the victory of achieving your goal that much sweeter. I wanted Canadians to know that you never fail in life unless you stop trying.

I had left Point Pelee, Ontario, Canada's most southern mainland point, ten months before on March 1, 1997, and now I was just hours away from successfully completing my journey. The joy and excitement of this long anticipated moment sent adrenaline pumping through my body.

The storm clouds had cleared and allowed me to see the sky for the first time in days. As I watched in awe, spectacular northern lights danced in the heavens. Glorious neon green curtains shimmered and waved at me as I cycled onward to my final destination.

Suddenly I was not alone. An armada of snowmobiles was heading towards me! The people of the Inuvialuit community of Tuktoyaktuk had heard of my imminent arrival on CBC North radio and decided to come out to greet me. I stopped to receive their grand welcome and, after posing for some pictures, with a full escort, I rode my tired bike on the final leg of my long journey, straight into the hamlet community of Tuktoyaktuk. The biggest full moon I had ever seen in my life hung low in the clear skies directly over Tuktoyaktuk, guiding me safely off the Arctic Ocean.

Because they had not known my exact arrival time, a welcome ceremony was scheduled for the next day in the Mangilaluk School. The entire community would be in attendance. However, for the time being, my first priority was shelter, so I cycled over to the Tuk Inn and checked in, leaving the darkness behind.

After stripping off all my gear my body gratefully drank in the warm air now surrounding it. It was the most wonderful feeling in the world!

The only phone in the small motel was in the office, so I called home and asked my wife, Carol, if she would receive a collect call from Tuktoyaktuk! Carol and our son James both screamed with excitement when they heard my voice and learned I was safe and had successfully completed my mission for Canada. I spent the next two hours on the telephone fielding calls from radio stations, newspaper reporters and television newscasts celebrating this Canadian achievement.

In the quiet of my room I said some personal prayers to thank God for bringing me safely to the end of the TO THE TOP CANADA Expedition. I opened my Good News Bible, and when I read these words they hit me like a baseball bat: *When that time comes, there will no longer be cold or frost, nor any darkness. There will always be daylight, even at night time. When this will happen is known only to the Lord.*

It felt like God was telling me I no longer had to fight the freezing cold or the total darkness. God would make the light shine twenty-four hours a day, and here I was in one of the only places in the world where this could happen—Tuktoyaktuk, the Land of the Midnight Sun!

I had now passed from the darkness to the light. It is my hope that my example will inspire Canadians to realize that all goals, even those challenging ones that will make Canada better, are possible with determination and love for Canada.

The simple lesson I have learned is that "hope" is like riding a bicycle. If you just keep pedaling it will take you anywhere you want to go!

~Chris Robertson
Stoney Creek, Ontario

Surviving the Ice Storm

According to Environment Canada, the ice storm of 1998 directly affected
more people than any other previous weather event in Canadian history.
~Susan Munroe

I remember the heartbreak of the first morning. I woke before dawn to complete darkness—no nightlight from the bathroom, no yard light from the driveway. Rain was drumming on the metal roof of the house, small branches were scratching at the windows and it was cold. I felt my way downstairs to the kitchen to add logs to the embers from last night's fire in the woodstove. I pulled up a chair, wrapped myself in a quilt and watched the logs catch and the flames flicker.

The relative quiet was broken with the first crack of a branch succumbing to the weight of the freezing rain. Seconds later came the crash as it smashed into the frozen ground, and just as quickly came the next crack, the seconds of delay, followed by the next inevitable crash.

There was a row of mature maples that had been planted when our children were small and we had moved to the country to grow our own food and enjoy the natural surroundings. Near the house were several old elms that had survived disease and drought and were particular favourites. Along the front were poplars and spruces, now full-grown and providing a barrier between the house and the road. Now, on this frightening winter morning, I sat alone in the darkness for two hours, listening to this relentless, still invisible destruction. Seven crashes per minute. I wept.

At daybreak my husband came downstairs and we went outside to survey the ruined landscape. Branches carpeted the ground around the house. The poplars were virtually without limbs and bent in half, their tops touching the ground. The remaining branches of the maples also touched the ground. Every piece of vegetation, every branch, every twig, every wire, was encased in ice the thickness of my wrist. It was an astonishing sight. Under other circumstances it would have been the winter wonderland of song, but now it was a terrible beauty.

We learned that day what it is to feel helpless. When the power goes out and there is no water and the house is getting colder and you have no idea how long this situation will continue and you have no way of finding out because there's no radio or television, and the phones are dead too, you quickly adapt. With a woodstove in our country home, plenty of accessible firewood, and a freezer full of food, we were among the fortunate.

Water was our most serious problem. We live in the country, and our water comes from a well. But electricity is required to run the pump that carries the water from the well to the house. We needed water to drink, wash and use the toilet. Early efforts to visit the edge of a field for the last purpose proved comedic. Hardhat perched on head, I slid across the uneven surface of solid ice littered with the debris of fallen branches towards my chosen destination behind a tool shed. I was dismayed to discover that the ice was too thick to break through in order to dig a hole that could later be covered. Compromise was required.

Mission accomplished, I crawled back to the house, optimistic that our power would be restored within a day. It wasn't. Out came the buckets. We collected the smashed tubes of ice that had broken off the branches when they hit the ground, and melted them to fill the kettle. On the third day, when the sun finally came out, huge sheets of ice slid from the roof. We filled the large canning pot that now stood on the woodstove to provide us with warm water to clean dishes and to take "bucket baths." Dishes were washed in the largest pot that had been dirtied that day. We didn't waste water by rinsing. A "bucket bath" was accomplished by half filling a plastic bucket with heated water, placing it inside the tub and then squatting beside it for a speedy, soapy wash in a bathroom that had reached a temperature suitable for refrigerating perishable foods. This dirty water was used for the next "necessary" flush. We believed each day would be the last without power. Meanwhile, life revolved around the basics of survival; planning the next collection of ice, arranging containers near the stove to melt the ice and saving dirty water to flush.

And then suddenly life changed through the generous spirit of a neighbor. Fred and Edith lived in a lovely house on a piece of land where they grew vegetables and raised pigs and chickens. Situated behind this new house was the old homestead, which Fred had converted to a workshop. Beside its uneven porch stood an old-fashioned outdoor hand-pump. Because this pump was still in good working order, Fred had been able to haul water to their new house right from the start.

Once the road had been cleared of debris and the surface sanded, Fred climbed into his truck and drove from house to house, inviting all his neighbours to help themselves to water from his well. Like everyone else we gratefully accepted his kind offer, and soon a steady stream of vehicles travelled up his lane to fill containers. In addition, Fred put out a large hand-lettered sign inviting any passers-by to help themselves to his water. How quickly we change our definitions of what is important. Clean water, which we normally take for granted, made all the difference. We could now cook, wash dishes and bathe easily. The baths were still conducted with a bucket, but now it was full and we could enjoy the luxury of feeling clean. We could flush.

But even more importantly, Fred's thoughtful gesture opened up new doors to neighbourliness. We pulled out the expensive roasts and frozen raspberries from the freezer and entertained our neighbours, some of whom we had never met before. People came with whatever they could contribute towards these communal meals, and everyone helped with cleanup. New friendships formed, and even more profoundly, a powerful, precious new sense of community was created, something I had never experienced in quite this way before. With the regular time commitments of life suspended, there was time to relax and to talk. Every night, a group of us went for a walk under a full moon that sparkled from a frozen, enchanted forest.

A week later, when the power finally came back on, I found I was not yet ready to face the real world. Later, when I looked out at our beloved trees, all of them broken and many destroyed, it broke my heart, but then I would remember the other things from that week that filled me with warm pleasure: sitting around a table glowing with the light from a dozen mismatched candles, enjoying dinners with our neighbours, the pride of accomplishment after preparing an elegant meal in the long-neglected oven of our wood stove, the tranquility and companionship of long days spent reading while huddled near the fireplace.

I remember the adventure of going to bed in sleeping bags on mattresses dragged from the bedrooms and arranged near the warmth of fires. I remember the breaking of ordinary rules as the cats slept with the humans and the dog tolerated their presence in the space of one warm room shut off from the rest of the frigid house.

But most importantly, when I look back on the Ice Storm, I savour the memories of the acts of generosity and kindness that created new friendships, the common experience of facing adversity, and struggling and triumphing together in survival that now binds our small rural community together with invisible threads of gold.

~Tanya Ambrose
Mallorytown, Ontario

The Winter Wonderland Wedding

If two stand shoulder to shoulder against the gods, happy together, the gods themselves are helpless against them while they stand so.
~Maxwell Anderson

The old wives' tale says that rain on your wedding day is a sign of luck. They'll even have you believe that spilling red wine on yourself and having a bird poop on you is also a sign of luck. In other words, any unfortunate experience is given a positive twist, so the person who experiences it doesn't feel as bad and others have something nice they can say to them about it.

If the old wives' tale is true, and rain on your wedding day means you and your betrothed will have a happy marriage, what can it possibly mean when two feet of snow fall on your wedding day?

None of this crossed my mind the morning of my wedding day—Saturday, March 8, 2008. Snow had started falling the day before, and that night, the night of our wedding rehearsal, the streets were a wet, icy mess. Not a single flake fell overnight, and early the next morning the sky was bright with promise. But then, in the quiet of the morning, the flurries began anew. Soon, what started as a gentle, picturesque snowfall quickly turned into a blizzard that nearly paralyzed all movement.

In stark contrast to my normally panicky predisposition and

despite the wild weather I became the calmest, most easygoing person that I've ever been. Miraculously I somehow tapped into a deeper part of myself where my frustration at my inability to control the weather to fit with the day I had envisioned as a little girl was hushed. I resolved that nothing was going to dampen my day or my spirits, not even this wet, heavy snow.

Moving about the house before any of the other women, I took a long, hot shower. The hair stylist and make-up artist both arrived and, before you knew it, preparations were in full swing. The bridesmaids and maids of honour had spent the night at my place, so the house was a flurry of estrogen and commotion as over ten women, all clad in jammies, robes and slippers, bustled up and down and to and fro as they washed, powdered, snacked and groomed. Once we were all gowned and jeweled, the photos would take place.

Unbeknownst to me, due to the weather, other things were not happening on schedule. The photographers had been late to the groom's place and subsequently to mine, and more importantly, the limo bus had gotten stuck in the groom's driveway in deep snow, essentially blocking it. That was my fiancé's opportunity to back out! But before he could change his mind, my father-in-law intervened. He jumped into his backhoe (how fortuitous!), wedding suit and all, and plowed a new driveway. The limo bus was out of commission, so, my groom, my in-laws, and the groomsmen all piled into various cars and trucks and made it to the church on time, and all in one piece! That same fleet of vehicles then came to my house to pick up all the ladies-in-waiting.

On the way to the church my resolve finally began to falter, and my nervousness began to build as rapidly as the snowfall. In all honesty I was not as worried about saying "I do," as I was about the empty church that awaited us. After all, the weathercasters were all exclaiming: "You would be crazy to leave the house today!" I had no misconceptions; since the snow had accumulated so quickly and unexpectedly, the plows had yet to begin the cleanup. I knew there was little chance that our guests could make it in time for the ceremony.

Nothing could have prepared me for the sight that awaited me in the church parking lot—it was practically full! I was amazed. It seemed that all our closest family and friends had managed to make it out for our big moment after all.

After the "I dos" were exchanged, a substitute bus had shown up to transport the wedding party to our photo site. "Plan A" had been to do the photos outdoors, "Plan B" was to go to the Tannery Mall. But with these conditions neither option was feasible, so we resorted to a "Plan C" and headed straight to the reception hall.

Our photo album is certainly not lacking in beautiful pictures. In fact, my favourite photo of the day was an impromptu shot of my new husband, best man, maids of honour and myself taking a quick turn outside in front of the hall. It was my idea to go outside for a few shots, but once we got there the wind was so icy fierce that we walked out one door and immediately walked back in through the next. In that moment the photographer caught us walking seemingly straight into the blizzard, pausing only briefly to glance over our shoulders at the camera. That one picture taken of those brave brief moments is my most precious. It appears to be black and white with the exception of the bridesmaids' blue dresses.

Once back inside we wrapped-up the photo-taking and pre-pared for the reception. My husband and I both have large families and were expecting 330 guests. But because of the unrelenting storm we did not expect the large crowd and had accepted that reality. After all, how could we expect our loved ones, friends and co-workers to risk their lives to come to a dinner and dance, dressed in their Sunday best, when what they really needed were knee-high, insulated boots, parkas and all the rest?

Well, for the second time that day I was proven very wrong. All but thirty of our guests arrived—we were absolutely dumbfounded. We shook hands, embraced and bantered with all our family and friends as they escaped the storm into the comfort of the hall. I was glowing indeed. Once the DJ introduced us as husband and wife we floated into the hall high on love and joy.

Three hundred people had made the dangerous, white-knuckled

trek just for the two of us. Despite the severity of the storm, almost all of our family and friends still came from the Greater Toronto Area, and surrounding small communities. Some traveled from out of the province and a few from even out of the country. They ranged from the very young to the very old. The memory of that day, with our entire family under one roof, will remain in my mind and heart forever. No "thank you" is adequate.

The forty centimetres of snow that fell that day may have made for very frigid, slippery conditions outdoors, but I can say without a doubt that inside the church and reception hall was a sacred and pure warmth and love. My husband and I were truly blessed that day, as we are today, in the knowledge that we are surrounded by an abundance of people who love and support us through both literal and metaphorical storms. It only took a white dress and a "real" Canadian winter day for me to realize that. Our wedding would have been a beautiful day no matter what, but those two feet of snow taught me a life lesson that I'll never forget.

~Lisa Molinaro
Oshawa, Ontario

The Snowball

There's no other love like the love for a brother.
There's no other love like the love from a brother.
~Astrid Alauda

As a young boy of eight it was a rare and coveted opportunity to be able to hang out with my older brother, Chris, and not feel like he would prefer that I be somewhere else. I can't say I blamed him. Our seven-year age difference placed me more than a little out of his peer group.

On one sunny winter day I was enjoying one of those rare experiences. Michael, one of my brother's friends, was struggling alongside my brother and me to roll an enormous snowball we'd been working on for some time. It was already twice my height and required special knowledge of snowball formation to be moved. We had, by trial and error, unlocked a secret to making impossibly large snowballs, and even with that knowledge we were struggling to move this monster.

The secret? Momentum. You dig out the bottom of the snowball on the side you want it to roll. When the snowball is properly sloped for rolling you station one guy on the uphill side, and one guy on the side you want it to roll, and you begin to rock it, back and forth; this is how the process gets its power. You keep doing this until it is really rocking, and then on the count of three everybody pushes together at exactly the right moment to teeter it over the breaking point for one full rotation. Then you have to do it again.

We were now fully engaged in rocking the snowball, and I was on the side to which it would roll. For a moment it stood still, looking like it might not go. Just one more inch and it would, but despite Mike and Chris's combined exertions, the snowball just teetered on edge.

I had moved to the other side to watch them push and could see desperation growing in their expressions. In a moment of sudden inspiration, I rose to my feet and raced towards the thing screaming at the top of my lungs like some furious war cry. Slamming into it at full speed, I hoped to provide the additional force it seemed to need to get moving. Pain shot through my shoulder from the impact, but the snowball did not budge. Caught up in the moment I shrugged off the pain and, wedging myself under the snowball I used my back to shove against it. Slowly it began to move, and as gravity took over we heard the gratifying sound of snow crunching underneath our creation as it rolled.

Now we had managed to achieve our original goal of positioning the snowball on the edge of a hillside where kids regularly went sledding. We thought we might roll it down the hill, but with the trouble we'd had just getting it to this point we were ready to take a break.

"That was hard, man!" exclaimed Mike, pulling an iPod out of his inside jacket pocket. He then lay down about halfway down the hill, with Chris sitting beside him.

I looked up at our work, which loomed high from where I was, just down the hill a bit.

I began to get an idea.

Mike was lying down with his eyes closed listening to music, and Chris was absentmindedly making snowballs and tossing them at a tree. They both sat in the path the snowball would take, if somehow it were to be pushed....

I began digging out the bottom of the snowball to get the leverage for the second stage of the operation. Without looking over his shoulder, my brother called out, "Greg, what are you doing to it?"

"I'm just... smoothing it." I answered innocently, with the first words that came to mind.

I continued to dig until I heard a crunch on the smaller snowball I'd used as a brace. Somehow, my brother and Mike had not turned around once to investigate, and stage two of the operation was ready to launch.

By now you have figured out what I was planning. The memory of the giant rolling ball in *Indiana Jones* had fired my imagination, and I was committed to seeing those guys' faces when they saw this thing thundering towards them. Lying on my back, I kicked the bracing snowball out from under the dug out side, then raced to the other to push with all my might.

The snowball began to roll down the hill. Chris looked up and saw it coming towards him, and when I saw the look on his face I finally began to consider the consequences of what I was doing. Seeing the snowball gaining speed had me wondering at the possible injuries that might occur when it ran over them. Then I remembered all the times I had worn that same look as Chris ran at me. We would see how he felt now that something more than three times his size was chasing him!

For some reason, my brother ran straight. He could have jumped to the side and out of the path of the giant hurtling towards him, but in his terror he tried to outrun the thing. He leaped over Mike who was still on his back listening to music, completely unaware of what was about to occur. Then, the runaway snowball rolled right over Mike's upper body and head.

A split second passed where I thought he might be seriously hurt, or even dead. However, he shot up from the spot where he had been compressed into the snow.

"Whoa!" he shouted, with a look of astonishment.

In the seconds it took for this to happen, Chris looked even more horrified. Why didn't he jump to the side? It was starting to not be so funny when he looked like he might cry.

The snowball caught Chris by the heel. He went down face first in the snow, his scream quickly muffled as it rolled right over him, thundering on to crash into the chain link fence at the bottom of the hill, causing the fence to bow under the weight and speed.

In the silence that followed I looked on in horror as Chris lay face down in the snow, not moving for a second. His body had been compressed into the snow—flattened like in the cartoons I watched. Maybe he was dead. But no—he was moving! Eventually he managed to push himself to his hands and knees.

He looked up at me then, perhaps noticing how scared I was of his reaction.

A grin suddenly split his face in two and he said, "You little jerk!"

I grinned back as I realized I would live to enjoy my prank.

All three of us tried to tell the tale from each of our perspectives all at the same time. "I was listening to a song when everything went dark!" exclaimed Mike.

"I knew he was up to something," said Chris.

"You should have seen your face, Mike," I said.

On the way home Mike asked Chris if he wanted to come over.

Chris looked at me and said to Mike, "Why don't you come over to my place and the three of us can hang out and play video games or something?"

"Sure!" answered Mike.

I happily plodded home through the snow between my brother and Mike. I knew this day would always have a special place in my memories.

~Greg Lamothe
Victoria, British Columbia

Curling Makes Me Canadian

Wherever you go in the world, you just have to say you're a Canadian and people laugh.
~John Candy

Recently, while I was travelling, a customs and immigration agent asked me my country of birth. I said, "Canada."

She said, "Do you have proof of citizenship?"

I said, "Yes, I watch curling."

"Thank you. Next!"

In my opinion, nothing makes me more Canadian than curling. Hockey, Mounties, maple syrup, back bacon, nothing (eh through zed) is more Canuck than curling. I was on the curling team in high school. Oh, sure, any guy into sports could play football. Any brainiac could be on the chess team. But I curled, baby I snapped those brooms, I pushed those brushes, I lifted those rocks until my body was granite. You yell "Hard, hard!" at me and I'm there for you, outside the house, in the house, out the back of the house. Curlers don't care where.

Well, those were my salad days. Now I mostly watch curling on TV. I love instant replay. You can't watch a good "raise take out" enough times. And of course, the telestrator—curling is such a fast-paced game, you need some guy with an electric pencil to explain what just happened. And you don't see the Nike swoosh on too many curling rocks. No, curling is above crass commercialism. Beer and cigarettes—those are the sponsors that curlers hold out for.

You know, maybe we didn't invent the game, or some years even dominate, but curling is ours, man. Canada—a big sheet of ice with circles at either end. A bunch of men and women in sweaters going back and forth sweeping.

People say, "I love Canada, it's so clean." Well, that's why. We know how to sweep. Canada. The C is for curling.

~Larry Fedoruk
Toronto, Ontario

This Miracle Was No Accident

There are only two ways to live your life.
One is as though nothing is a miracle.
The other is as though everything is a miracle.
~Albert Einstein

It was just another typical Canadian winter day; the falling snow blocked out the sun creating a dark, drab morning. The wind challenged the car to keep its course and, in the end, joined the other forces of winter—slippery roads, poor visibility and slush to take our little Neon off course.

"How's my driving? Do you feel safe? Should I turn back?"

"No," my wife Jennifer replied, "I really want to see this show in Toronto. I have faith in your driving."

We were coming down the hill at Cookstown, southbound on the four-lane 400 highway, notorious in winter. Suddenly there was a noticeable increase in the force of snow whipping against the windshield. Inside, the car began to fog up, so I ran my finger down the side of the windshield to see if defrost was needed.

It was just a couple of seconds but that's all it took.

When I turned my attention back to the road, I felt the car stagger slightly to the left and then to the right. As if watching from a distance, as if shock had removed all emotions, calmly I said to Jennifer, "We're going to hit that bus."

We were in the far left lane; the bus was in the middle. Our little Neon slid into the side of the bus about midpoint.

Suddenly Jennifer was cheek-to-cheek with the side of the bus. She screamed in horror. Bouncing off the bus, our car then ricocheted onto the barrier in the middle of the highway. I hung on to the steering wheel and waited for whatever was to be our fate.

From the barrier we rebounded back to the side of the bus. Jennifer shrieked. Then back to the guardrail again.

On our third return, the bus had moved far enough ahead that we just caught the rear bumper, which caused the car to spin 180 degrees so we were now facing oncoming traffic. All I could see through the snow were the headlights of a transport truck bearing down on us. There was nothing I could do but wait to be demolished.

Jennifer whispered to herself, "I guess this is how it feels just before you die. I wonder if it hurts."

In that instant, before I could panic, I heard a voice inside my head. "Relax, let go and everything will be alright." So I took my hand off the steering wheel, took a deep breath and just sat there.

By the grace of God, we somehow ended up on the side of the road facing in the right direction in our now beat up Neon.

Since the car was not completely off the road, I restarted it and moved us safely onto the shoulder. It then stalled again, never to restart. We were not hurt at all.

A tow truck driving by stopped and after hooking us up, brought us back to town.

I don't know how the transport truck missed running us down, and I don't know where that voice inside came from, but to both Jennifer and me it was a miracle. It was some force from somewhere that looked down at that moment and, after telling me to relax and let go, somehow rearranged the traffic on that cold, snowy day so we could live to tell this story.

Those two minutes of our lives changed us forever. Now when

stress or danger confront, I simply let go, relax and know that everything will be all right.

~Ross Greenwood
Orillia, Ontario

Cornet Serenade

You have not seen Canada until you have seen the North.
~*Pierre Elliot Trudeau*

Just before Christmas of 2008, our band, The Porkbelly Futures, returned from a three-week tour of Canada's western provinces. It took us from our home in Toronto all the way out to Nanaimo, British Columbia and back, with many stops along the way.

Stuart Laughton, our multi-talented guitarist/harmonica/pedal steel mandolin/trumpet player, and myself, drummer and singer, were charged with the responsibility of getting all our gear out to our first gig in Twin Butte, Alberta. The other band members, our bass player Chas Elliott, Rebecca Campbell our vocalist, and Paul Quarrington, our lead vocalist and guitarist, would meet up with us along the way.

On November 9th Stuart and I hopped into our van, lovingly called The Pig Rig, and after first driving north to the Trans Canada Highway, we pointed the Pig Rig west.

It is interesting to note that many parts of Canada are, in fact, two different places depending on the season. While they act one way in summer, spring and fall, they are generally completely different in character in winter. This was never more evident than when we discovered just how few gas stations were open between Sault Ste. Marie and Wawa during winter. With driving up and down hills pulling the weight of a fully loaded trailer, we had underestimated the increased rate of fuel consumption. You guessed it, we ran out of gas twenty miles south of Wawa. When we pulled out the cell phone to call CAA, there was no cell service.

Traffic was totally non-existent. No one drove by. Not a single vehicle. The snowy stretch of deserted highway and the surrounding expanse of wintry pines along the north of Lake Superior never felt more indifferent and hostile than they did at that moment.

It was getting colder and colder. Daylight was waning. At this point, for some reason, Stuart decided to serenade the pines with his cornet.

Eventually someone had to come by.

And, eventually someone did. It's probably not every day that drivers see someone practising their horn in the middle of Canada's frozen north, so the curious driver slowed down, came alongside and rolled down his window.

With a smile on his face, Stuart leaned in and uttered what had to be one of the best quips of our tour… "Any requests?"

The driver of the car started laughing so hard we barely understood him as he told us that his brother-in-law owned a gas station just ahead on the outskirts of town. He'd send him back with some gas. He was as good as his word. Sure enough, the man arrived with the gas and soon we were back on the road—with the heater on full!

Nothing unites Canadians more, it would seem, than a little strife, the winter, and of course, some music!

~Martin Worthy
Toronto, Ontario

O Canada The Wonders of Winter

More than Just Neighbours

Bless thou to be mine eye.
May mine eye bless all it sees;
I will bless my neighbour,
May my neighbour bless me.

~Celtic Prayer

14

Healed by a Snowstorm

Because that's what kindness is. It's not doing something for someone else because they can't, but because you can.
~Andrew Iskander

The blizzard over Winnipeg lasted all day and all night. Through the kitchen window, I saw only a blanket of uninterrupted white. The cotoneaster hedge, the cedar fence, my rock garden, even the young blue spruce that Don and I had planted the previous spring were cloaked in heavy layers of snow.

Don had been away caring for his parents for two nights and I was missing him. I knew he was okay, because he had called as soon as he had arrived. He would stay with his folks until other support could be put into place. Like the blizzard, his parents' deterioration was sudden. One day they were healthy, independent and self-reliant; the next, they were frail and needy, unable to manage. Don and his sister had great difficulty adjusting to this change. What to do? Where was the right balance between helplessness and autonomy?

Still staring out the window, I tried to shake off the melancholy. My thoughts wandered to the still unresolved problem with our neighbours—a minor irritation perhaps, in view of this new crisis, but nevertheless, an ongoing frustration. My jaw tightened.

For the last fourteen months we had been awakened every single day before seven by the sound of the grand piano next door. The eldest child was taking piano lessons, and dutifully practised every morning. Unfortunately, due to the proximity of our houses and the location of the piano, it sounded like it was in bed with us.

We had no objection to the boy's practice; after all, our own now-grown daughter had also taken lessons. But the earliness of the hour, which included weekends, grated on our nerves.

We had both spoken to our neighbours, and I had written them notes about the problem, but to no avail. Things had grown tense. Our pleadings were met with tenacity and the position that it was "their" piano inside "their" house, and they would do what they wanted. It had degenerated into a standoff. Apart from considering some noisy retaliation, we were out of ideas, and dog-tired.

Why couldn't we work this out? After all, we had lived side by side for ten years, mostly in a friendly, accommodating relationship. I shook my head, and refocused my thoughts, shifting my gaze to the monotonous white landscape of the back yard. I stared at it absently.

Suddenly a bright patch of colour appeared near the corner of the garage. Then, a head appeared beneath this rainbow-striped blob. Sluggish and tired, it was a moment before I grasped what I was seeing... and hearing! The scraping sounds of a snow shovel made me realize, with a jolt, what was happening. Mack, my neighbour, father and defender of the piano-playing prodigy... was clearing my driveway! I rubbed my eyes, and checked again. There was no mistake!

Climbing into boots and parka, I headed out. Mack had finished the sidewalk and was starting on the driveway. A huge smile broke across my face as I made my way to the driveway. Then, unable to stop myself, I threw my arms around my unpredictable neighbour and just held on. After a moment, I felt the hug being returned, and there we stood in a snowy embrace on the partially shovelled driveway.

For the first time in months, we spoke. In between comments about the weather, we made inquiries about each other's families and discussed plans for the upcoming holidays. I wondered if I was doing the right thing when I invited him in for a cup of coffee, but he said he'd like that as soon as he finished the job.

A few minutes later we were visiting over steamy mugs of Colombian dark roast. Mack, sensing my confusion at his unexpected behaviour, looked down at his coffee self-consciously.

"Wondering why I was out there shovelling your snow, eh?"

"Well, frankly, Mack, yes! It was a bit of a shock considering how things have been," I replied.

"Well, it's because of your car in the driveway. No, I mean, because your car's not in the driveway. First, I figured you and Don were away, but then I noticed you were home alone. So I asked the Baileys, and Carole told me about Don's folks."

Mack paused to gulp his coffee then continued awkwardly. "Anyway, that storm dumped a lot of snow, and you being home alone by yourself, and Don, having enough on his plate with his mum and dad… I mean, I was out there shovelling anyway, I thought I might as well…" His words drifted off. Stiffly, Mack raised his cup for another swallow of coffee. After a few moments of embarrassed silence, I reached out and took his hand.

"Thanks for caring, Mack. Thanks so much," I whispered, my eyes overflowing, and my heart full. Months of hostile feelings disappeared, in an instant. With Mack's generous act of friendship, all the bitterness seemed to evaporate.

"Sure, no problem. Well, I'd better get home. My wife will wonder what's happened to me. Thanks for the coffee." And with that he hurried out the door.

When I awoke the next morning, I rolled over, alone in the bed. Don would not be home until after supper. I turned over for a better view of the clock expecting to see the display read 6:15. Unable to sleep in anymore, I steeled myself for the daily piano recital that usually woke me shortly after 6:30 a.m. To my amazement, the clock read 8:37! Unlike every morning for months, I had not been jolted awake by the strident notes of a piano. I thought that perhaps sheer exhaustion had prevailed and I'd simply slept through the daily musical ritual. However, the next morning was the same, and the one after that. As the days went by, I was overjoyed to realize that mornings could once again be counted on to be peaceful oases of quiet, at least until after 8:00 a.m., and on weekends, piano practice didn't occur until after lunch.

In the weeks that followed I reflected on the poignant life lessons I'd learned. An unexpected December blizzard and act of God had arrived suddenly to blur the hard edges of the world. In a parallel fashion, the snowstorm had also softened and blurred the hard edges of my anger.

An act of neighbourly kindness, unexpected and unsolicited, had unblocked the flow of love, and the hatchet, quite literally, was buried. Friendship and harmony had been restored as miraculously as the fall of snowflakes on that quiet wintry day.

Love is such a mighty powerful force—I had just learned this first hand. I had to have faith that if there was this sort of goodness in the world, anything was possible.

~Sharon Melnicer
Winnipeg, Manitoba

15

The Heart of a Community

*In the country, community is a loosely defined term that starts with family,
and tends to spread itself around through a network of marriages,
friendships and other relationships.*
~Marsha Bolton

My cousin Rosaire Desrosiers was a young man when he and his wife Alice left their farm in Ste. Anne Manitoba, for a day of Christmas shopping in Winnipeg. With confidence and smiling faces, they kissed their six children goodbye that November afternoon in 1954 as they left Rosaire's fourteen-year old cousin Simone in charge.

Late in the day, Simone busied herself with the evening meal, preparing a rather elaborate spread while the children watched and played. As she worked, the wind whistled through holes in the walls where insulation should have been. But the children didn't mind.... this was their home, a place where the family celebrated life with laughter.

As they finished their supper that evening, the lights went out with a deafening bang. Louis, the eldest at eight, went off in search of a flashlight to further investigate the problem. As he fumbled around the closet, he found it odd that something resembling a pair of cat's eyes was being reflected off the ceiling.

Simone realized in an instant what those reflections were. Without hesitating, she wrapped the baby in a blanket and yelled for the other children to get outside quickly. The roof of the house was already engulfed in flames. With snow on the ground and no shoes on their feet, Simone hurried the children to her parents' farm fifteen minutes away, carrying the baby in her skirt to keep her warm. Turning only once, she shuddered as the house disintegrated entirely in flames. What a close call, she realised with a breath of relief. At least she had got all six children to safety.

When Rosaire and Alice returned that night, they went into shock when they found their home in smoking ruins. Although they thanked God and Simone countless times for their children's safety, both Rosaire and Alice knew that difficult times lay ahead. All that they had ever owned was lost. With little insurance to rebuild, Rosaire despaired at the apparently hopeless situation. He and Alice found little to laugh about now.

Realising they had nowhere to go, Rosaire's father, Magloire, gladly opened his doors to his son's family. The children adored their pépère. Although it was a temporary solution, Rosaire knew that his young brood would benefit from the attention lavished on them by their grandfather.

Yet, even with Magloire's assistance, Rosaire was desperately in need of money. The recently purchased Christmas gifts were returned and the small insurance policy cashed. Even then he knew there was not enough to rebuild, and was resigned to renting a home.

Then, Johnny Goosen, an old school friend, came over to chat. Johnny's solution was simple: "You buy what material you can, Rosaire, and we'll all help you rebuild."

As the lumber began to arrive, so did the truckloads of people wanting to help. One truck after another showed up with family, friends and neighbours; people from both French and Mennonite communities. Together they worked in the cold and snow to build the Desrosiers a new house.

When one job was completed, Johnny Goosen would put in a

word at his church for someone specialising in another trade. Sure enough, the next morning, a plumber or electrician would appear.

With Christmas only one week away, the work was suddenly finished and the Desrosiers were finally home!

As the last of the workers left, Rosaire and Alice sat back in amazement in their new kitchen. So much had happened in the last two months, and they were so grateful. But, having spent all they had on building materials, they had no money left for gifts to put under the tree.

Even after all they had been through, Rosaire and Alice still did not want Christmas morning to be a disappointment for their children. They decided to share with their children the joy that they felt from the generosity of all their friends and neighbours. Each night they worked feverishly, using imagination and leftover pieces of wood to build a dollhouse, a wooden horse, and other beautiful gifts. They were determined that Santa would come to their home after all.

Unbeknownst to them, their son Denis was watching. He would position himself nightly at the top of the stairs and watch the two elves at their secret work. And then suddenly, with two days left before Christmas, Rosaire and Alice stopped their craft, leaving some projects incomplete. This mystified Denis, but he didn't dare ask why.

On Christmas morning the children awoke to a tree magically laden with beautiful gifts and sweets. Denis noticed that many of the gifts had not been part of their parents' workshop, and quietly wondered where they had come from. Rosaire and Alice decided to keep the secret safe for the time being, as they watched their children's overwhelming joy.

It was only years later that Rosaire finally told Denis and the others the secret about that day, his eyes brimming with tears. Two days before Christmas, the local parish priest Father Laplante had arrived as an emissary. Apparently, the community's generosity had not stopped with the building of the house. They had also collected enough gifts to ensure that the Desrosiers children had all their Christmas dreams fulfilled. And so the late night work had stopped.

Good to his word, on Christmas Eve, Father Laplante had arrived at their door with satchels of presents contributed by the many well wishing families and friends.

Years later, as Uncle Rosaire reflected back on the events that transpired that cold winter of 1953, he was still moved to tears when he remembered Simone, who is my mother, Johnny Goosen, and the countless others who gave so selflessly. The Desrosiers found great joy that year, not because the people gave with their money, but because they gave with their hearts.

~Paula Meyer
Winnipeg, Manitoba

The Shiny New Snow Shovel

A good neighbor is a priceless treasure.
~Author Unknown

When I moved into my first home in Toronto, my father gave me a shiny new snow shovel. "Here," he said, as he handed it to me, "now that you own a home, you're going to use this a lot over the next four or five months." Then he and my mother drove home to Montreal.

For the next couple of weeks, I checked the weather report carefully, hoping for snow. I had a shiny new shovel to break in and shoveling my own walk was yet another sign I was truly a homeowner—and an independent adult.

When the forecast finally heralded snow, I was thrilled. I woke up early and glanced out the window. Snow! I opened the front door, ready to shovel, only to find that my sidewalk had already been done. I looked around but didn't see anybody.

The same thing happened several times over the next three weeks. I began to wonder if I had magical sidewalks and snow simply didn't stay on them. Or maybe the snow-shoveling fairies were hard at work.

Then one Saturday morning, I rushed outside to find my neighbor shoveling my walk. When he saw me, he smiled. "Sorry I'm late today. Had a bit of a lie-in."

So much for magical sidewalks and snow-shoveling fairies. My vanishing snow was due to the hard work of my neighbor who was at least sixty-five, perhaps seventy. "Thank you," I said. "That's really nice of you to do this, but you really don't have to."

He threw the last shovelful of snow onto my lawn. "I'm retired. What else do I have to do?"

Disappointed that I didn't have a chance to use my new shovel, I mumbled another "thank you" and went back inside.

A few hours later I knocked on his door. "Hi," I said. "We haven't been formally introduced. I'm Harriet."

"Come on in and meet the wife," he said. I followed him into the living room. He motioned me to a chair. "I'm Al and this is the wife, Peggy."

I handed him a big tin of cookies. "This is for you. A thank-you for the shoveling."

At their insistence, I stayed long enough to have two cups of tea and eat some cookies. We chatted and I found out all about their kids, their grandkids, and petted their Yorkshire terrier.

When I said I had to leave, Peggy walked me to the door. "Please come again," she said. "It's so nice to have visitors. Our children live out of town, so we don't see them often." She lowered her voice. "And thank you for letting Al shovel your walk. It makes him feel needed." She paused. "And it gets him out of the house."

From then on, I visited them about once a week, but I always brought my own cup of tea. "So you don't have to get up and make me one," I said. It became our joke.

For a first-time homeowner living on her own, with no family in town, the Browns were the perfect neighbors. When my telephone wasn't working, my mother called them so they could knock on my door and tell me. When I accidentally left my keys in the door, my mailman left them with the Browns for safekeeping. When my cat got stuck on their roof, they let me dangle out their bathroom window to call to her. She, of course, ignored me but managed to find her way down a couple of hours later.

For the next six years, Al shoveled my sidewalk every winter, and I thanked him with cakes, cookies and company.

Then one day it snowed and my sidewalk remained unshoveled, as did my neighbours'. Their car was in the driveway so I figured they were probably home. Maybe he slept in again, I thought. Or maybe he's not feeling well.

I grabbed my shovel, still shiny after six years of non-use, and cleared a path. After I did my front walk and sidewalk, I continued shoveling right up to their door.

Shovel in hand, I rang their doorbell to see if everyone was all right. Their daughter answered and told me her father had had a stroke. That stroke turned out to be the first of many mini-strokes that sapped Al's emotional and physical health.

For the next year, I shoveled for both of us and continued my weekly visits. Most days, Al remained upstairs in his bedroom, but Peggy and I talked and sipped tea.

Eventually they moved in with their daughter in another city and we lost touch. But whenever I shovel snow, I think about them and their generosity of spirit that made moving into my first home so enjoyable. Some people say fences make good neighbors. For me, it was a snow shovel.

~Harriet Cooper
Toronto, Ontario

Ring to the Rescue

*No animal I know can consistently be more of a friend and
companion than a dog.*
~Stanley Leinwoll

I n the early 1940s my father, Alvin Eklund, lived in the Twin
Butte district of Southern Alberta. He was a rancher, and a
farmer. When it came to animals, he was known as one of the
kindest men around.

In summer he and his friend Owen Leavitt moved their sheep
into the mountains. In winter, my dad brought his herd down into
the farming districts of Hill Spring and Glenwood where he rented
grain fields to run his sheep. It was almost impossible to handle
sheep without dogs to help, so both my father and Owen had very
good dogs.

Ring was my dad's dog. Ring was a dog you could send out
around the sheep in the brush, and if he found one that was caught
or unable to return to the herd he would bark until someone came to
his aid. Ring would go up the mountain and bring sheep down that
were so high they could scarcely be seen. He could be sent ahead to
turn the flock either way at a signal, or he could be left to drive from
the rear of the flock while the herder drove a small bunch in the lead.
Ring would bunch the flock in a tight circle and hold them until you
relieved him of the chore.

One winter my father stayed with Owen while his sheep grazed in fields two miles away. It was January, and of course very cold at night. Dad began complaining of not feeling well. Owen tried to get him to stay indoors, but my father would not stand for pampering. After a few days had passed he was still sick, but he really wanted to go home to his ranch in Twin Butte.

Owen tried to dissuade him, as at that point he had no family and lived alone. His nearest neighbors were about two miles away. But he said that if Owen would take care of his sheep, he would be back well and able in a few days. So he left for home with Ring at his side.

About a week went by and Owen had received no word from Alvin. Then one morning—early, about seven o'clock, Ring came scratching and whining at the door. When Owen went to see what he wanted, he barked a few times and started back out to the road. When Owen didn't follow Ring came back, and whined and barked again.

Quickly realizing what he wanted, Owen said, "I understand Ring, I'm coming."

Owen later said, "There was about fourteen inches of snow on the ground, and it was twenty-five miles back to Alvin's ranch. I thought I'd better get some help to go with me, so in a short time Ted Green and I hopped in my car with Ring, and set out for Alvin's ranch. We brought a big snow shovel along to dig the snow away. We couldn't make very good time as the snow was pretty deep for a car, but at last we were on the hill above Alvin's ranch. I'll never forget looking down on the scene of that little ranch all covered with white, not a single track anywhere except those Ring had made coming out. When I saw smoke coming out of the chimney, I said to Ted, "Well he's still alive."

"When we got down to the house and found Alvin, he was scarcely able to stand. He just stood and looked at us with tears running down his cheeks. He wasn't able to say a word."

Owen and Ted tucked their friend in the car and brought him back home with them. It turned out he had smallpox, and was sick for a very long time. Alvin later told them that when he got too sick to go to the door, Ring would scratch on the wall under his window several times a day and he would talk to him.

"I must have lost track of time," Alvin told Owen, "because when I finally realized Ring was gone, I hoped and prayed he would go to you. My neighbours wouldn't have understood him—they didn't know I had come home."

Ring had braved the deep and treacherous snow, travelling twenty-five miles to go for help without hesitation. And he knew exactly where to go. He was a hero to all of us from then on. My dad, of course, recovered, and none of us will ever forget Ring's incredible heroic act of love.

~David A. Eklund
Lethbridge, Alberta

18

A Generous Heart

You have not lived today until you have done something for someone
who can never repay you.
~John Bunyan

My in-laws loved to travel and every winter would visit different countries. While they were gone some friends moved into their house so it would not be left empty. When Dad and Mom returned, their friends would then pack up and head south for their own time away. This arrangement worked very well for many years.

Sadly, Dad was stricken with an incurable illness and it looked as though those trips would no longer be possible. Wanting to enjoy a final cruise with him while he was still able to recognize and enjoy their trip, Mom went about taking care of the details. Unfortunately, the couple who usually house-sat for them assumed that traveling days were over for Dad and went ahead and made their own plans to go south for the winter. This left my in-laws with no one to look after their home.

Other family members had jobs or young children in school, making it impossible for them to come and stay. Our children were older, and I didn't work outside of our home so it was decided that it would be easiest for me to re-arrange my schedule—I would be the one to house-sit.

I wasn't thrilled with the decision. I'm used to streetlights shining in my windows at night, the continual hum of traffic, stores that are open 24/7, and the comforting knowledge that I'm surrounded by other city dwellers. The thought of staying alone in a country home for an extended period of time made me anxious.

In addition, I had just been diagnosed with multiple sclerosis, a debilitating neurological condition. Because of this diagnosis and not knowing much about the disease, I was feeling pretty scared. How would I cope being on my own if I had an episode? Someone staying with me would have made this commitment easier to face, but there was no one available and I felt I had to do it. Despite my fear, I simply couldn't let Dad and Mom down. When everyone realized how difficult it was going to be for me to be on my own the entire time, it was agreed that I would return home on the weekends.

I tried to keep myself busy. Each day I walked down to the bottom of the driveway to collect the mail, I crafted a wall hanging and sewed curtains for four large windows, filled the bird feeders, chased away the raccoons, cleaned the house from top to bottom, watched an occasional TV show and spent a frustrating couple of hours trying to get on dial-up Internet. Chatting with friends and family on the phone helped sustain me, but these conversations and the simple chores didn't totally fill my time. Basically I did whatever I could to keep my mind off the fact that I was there alone.

Come Friday I would head back to the city to meet up with friends and spend time with my husband and our family. On Monday, the car filled with groceries, I'd make the drive back to my in-laws house.

During my third week in the country the temperature dropped and a massive snowstorm set in. The driveway filled in quickly with wet, heavy snow. I hadn't seen that much snow since I was a child, and as lovely as it was, I feared that I wouldn't be able to get out. It was very cold and every day the snow kept falling. On Thursday night it started to rain. The rain turned to sleet and covered everything with a thick coating of treacherous ice. With a sinking heart I knew I wouldn't be going home that weekend. Disappointed and feeling very low, I worried about having enough food. What would I do if the power went out? What if I fell? It continued to sleet and I spent a restless night wondering what the next day would bring.

Friday morning I awoke to a winter wonderland. The trees were weighed down with ice and everything sparkled. The sky had cleared, and looking out over the deck through the forest I could see that a snowplow had cleaned the road, but the surrounding countryside was blanketed in a deep hill of unbroken white. I felt utterly helpless.

Suddenly I heard a noise I didn't recognize coming from the front of the house. I ran across the room to the window and saw a man I had never met shovelling the driveway. The noise I heard was him trying to break through the crusted ice with nothing more than a shovel. Who was this guy? Why was he shovelling the driveway? I was almost afraid to ask if he had the right address because I wanted the driveway cleared so badly.

As I stood there watching, the realization sank in that I might be freed. Relief flooded over me and tears sprang into my eyes. After taking a moment to compose myself, I put on my coat and boots and went out to help him. It took an exhausting four hours to clear that driveway and because my enthusiasm was greater than what I could actually accomplish, he did most of the heavy work. It turned out he was my in-laws' closest neighbour and before they left Mom had let him know I would be staying at the house while they were away. She also explained to him how important it was for me to go back to the city on the weekends.

Apparently he had his eye on the house and was watching out for me. Earlier that morning when he had walked around the property he saw the state of the driveway and realized I wasn't going anywhere. Out of the goodness of his heart he generously took on the task of ensuring it was cleared so I could get home. After the driveway was clear he waited until my car was loaded and I was ready to leave, and made sure I was safely on my way.

When I looked back through the rearview mirror I saw him still standing there by the garage, waving goodbye. My heart was filled with thankfulness towards this kind man and his selfless act. I drove home feeling on top of the world.

~Jennifer E. Bailey
Toronto, Ontario

Victory Victoria

If we could predict the weather perfectly,
it would take all the fun out of being Canadian.
~David Phillips, Climatologist for Environment Canada

December 1996 was colder than usual and a soft, heavy snowfall on the 23rd had folks, children especially, looking forward to a rare white Christmas. The residents of Victoria, British Columbia have often been accused of smugness as they enjoy the year-round good weather and mild climate of Canada's "banana belt." So when the unusual snow continued with a blizzard warning on December 28th, Victorians weren't prepared.

Before that holiday season was over, Victorians wished they would never see snow again! In the "Storm of the Century," between December 21st and 29th a total of 124 centimetres of snow fell, with 64.5 falling on December 29th alone. The little city that seldom sees snow lay covered in two-metre snowdrifts.

I called my mother, who lived in a downtown nursing home. At eighty-seven, Mum was in poor health, but her mind was active and unaffected. "Mum," I said, "We're completely snowed in, and the plows have to concentrate on the main roads. It may be a few days before we can get out to see you."

We were concerned. My mother had been battling the flu, and in the immediate aftermath of the storm, not even antibiotics were being delivered.

On the morning of December 31st, the phone rang. It was the nurse in charge of Mother's care. "Mary," she began, "the flu has turned into pneumonia. Your mother is dying, and she is asking for you. Is there any way you can get down here?"

My heart sank, because I knew there was no way I could get there. Well off the beaten track, our quiet neighbourhood was a low priority for snow removal. Like thousands of others in the city, we were trapped.

Friends suggested we contact C-FAX, one of the local radio stations. C-FAX had cancelled its regular programming and was now a communications centre for news updates, volunteer co-ordination, and health and safety tips. It had become Victoria's lifeline.

"Can you help me?" I asked them. "My son and I are stranded and we have just received word that my mother is dying."

For the next forty minutes we waited patiently, praying for a miracle. Then the telephone rang and the voice on the other end of the line said, "Mrs. Turner, if you and your son can navigate to the end of your property, we have an army truck waiting to take you to the nursing home!"

The gift of strangers. That was the most blessed ride of my life. Between the doses of morphine, Mother was aware and coherent. My son John was able to say his goodbyes to Grandma. I read Mum's Christmas mail to her and we reminisced and comforted each other.

When Mum passed away at 2:00 a.m., New Year's Day, I was able to release her in peace.

Many other small miracles occurred during our storm. Whole neighbourhoods came together and were strengthened. The able-bodied grabbed shovels and dug out those not able to help themselves, and medicine and grocery deliveries were arranged for the elderly and shut-ins.

In our family there was a death. In another there was a birth. When Joy and Michael Egilson's daughter was born in their home at the height of the storm, the neighbours strapped mother and infant to a toboggan and formed a chain to bring them to the safety of the ambulance.

The experience of the storm changed the heart of Victoria. In the Blizzard of '96, I discovered I was not alone.

~Mary Turner
Victoria, British Columbia

Storm-Stayed

Home is a place you grow up wanting to leave,
and grow old wanting to go back to.
~John Ed Pearce

"Storm-stayed?" my husband replied with a questioning glance. "That's an odd expression." But that's what my family called it whenever you were unable to make it home because of one of those infamous winter snowstorms that regularly afflicted Southwestern Ontario when I was growing up. For children, this occasion inspired an exciting impromptu pajama party; for teenagers, the opportunity to hang out just a little longer with their friends. For adults, it was an inconvenience, but also the chance for some shared company or an extra game of cards on a blustery night. Being storm-stayed at school, however, was a whole other story.

I was ten years old and attending elementary school in a tiny village about two miles from my family's farm, when a fierce winter storm hit. (And by tiny village I mean a church, a general store that doubled as the post office, a feed mill, a small cluster of houses, and our school.) The buses had delivered us safely to school that morning, but the wind and blinding snow had come up so suddenly that we were unable to be transported home. By early afternoon it was clear that something had to be done with the entire student population and staff of the school.

The school facility could not accommodate everyone, so the

inhabitants of the village rose to the challenge of providing shelter for as many people as they could. Students who lived in the village gathered together a few classmates to spend the night at their houses, and I was chosen. Yes, chosen! I felt so relieved to be among those who would not have to sleep on the hard gymnasium floor under the watchful eye of the principal. Selfishly, I gave no thought to my three sisters in the other classrooms, and didn't stop to wonder where they might end up spending the night.

Along with four other children I made the trek through fresh, deep snow, literally following in the footsteps of our classmate Joan, whose home would be our camp-out site for the night. I felt like a miniature explorer, braving the elements in search of some mysterious destination. Even in the semi-protected streets of the village the snow was heavy. Worried about losing my way, I never took my eyes off Joan's red toque bobbing along in front of me, collecting a thicker layer of snow with every step she took.

When we reached the house and shed our heavy winter clothing, we were instantly welcomed and warmed with hot chocolate. Five sets of fingers curled around steamy mugs as puddles began to form around five sets of boots in the front hall. The rest of the day was spent playing board games and, when our clothes were dry enough, creating intricate forts in the backyard snow. That night, all of the extra blankets and pillows in the house were pressed into service to keep us warm and comfortable. I had never been storm-stayed in an unfamiliar place before, but so far, the whole situation was a thrilling adventure.

And then the storm continued. The wind howled all the next day bringing with it whiteout conditions and massive accumulations of snow. Our backyard forts became great shapeless lumps. Highways were totally impassable. Hydro lines went down. The local news station offered little hope that things would clear any time soon.

By the third day, the sight of more snow outside the windows seemed to elicit a collective groan from everyone in the house. I was tired of board games and sick of playing cards. I had no desire to pull on my damp boots and trudge through thigh-high snowdrifts. I hesitated to confess that I was homesick. Joan's family had been wonderful, but they weren't my family. I missed my own warm kitchen, the familiar faces and food around our table. I wondered where my sisters had been staying and if, somehow, they had been able to make it home yet.

With my face pressed up against the kitchen window, I peered hopefully at the sky. No glimmer of blue. No weak ray of promising sun. No break in the interminable wall of white. Feeling my chin begin to quiver, I swallowed hard to stop the ache that was growing in my throat. My eyes filled with tears and my shallow breaths began to create a small circle of fog on the cold glass in front of me. I looked at it glumly without the usual impulse to draw a little happy face or trace my initials in the fog.

The voice of Joan's mother caught me off guard. Using my sweater sleeve, I quickly dried my eyes. After all she had done over the past few days, I couldn't let her see me crying. It took a moment before her words really sank in.

"Judy, your dad is on his way," she announced.

I didn't stop to ask any questions as I flew to the front hall to retrieve my coat and boots. My soggy toque was still in the coat sleeve where I had stuffed it after our most recent expedition outside into the winter wonderland.

Fully dressed and sweating slightly, I was waiting by the door when I heard the distant drone. Minutes later, my dad pulled up beside the front steps on his snowmobile, encrusted in snow from head to toe. I had no idea how he had found his way through this blizzard, or why he had decided to set out at all. After we had both thanked Joan's family, Dad handed me my helmet and I squeezed it on. I then climbed onto the snowmobile behind him and wrapped my small arms tightly around his waist. I didn't let go until we had reached the safety of our own front steps.

That evening, as the storm continued to bluster outside, we all sat down together at the kitchen table to enjoy our mother's warm, comforting meal. Mom told me later that Dad had driven to the village and back four times that day, gathering his daughters one by one and bringing them safely home. The roads were still closed, but he had blazed his own snowmobile trail to carry out his mission.

I have been snowed in on several occasions since then, but never for such an extended period of time, and never with such a timely and, in my eyes, dramatic rescue. It seems to me now that the best part of being storm-stayed is coming home again.

~Judy Carter
London, Ontario

21

Winterpeg

What this world needs is a new kind of army—the army of the kind.
~Cleveland Amory

It was 1989 and I was teaching adult upgrading in Winnipeg's inner city core area. The school division had arranged for staff parking at a small, gravel-paved lot at the end of the same block as the school. In "Winterpeg" temperatures often dip as low as -30 degrees Celsius with high wind chills, so being able to plug in my car there made my life easier. So did the fact that I didn't have to parallel-park on the street—a challenge for me because of poor depth perception.

The first day of school in January, the principal's announcement made my stomach clench. "The city is expropriating our parking lot to make room for new development," she announced. "As of tomorrow, the lot will no longer be available and you'll have to make your own arrangements."

The next day, I arrived early to find a suitable parking spot. I had already decided against parking across the street from the school; an unbroken line of vehicles squeezed into every inch of space along that curb. As well, a two-hour parking limit because of the nearby hospital was strictly enforced; any car violating the rule had its tires marked with chalk and a hefty fine imposed.

A block away I found ample parking, but had to move my car twice during work to avoid being ticketed. This entailed having to watch the clock, leaving my class unattended, putting on winter clothing, walking to the car, starting it up, running the engine for several minutes, then finding another parking spot, walking back to the school, thawing somewhat and finally continuing the lesson. At least fifteen minutes of wasted class time—if everything went smoothly.

I parked there until a fifty-dollar fine made me resume my search. Then, just a few blocks north, I found a street with unrestricted parking and only a few cars lining the street. The houses struck me as different from those closer to the school; they seemed better kept, with brightly coloured paint and religious icons adorning the front doors.

No sooner did I park than the curtains of the nearest house pulled open a few inches. A bald, elderly man with dark, piercing eyes peered out the window at me. When I left the car, he still hadn't budged; I felt as if he were watching me.

At the end of the day, there he was again at the window. Was this a coincidence? Maybe. It made me vaguely uneasy, but not enough to move the car elsewhere; the spot was too convenient. And so it went, the same routine twice a day; his keeping careful track of my arrivals and departures. Although it made me uneasy, I tried not to give the situation too much thought.

One day, the man didn't appear at the window. Then, just as I was warming up the car he turned the corner, limping along, a cane in one hand and a bag of groceries in the other. I smiled and waved; he nodded solemnly. His response deflated me; I'd hoped he might be friendlier. Then back to the same pattern. The silent stare twice a day repeated itself the next week.

The following Monday I returned to my car a bit later. The man didn't appear by the curtains, nor did I see any parked cars on the street—including mine! In fact, where was it? Had someone stolen it? That seemed unlikely. In any case, something unusual about the road itself caught my attention; the pavement was very glossy, like a skating rink embossed with tire imprints. And there on the road right in front of me, a huge icy mound stood gleaming in the late afternoon sun. Gazing at the long, squat shape, I imagined a frozen Ice Age mastodon underneath... or... possibly something else. At that point my brain finally clicked in.

A water main must have broken earlier in the day — right near my car — and it got drenched, its entire surface now covered in solid ice, including the windows. What to do? Searching my purse, the only tool I had was a nail file, and with that I began trying to chip away at the ice near one of the doors, while the -30 degree Winterpeg wind stung my cheeks. Talk about tough slogging. After twenty minutes I had managed to dislodge only a few chunks of ice near the passenger door. I was beginning to despair, realizing that at this rate, it would take hours to open my car and get home. My gloved fingers were starting to feel numb. Even if I managed to open the trunk to retrieve the scraper, how would I ever de-ice the front window?

I was considering knocking on the man's door when suddenly he appeared briefly at the window, to retreat almost immediately. So much for that option, I figured. I could call the Motor League from the nearby hospital, but the truck would no doubt take hours to come in such cold weather.

Suddenly the man burst out of his house and came up to me. "My name Paulo," he said in a low voice. "I no speak good English. You wait here."

He then went and knocked on his neighbour's door. I could not identify the language he was speaking: Italian? Portuguese? Then he went to the next door, then the next, and then the next until he had called upon five of his neighbours. As he went from door to door, I felt like I was witnessing a miracle in progress.

In no time, men were pouring out of their houses with picks and pails of hot water to help free my car from the ice. Then Paulo limped over to a store around the corner and enlisted their help as well. Soon there were eight men of various ages working on my car, trying to break through the ice. I stood there watching; watching the buckets of hot water melt the ice little by little like some magic potion, the blue of the chassis finally showing through. In the meantime, Paulo disappeared inside his house, only to emerge a few minutes later with a large mug of hot chocolate — for me.

The de-icing took at least forty-five minutes, after which my rescuers all cheered "Bravo!" Feeling heartened, and truly grateful, I thanked them all and shook their hands before taking my leave. Driving off, I glanced in my rear view mirror to see them all still waving. What a sense of community I'd just experienced—I was truly impressed, and truly touched. Wow, had I misjudged that man. I knew the next day when I drove up and Paulo appeared at the window—watching over me with care—I would smile and wave at him—as a friend.

~Bev Sandell Greenberg
Winnipeg, Manitoba

Chapter

3

O Canada The Wonders of Winter

The Great Outdoors

…as long as there are fascinating new places to explore, new pathways to discover through the forests, new stars to notice in the wilderness sky, new experiences to share, and books to read, I will— God willing—remain a happy man.

~Pierre Elliot Trudeau

22

Winter Campus Bannock

There is something that all Canadians know, the feel of the wild
even in the heart of the city.
~Wade Davis

The first thing I did when I awoke was look out the window to predict the day's weather. It had rained all night and a thick mass of low grey clouds still remained, confirming my notion that this day was going to be a big flop. I couldn't image the undergraduate students I was teaching coming to campus dressed warmly enough to sit outside for a class in December, especially when it looked like it was going to sleet.

The previous week I had asked them what they wanted for the last tutorial of the semester. One student responded by describing a scene of Native women making bread on a stick, something she had seen while visiting Moosonee on the Polar Bear Express the previous summer. These students all knew I had lived and worked in the north, and they hoped that I would recognize what was being described.

"It's bannock," I responded. "It's like a bread without yeast. If you'd like to learn how to make bannock around a fire, I think it might be possible." In the discussion that followed several students volunteered to bring the needed supplies to the next class.

Later, I began to consider how the concrete campus we all attended for this class on environmental issues was not really conducive to a campfire setting. However, there was one tiny remnant of a forest that looked out of place and abandoned, surrounded as it was by high-rise buildings and concrete residences. This was where we would gather for our class.

That morning, as I outfitted my pack with a big fry pan and flipper, I started thinking about everything that could go wrong and really began to lose my nerve.

Before we could embark on our little adventure, there was a lecture from the professor to be completed. During the two hours in the windowless classroom I frequently wondered about the weather outside. Had it begun to rain or sleet? What were the prospects of finding the dry tinder needed to get a fire going after a night of rain? Would anyone show up in suitable footgear to stay warm? How many of these students were really planning to attend this final class in a cold, wet soggy bush?

On the way out, a few students who had not attended the class joined us. With cheerful enthusiasm they said they had just wanted to come to tutorial so they could learn how to make bannock. Their positive comments and faith restored some hope to my pessimistic attitude on the outcome of the venture.

I usually only made bannock along isolated shorelines deep in the heart of the Canadian Shield countryside, but as we walked along pavement beside towering concrete walls to the edge of the woodlot, I sensed that this bannock making experience was going to be more urban than wilderness. We all tramped down to the woodlot under the grey damp sky and found a clearing in the middle to build our fire. Even in the middle of this tiny patch of forest, all the surrounding buildings could be seen as if they were fencing us in. As the students began to collect firewood just to keep moving and stay warm, with the help of two other students I started to mix up some bannock batter. It soon became apparent that the fire crew was struggling with getting the fire going, so I gave a mini lesson on fire building.

Finally our little fire began to burn. As I watched the smoke start to rise in bigger and bigger billows I wondered how long it would take before the campus security guards noticed and came running.

Would we be able to plead innocence to them, or bribe them with a piece of fresh bannock?

Then suddenly, with no warning, the enchantment happened.

The largest snowflakes I have ever seen in my life began to float down, and within less than a minute every towering concrete academic structure faded from our view and we could no longer see beyond the edges of our little forest. In seconds, we had all been transported deep into the Canadian wilderness.

The fire crackled and grew as we twisted bannock around sticks to bake near the fire's warmth. We pooled our knowledge, sharing how we could cook bannock in a variety of different ways. I offered around some moose jerky I had brought back with me from the far north, and got a few stories going. Our imaginations were captured as we shared tales of well-loved canoe trips and other travel adventures.

As the bannock turned golden, we continued to talk and share the fire's warmth while our eyes and noses caught snowflakes. Soon, we were sipping hot tea while we tore off pieces of raison bannock, savouring every morsel. As I looked around the campfire circle, I saw cheery faces chatting and laughing. No one seemed cold and my own hands were doing fine while poking at the fire occasionally with a stick. As the students gazed into the campfire, it reflected back upon their rosy faces. This was an ancient education full of the wisdom never found in lecture halls, but experienced in the bones. We talked of the important things in life: those things that seem most significant after a long day spent canoeing, portaging or hauling a toboggan.

Eventually it was time to go. Our newly bonded group was reluctant to leave our little winter oasis, but lectures and exams awaited beyond the forest's edge. One by one they headed off to classes in various lecture halls with their clothes saturated in the fragrance of a fresh campfire. Regretfully, we packed up the fry pans and doused the remaining flames with the last of the tea. We made sure the fire was out by scooping up some of the freshly fallen snow and the resulting hiss seemed to sigh "sorry you have to go, come back soon." I overheard many remarks about how this had been one of the best classes they had ever had. We laughed as we thought of new names for this university course: Bannock Making 101 or Winter Survival Skills on Academic Campus Terrain.

As we walked away from the forest, the snowflakes began to cease just as suddenly as they had begun. By the time we reached the pavement the sun had emerged, welcoming us with sunshine and blue sky. It was as if this little remnant of a forest had been enchanted all along and just needed a campfire, a few good stories and some laughter to remind it of its true heritage.

~Zabe MacEachren
Kingston, Ontario

23

The Harrowing of Hell

It is wild out there—there's a lot of misery on the weather map from coast to coast to coast. We'd sent out search parties looking for winter and we finally found it, and it's here, and it's beginning to bite us deep and hard.
~David Phillips, Climatologist for Environment Canada

Yet again you're awakened at 3 a.m. by the psychotic chirping of a huge machine backing up. It sounds like a duck being skewered without anesthetics. Yes, this is the snowplow; it arrives once again to clear the mini-mall lot behind your house in Vanier, just outside Ottawa. These snowplow operators seem constitutionally incapable of plying their trade here except between 2 and 5 a.m.

As awful as the chirping was, it's like melodious flute music compared to the feature event—the actual operation of the plow itself. A dozen times a minute, this battering ram on steroids revs up to 110 decibels as it pushes its load of snow over, under, around and through a lot half the size of a football field.

The plow operators must have been the stars of their auto mechanics stream in high school, you sourly reflect while debating taking a sleeping pill… the sort who put 400 horsepower motors into old Chevrolets, and squealed their tires wherever they went. Fearing that the pill will leave you too groggy to work, you opt instead for a generous slug of brandy.

Eventually you manage to nod off, only to be awakened to an

even more hideous noise. This is the scraping operation, where the plow actually bares the asphalt pavement, a process known as harrowing, shooting up a trail of sparks in the process.

Is it absolutely necessary to harrow this asphalt hell a fourth time? Midway through the fourth circuit the blade scrapes extra deep, resulting in a screech like an elephant undergoing root canal work and sending sparks fifteen feet into the air. Your lifelong support for strict gun control crumbles in the midst of this winter torture chamber.

You must do something, anything, to stop this horrific din and preserve your sanity. It's nearly 5 a.m. The fiends have been at it for two hours now. Rashly, you chug the rest of the brandy before racing to the living room screen door and opening it, disregarding the -25 degree temperature outside. Waving the empty bottle furiously, you roar a long volley of the foulest curses you can muster. The man just ignores you; the woman has the effrontery to laugh at you.

Aren't any of the neighbours bothered by this? Or have decades of late-night snowplowing left them all completely deaf? You're sorely tempted to fling the empty brandy bottle at your tormentors' heads. Instead, you yell out the screen door, "Don't you know some of us have real work to do tomorrow?"

"That's your problem, buddy," the simian plow operator says sourly. "Call the cops if you want."

"That's exactly what I'll do. And I'm not your buddy."

But when you call the cops, they say they can do nothing. "You should speak to the bylaw enforcement people," they say. When you finally get through to the bylaw enforcement people, they say the plow operators are perfectly within their rights.

"But isn't there a bylaw prohibiting loud noises after 11:00 p.m.?"

"There is, but snowplow operators are exempt from it."

"Even on a private lot?"

"Even on a private lot!"

"How's anybody supposed to get any sleep around here?"

"You can put in earplugs. Or move."

Slamming down the receiver in disgust at the bylaw staffer's sheer idiocy, you chug some Scotch, the only spirits you have left. Then inspiration strikes. As you're gloomily considering burning sick leave, you spy a cardboard box containing several cans of old tennis balls. In passing, you notice that the box also contains a dish belonging to a dog that formerly lived here. After emptying the cans of balls into the box, you again head toward the living room screen door.

"Last warning!" you call out surprisingly calmly to the snowplow operator, who's once again into his spark-shooting routine. "Better stop right now, or I'll do something you won't like."

"And what might that be?" demands the simian.

"That's for me to know and you to find out!" you say, starting to lob the balls out into the parking lot.

"Why are you doing that?" the man soon asks. The note of uncertainty in his voice is music to your ears.

"You'll find out soon enough," you say calmly, lobbing a couple more balls through the door. Then you call out in the general direction of the back stairs.

"Heinz! Sic balls, Heinz!"

"Who's Heinz?" the man demands. The smell of fear… how delicious it is.

"Just my little Rottweiler," you say, waving the empty dish for added effect. "I try not to feed him too much. Gotta keep him lean for hunting, you know. Heinz! Vorwärts! Du hass Arbeit zu tun!"

"What crazy language is that you're speaking?" asks the simian, who has stopped the plow and is devoting his full attention to what might be leaping out the sliding door.

At this you lower your arms in disbelief and start laughing—a full-bodied roar straight from the belly. First you slap your thighs; then you start rolling around on the floor. Now the snowplow operator is no longer questioning your sanity; he's fully convinced you've abandoned it.

"Heinz! I said Vorwärts!" As you shout out more of your movie German, you lob another half-dozen balls into the lot.

"I'll get you for this. You're littering!" the man wails.

"Littering? Don't make me laugh! You, the prince of every brand of pollution known to the human race, have the nerve to talk about having me charged for littering. Go right ahead—and I'll let people know what you've been doing around here. Tell your partner she can pick up the balls if she wants. Or has she gone home to bed, as any sane person would have done hours ago?"

"None of your damn beeswax."

"Temper, temper! Don't get nasty, or I'll have to take the next and final step."

"What's that?"

"Heinz is still chained up—luckily for you. I've just been trying to get his attention. But if I hear another word out of you, the chain comes off. Like I say, I don't feed him too much. When he's been bad, he has to catch his food himself. And he's been very bad lately."

"HEINZ! Mach schnell!" you shout in a voice that could rouse the dead. Then you walk purposefully toward the back of the house.

"Betty! Get in your car and get the blazes out of here!" The man shouts to his partner, who turns out to have been taking a lengthy smoke break at the far end of the lot. "We got ourselves a bloomin' nut case here!" As you laugh once again at this delicious bit of irony, he starts to turn the cumbersome plow around, in the process narrowly avoiding a collision with a huge, dark dumpster. Then, with a screeching of tires that would have done James Dean proud, he's off.

"And a Merry Christmas to you!" you shout out at the man as he speeds away, his partner in crime not far behind. As for you, you have a bit of celebrating to do. So you toast your deliverance with a final glass of Scotch. The hair of the dog, so to speak.

~Jon Peirce
Dartmouth, Nova Scotia

Own the Podium

I think it's only right that Canada should own at least one podium.
It's a big country.
~Author Unknown

John Furlong, the CEO of VANOC, the organizing committee for the 2010 Winter Olympics, is reportedly going to head Canada's Own the Podium program. Although Canadian athletes came through with a record number of gold medals in Vancouver, they did not win the overall medal tally. So if we really want to "own the podium" in 2014 in Sochi, Russia, perhaps Furlong should lobby to add some new events that we Canadians excel at to the roster of the next Winter Games. Events like:

Jumpstarting

There's no doubt that ski jumping is a dangerous and exciting sport to watch. But for a pure adrenaline rush, nothing tops the Canadian sport of jumpstarting. Each competitor is given an operational late-model vehicle and has to jumpstart a stalled car with a dead battery. This timed event requires a multitude of skills including locating the jumper cables, finding the hood latches and hooking up the cables. Do you ground the second cable, or connect it to a terminal? Do you leave your vehicle running while you try to start the stalled car? There's heartbreak for those who make the wrong choice. But gold awaits the savvy driver who can "turn over" an engine in record time.

Driveway Shovelling

Sure, curlers have to sweep. But there's really no better Canadian winter activity than snow shovelling. Like many Olympic events, this one has different divisions: the single-lane driveway shovel, the double-lane driveway shovel, and outdoor hockey rink snow clearing, a thrilling team event that requires co-ordination and co-operation. Finding that delicate balance between adequate dress and needed flexibility presents a challenge unknown in any other sport. A lost mitt or a frozen plug at the end of the driveway can spell the difference between gold and silver.

Ice Scraping

It's 7 a.m., -10 degrees Celsius, and the car is parked outside with half an inch of freezing rain coating its windows. How fast can you clear enough visible space to allow you to safely navigate the car through five miles of downtown traffic? Do you let the car's defroster do most of the work and lose valuable time? Or do you clear two square feet on the driver's side of the front windshield, and hope for the best? Those fastest out of the driveway are not always the first to cross the finish line, as the scattered ice-covered wrecks along the course will attest.

Washer Fluid Filling

Much as skiing gave birth to snowboarding, ice scraping begat washer fluid filling. Faced with a slush-filled obstacle course replete with water hazards and fountains, car-driving competitors try to gauge how much windshield washer fluid will get them to the finish line. Without the benefit of funnels or hoses, they must pour as much washer fluid into the reservoir as they feel they need. Then it's off to the races to see who can make it to the end without overusing the wipers or stopping for refills. One thing is certain: those who forget to top up their washer fluid at the starting line will not be medalling in this event.

Sidewalk Shuffling

A one-kilometre stretch of downtown sidewalk is hosed down overnight to present the trickiest slalom course in the world of recreational sports. Running next to a slush-filled street, the course tests the competitor's ability to stay upright while still avoiding waves of vehicle-launched icy, salty spray. This is a timed event, but there are also crucial style points awarded for fewest falls, fractures and clothing stains. Not only does the winner have to cross the finish line, he or she has to look good doing so.

Toddler Dressing
This is an early morning event requiring a combination of physical skills and patience. Presented with a two-year-old ready to be transported to day care, the parent-competitor has to first locate the various elements of the child's outerwear, including the snowsuit, scarf, toque, boots and both mitts. Much like Greco-Roman wrestling, the participant may use any of a number of non-choke holds on the child while simultaneously putting on each item of clothing. In the event of a tie, the finalists will battle it out by seeing who can buckle the toddler into a child's car seat the fastest.

Tire Changing
If there's one winter activity Canadians excel at, it's tire changing. Starting from a basement location, each competitor must haul up four winter tires to the family sedan in the driveway. Each wheel must be jacked up, and all four summer tires replaced with the winter tires. The summer tires must then be returned to the basement for winter storage. Two laps around a predetermined course will fully test the competitor's work. Lost lug nuts, wheel covers or car jacks can spell disaster for the participant or the car.

Faced with events like these, international Olympic competitors would not stand a chance against us hearty, winter-savvy Canadians, providing us with the best chance to "own the podium" at the next Winter Olympics.

~David Martin
Ottawa, Ontario

Bruno's Bruin

Camping: nature's way of promoting the motel industry.
~Dave Barry, Only Travel Guide You'll Ever Need

Being an avid outdoors person living in British Columbia, I agreed to be Bruno's guide on a backpacking climb in Manning Provincial Park. This is bear territory and he was anxious to "experience the wild" as he put it. Safeguarded with bear-bangers: "Sure thing to scare 'em off!" he pronounced, he demonstrated the shattering 'bang!' and brilliant red flare. I rolled my eyes; I never had use for these. At six-foot-three Bruno is a big guy, but I quickly realized just how fearful he was of these powerful animals. For my part, and you may laugh at this, I like to talk to bears. Silently. Ask permission to cross their grounds, while clanging Santa bells from my pack for extra measure.

It may have been July when we started, but up on Lone Goat Mountain it was winter. At day's end, tired from an arduous climb, we were greeted by a huge sky wafting delicate snowflakes. Beautiful! Rapidly though, storm conditions set in. Hurrying, we made base camp, melted snow for water, and soon had a freeze-dried meal boiling on the high altitude stove.

Again, Bruno explained how to use the bear-bangers before carefully positioning them along the inside edge of the tent. "For a quick grab," he said. "You never know." He looked at me, eyes clearly anxious, his voice tense.

"Stop worrying," I re-assured. "Bears are smart, and with all this snow pelting down, they'll be hunkered down already."

"But what if they're not? How can you be sure?"

With a sigh of exasperation, I almost scolded. "They will be! You can count on it!" Oh, this guy! Really! Why did I agree to bring him?

After we gulped down supper, my nervous companion fidgeted with our food bag to get it on the highest tree branch, calling over his shoulder. "Did you put the chewing gum in here too?"

"Yeah, yeah. Sure," I answered, rolling my eyes.

Returning, he removed his boots and climbed into his sleeping bag. I followed suit into the tent, taking the lee side. Thank goodness I did, too. We settled in, accompanied by the sounds of a now raging blizzard. The wind whacked against the tent and whistled over the Lightning Lakes far below, like a banshee in a foul mood.

Yanking down my wool hat, my last words were, "Imagine the view of the Hozameen Range peaks, come morning." At that, we were soon asleep in the dim light of our shelter, but not for very long.

I woke that night with an abrupt start. Above the ruckus of the blizzard, was that a moan? A grunt? I lay perfectly still and listened. Then I noticed something else. There was pressure against my right thigh, a bristly textured one, a hot-spot contact from outside of the tent's nylon wall.

"Oh, my God! Oh, my God!"

Any doubts as to what was transpiring dissipated with what came next. An eardrum-blasting snore! "Oh, Lord above!" The guttural in-breath, followed by the loud swooshes of out-breath set up waves that brought a revolting smell of yucky breath. This was no small animal; it brought to mind an oversized hog. But there were no hogs to be found up here. In a flash, my thoughts flew to Bruno. He was going to freak out! For sure, for sure, he would. Luckily, I detected no movement from his side. But if he woke up... Cripes, he would scream, jump for the bangers. What if he set them off in the tent? Our bacon would be cooked!

Gently, I elbowed Bruno and said with pretend bravado. "Shush!

Don't make a sound." No stirring, no reply. Wow! He was showing such restraint. I couldn't believe it! Good on him! Taking his silence to mean he'd do nothing rash, I turned my attention to assessment, damage control. This had to be a bear, and a big one. Black, Grizzly, or Kodiak, I didn't know, and it didn't matter. Snuggled against the tent, it would be asleep on its side. If suddenly disturbed, it could turn over, lash out. It would fling its great paw, with even greater claws, smack on the soft part of my midriff. I would scream, send it into confusion and further mauling. We would be goners.

I knew I couldn't pull away. Why hadn't Bruno taken this side? He was burly, and instinctively I wanted him to rescue me. With no shame at all, I desperately whispered. "Help! Help! Bruno. Do something!"

Bruno's calm perplexed me. What a show of restraint! At a complete loss, I finally resorted to my "tried and true" method with bears. Meekly, I commenced the mind-to-mind approach.

"Bear, you'll find better protection down the mountain! Big trees. Down. Go down!" I repeatedly urged. And then, unbelievably… success came. Finally. The contact against my thigh slackened. The hot spot cooled. The tent bulge disappeared. The taut nylon wall began to loosely flap. I wanted to yell with joy!

Rolling towards Bruno I yelled, "He's gone! He's gone! The bear's gone! Still nothing. And then I realized. All along, Bruno had accompanied Mr. Bear, forming an orchestra of snorers! Dumb-struck, I realized I had faced the ordeal totally alone! I wanted to beat Bruno to bits, there and then. Pummel him good. Grabbing him I shook hard, but to no avail. Finally, exhausted, I collapsed back on my sleeping mat.

At daybreak, when I finally shared the details with a yawning Bruno, they surely did send him leaping out like a jackrabbit—with my expletives chasing after him. "You no good son-of-a-gun! Bear-bangers! Ugh! You did nothing!"

"Where? Where? I don't see any tracks!"

To my dismay there were no tracks on the lee side, only fresh snow. But… we both saw them at the same time. Reaching down, Big

Bruno plucked three course dark hairs from the snow. With his eyes glued to them, cradled in his palm, he said. "How about we go back today?"

I smiled wryly. "Yeah. You non-defender of damsels."

"Honestly, I would have," came his earnest reply. Spread before us, the Hozameens sparkled like giant diamonds.

~Patricia A. Donahue
Vernon, British Columbia

My Downhill Racing Career

Eighty percent of success is showing up.
~Woody Allen

I am not an accomplished skier. In the hierarchy of skiers I probably fall into the category of advanced duffer. I first donned a pair of skis at age fourteen when I was visiting Brussels for my brother's wedding. His fiancée's father and her two brothers took me to the Ardennes. The long wooden skis they rented for me had no steel edges and were attached to the old lace up boots by something called rat trap bindings. I spent the better part of the day in a state of terror. I quickly learned to stop by means of the snowplow, which became my preferred manner of descent.

It was 1953 before I went skiing again, and actually bought a pair of wooden CCM skis in the Laurentians. Still no steel edges, I learned the telemark and how to turn using a stem Christie, which I used for years until a ski instructor on Grouse Mountain taught me the more simple and elegant parallel turn.

In the early 1980s a group of enthusiastic lawyers in Vancouver decide to hold an annual law firm ski race. Each firm would enter a five-member team, which had to include at least one woman and one member over fifty. One morning, four members of my firm strode into my office and explained the rules of the race to me. They also explained that, since I was the only lawyer in the firm over fifty who could ski, I was drafted as the fifth member. Saying no was not an option.

On race day I travelled with the team from Vancouver to Blackcomb. The race was scheduled for 2 p.m. so we spent the morning enjoying the slopes. I soon realized that the rest of my team were experts compared to me. A small woman, also on skis, was busy organizing the race, shepherding racers into the gates, supervising the starter and organizing the timing of the racers. As the morning wore on, I grew increasingly apprehensive.

There were two runs and so two starting gates. Two racers would race at the same time. A rope divided the tracks, and each track had a rope on the outside: so there were three ropes and two tracks. Each time a racer finished, his or her time was announced. By the time it was my turn the best time was down to one minute, forty-three seconds, a time achieved by a Norwegian lawyer who confessed he had started skiing at the age of three.

The day, which had started out mild, began to grow colder, and the tracks became icy. By the time it was my turn to race the earlier contestants had gouged serious ruts at each gate. I was anxious, but the rest of my team exhorted me to get to the finish line as best I could and not worry about my time. It was, they insisted, more important to finish and not be disqualified than it was to make good time. Only the times of the fastest three would count, but if I did not finish it would compromise the times of those three.

I was ushered to my starting gate. I looked over at the track next door and saw that Hamish Cameron was my racing opponent. He looked supremely confident. We grinned at each other. The command to go was given and off we went. I immediately realized that the course was far steeper than I was used to. I habitually chose gentle, wide sweeping slopes that caused me as little challenge as possible; slopes that had been groomed to perfection by the nocturnal snow cat. This slope was a black diamond affair and I was soon accelerating out of control. My heart was pounding at an alarming rate, not from exertion, but rather from the sheer fright of staring down at a slope that appeared to be about sixty degrees of churned up snow and ice.

I knew I would never be able to descend that hill at the kind of speed needed to register a respectable time.

When I reached the first gate I was horrified to see that earlier racers had gouged a deep rut around the poles. In a desperate attempt to regain some control before negotiating the gate, I resorted to my old snowplow routine to slow myself down. I staggered through the gate, gathered myself together and set off towards gate number two. Hamish, who had already reached it, seemed to be negotiating it in grand style. I was, by now, in a considerable panic and feared at least one broken limb, perhaps two.

When I saw Hamish barrelling down to gate number three I decided to go for broke and set off to try and catch him. It was at this point, as I reached a speed I swear I had never experienced before, that I glanced over the rope to my right and noticed that the small woman in charge, the one who had started us off, was now skiing down right beside my track. She was gesturing to me, beckoning me on and shouting, "Come on, faster, faster!"

She was going faster than I was, and then I realized that she was actually skiing backwards. Backwards: faster than me!

I finally made it through the last gate and saw below me a hundred yards of steep, wide snow straight down to the finish line. I thrust my poles under my arms and went into a tuck that I'd seen real racers use. Hamish won, but I had at least gained some ground on him.

The small woman, who had accompanied me backwards down the track, was already at the finish line. She grinned. "Well done," she said and grabbed the rope tow and was instantly whisked back up the hill.

I shuffled over to Hamish and congratulated him. "Hamish," I asked, "who was that woman skiing backwards beside us?"

"Oh, didn't you recognize her?" he grinned." That's Nancy Greene! She runs Blackcomb's customer relations department."

~David Roberts
West Vancouver, British Columbia

Editors Note: Nancy Greene (Raine) skied for Canada at the 1968 Winter Olympics and won the gold medal in giant slalom, and the silver medal in Slalom. She went on to become Canada's most decorated ski racer in history.

27

What Goes Up

Skiing combines outdoor fun with knocking down trees with your face.
~Dave Barry

Skiing was never one of my strengths. Oh I liked it well enough, as long as I felt I was in control. However, I frequently found myself not in control. Perhaps if I had started in my youth I wouldn't have had quite so many… "unusual" events linked to the slopes.

It always seemed strange that skiing did not come easily to me. I'm a dance and fitness instructor and, as my mother frequently pointed out, "Ellie, you have the rhythm and the strength!"

"Yes, that is true, Mom," I'd reply, "but I'm scared. I know all the moves and understand the strategy, but I'm still skiing mechanically, like a programmed robot with a stiff body to match. Maybe I should just stick to dancing!"

On this particular day, I was wearing a beautiful new ski outfit when I headed out for a day on the slopes with my partner. I looked great! The day started out in the usual way—with me having a small spill. This was normal. I found myself skiing too fast and got nervous, so I threw myself to the side. Then, not wanting to look like a coward, I agreed to get off the beginner slopes and be a bit more daring.

We chose a medium slope. My partner was skiing just a few meters ahead of me, and when he took a narrow curve, I followed him. Well, let me qualify that. I almost followed him. We were travelling at a good pace and I didn't want to lose him. But speed and I do not make a good match, and I simply shouldn't have tried to keep up.

Well, I didn't quite make that narrow turn, and, instead of going down, I found myself racing sideways across the slope. Suddenly there was no snow under my skis because my momentum had propelled me right off the run and I was now flying through the air heading for a clump of trees. I was airborne! When I finally stopped moving, I didn't know whether to laugh or cry.

Soon I heard my partner's anxious call, "Ellie, where are you?" When he noticed I was no longer following him he had to backtrack, a process that involved awkwardly sidestepping back up the slope.

"I'm here." I called out.

"Where is here?"

Well I was reluctant to tell him because my skiing finale, abruptly and surprisingly, had deposited me unceremoniously high up in the branches of a tree. I was wedged up there, a few meters above the snowline, with one ski extended on either side of the trunk, and me appearing to be an avid tree hugger.

Looking down I noticed that sticky tree sap was now smeared across the front of my beautiful new ski outfit. However, I was mostly surprised and more than a little grateful that both the outfit and my body seemed to have survived the flight and unusual landing.

"I'm kinda treed," was my response.

I'm glad I couldn't see his reaction to my news because I knew that when he finally spotted me, he'd quickly realize there was really no way he could help me. Extricating myself from the clutches of this tree was something I was going to have to handle alone.

It took me a while to figure out how to un-wedge myself and then climb down out of that tree. It was during my descent that I seriously considered hanging up my ski boots and sticking to the dance floor.

~Ellie Braun-Haley
Calgary, Alberta

It Was Only a Snowball

Great is the human who has not lost his childlike heart.
~Mencius

I leaned forward in my chair, listening to the plea from the young offender standing before me. "Please sir, it was only a snowball. I didn't mean to hit her."

I had just dealt with two other offenders for pushing people off snow hills, and I knew there were several more children waiting outside my office, preparing their explanations for violating playground rules.

It was early January and only my third day as principal at a public elementary school in Ontario's mid-northern snow belt. Just prior to Christmas I had been appointed to replace a retiring colleague, and had assumed my duties following the holiday break. I had hoped to make a good first impression with staff and students and develop a positive working relationship with all, but so far dealing with discipline problems following recesses had consumed much of my time. Things had to change!

Winter conditions on the playgrounds of Canadian elementary schools are generally harsh and create significant problems. Deep snow and constant below freezing temperatures are not conducive to children's outdoor play. My new school in Orillia was in the lee of Georgian Bay making us subject to frequent "lake effect" snow squalls that deposited large quantities of heavy wet snow.

From September to late October the students enjoyed playing on the grass and tarmac. Baseball, soccer, football, basketball and tag games kept them active and busy, while the teachers on recess duty circulated, interacting and keeping order. But in early November, snow and freezing weather would arrive, changing conditions dramatically and forcing us to cope with months of winter conditions. Although the school's entrance and walkways were cleared, the yard was snow-covered and students, deprived of their usual recess activities, became bored and prone to testing the rules. To compound matters, injuries resulting from students being hit by thrown snow or hurt while playing "king" of the snow hills had resulted in new rules forbidding these activities. This resulted in the line-up now outside my office.

As a "rookie" principal I did not want to be found violating policy, but the children clearly needed activities to keep them active and out of trouble.

As Canadians we have survived and thrived by learning to embrace winter and work and play with it. That tradition gave me an idea. My first plan involved my custodian and some of her metal garbage can lids. After school she and I took a half dozen and hung them from the baseball cages on the playground. We couldn't resist testing them. I can't imagine what passing community members, students, or departing teachers thought when they saw their new principal and the school's custodian throwing snowballs and high fiving when a gratifying clang signaled a hit. Those ball diamonds would become legally designated snowballing zones.

Next I inspected the "problem" snow hill at the rear of the schoolyard, the result of tons of the white stuff being plowed from the neighbouring Hydro Electric Service yard. It was at least two stories high, but very broad with many peaks and valleys, and of course it grew with every snowfall. It was a wonderful piece of natural playground equipment. We needed to use it as such.

The next morning I held a quick staff meeting before classes began. I explained my plan, and the teachers, seeing support for innovation, got on board and added ideas of their own. We followed up with a special student assembly, explained the new rules and sought their input. Many junior pupils wanted an area where they could build snowmen, sculptures and forts without fear of them being ruined by others. What a great idea!

The basic rules were kept simple and strict. If you wanted to throw snow you were welcome to use the target area only, and fire away until your arm fell off. Playing on the "Hydro Hill" was now encouraged, as long as a teacher was standing on top and you kept your hands off others while doing so. And a special area for building with snow was established. Some senior students volunteered to help the younger kids, and prevent interference with their creations. At recess that morning the plan went into effect.

I was stationed on top of the hill, while other teachers on duty supervised the new areas. It was soon clear the kids were all having a great time, but the bonus for me? Afterward, there was no post-recess line-up of offenders outside my office. Not only did outdoors behaviour cease to be a concern, classroom performance and school morale improved.

During my ten-year tenure at the school we faced and successfully overcame many learning and social difficulties. But to this day, I reflect most on resolving my first administrative challenge by embracing winter with a truly Canadian solution.

I must admit, I enjoyed being "King of the Hill," joining my students in the target zone, and thankfully having an acceptable explanation when my superintendent telephoned to investigate a complaint that the principal was throwing snowballs!

~John Forrest
Orillia, Ontario

A Ski Day with Dad

Not bad for a Canadian, eh?
~Steve Podborski

People must wonder when they see him. Did he make a mistake? Maybe he took a wrong turn. Surely he's not meant to be at the Sunshine Ski Resort. That poor old fella can hardly walk.

That poor old fella, he's my dad.

He's eighty-one years old. He skied forty-six times last season. His right knee is snuggled in a titanium brace, his left knee in a magnetic wrap, a double hernia belt holds in, you got it, the hernias, and most times he forgets to wear his hearing aids.

"How's it going? Last day of the season," I remark while I snap on my helmet.

"Skis, boots, pass," he mutters. That's his mantra before he leaves the parking lot. He forgot his ski boots once, back in Germany in the late forties. He got all the way to the top of the tram, walked out with skis and poles and looked down at his feet. Oops, he had on his after-ski boots. That day he didn't get to make the inaugural run in virgin snow; no first tracks for him.

"I'm hurrying," he says as he glances at all the cars parked beside us.

"No rush. The snow's not going anywhere," I assure him.

"We want first tracks," he whispers. His white, well-trimmed moustache twitches as he heaves his red parabolic skis onto his shoulder and grabs his poles.

"What are you waiting for? Let's go." His uneven, jerky stride takes him around the frozen tire tracks as he digs the hard toes of the ski boots in for traction.

I tense up when he falters. His poles are quick to stab the ground. He regains his balance and pauses. His ski jacket rises, then falls. An arm swings forward and he clomps on. Next are the steep, ice-crusted cement stairs. I cringe and hold my breath. He shifts the skis on his left shoulder, puts the poles in his left hand and grabs the railing with his right. It's a tedious process. I follow but not too close so he doesn't feel pressured to go faster. At the top of the stairs he turns his head to check around before he puts down his skis. He shuffles over to the gondola's line-up. Once we're settled inside the gondola, Dad continues his methodical checks.

I sit quiet.

In less than twenty minutes we'll be at the base of the ski resort where eight high-speed quad chairlifts can whisk us to the top of numerous runs.

I swallow hard. My ears pop. A raven soars above as we bump over the rubber tires on the tracks of another tower. Far below the tips of the spruce and pine trees resemble green daggers.

Dad finishes off with tightening the buckles on his boots.

Only then is he ready to discuss our plan of attack: where to ski first, what run will have the best snow, maybe even new snow. It's a tactical analysis that requires a great deal of serious deliberation.

A sudden wind sways the lift. It gives a brief sense of weightlessness, like when you jump up just before the elevator stops. I look down. Ten stories below the snow twinkles with mini-rainbows.

"It'll be cold." Dad pulls up his neck tube. We re-strategize our run selection to take into consideration potential wind drifts.

At the top Dad hauls his skis off the ramp and onto the snow, pulls them apart and clicks his boots into the bindings.

The transformation occurs. With the ease and grace of a seasoned racer he slides up to the chairlift line-up. Once the bar is down, Dad's shoulders drop. His breath comes out in slow white puffs. I point to the thick hoar frost that sparkles on the limbs of giant larch trees that pass by at eye level. The faint Christmas tree aroma of spruce and pine trees tickles our nostrils. Fresh corduroy runs groomed to perfection spread up to the peak of the Great Divide, an elevation of 8,900 feet. At the top, Dad adjusts his goggles and pushes off.

I watch him. He's in his glory. He's at home. At ease. Doing what he does best. Descending the mountain with the grace of an old European-style skier: a quiet upper body, close-together legs, precision parallel turns. He glides down the slope. He's easy to pick out amongst the more contemporary rigid forms that appear to be riding broncos as they make their way down, across and sometimes even up the hill.

It's a treat to watch him.

After a few turns I follow.

"Race you!" Dad tucks low, carves tight, back and forth. Must be a slalom race this time. He schusses through a finish line.

Run after run. Racing. Laughing. Playing. Jostling for the lead.

We take off into the moguls for a bit but not too long. His mind can tackle anything but his knees can't. We veer off to a smoother run.

While we ride up the chair, Dad nods at the thin wisp of clouds that cling to the summit of Mount Assiniboine. "She's wearing her crown," he remarks.

He's seen these surroundings a thousand times. He never gets bored. As a warden in the National Park, he'd spent his career working in the backcountry. If you don't acknowledge the mystic lighting on a peak he'll point it out for you.

"Look at Quartz Ridge. Looks like it slid last night." The grey-black speckled snow he studies appears to have peeled off a layer of the mountain.

"Remember the big avalanche?" Dad states more than asks.

I shake my head and grin under my scarf. "No. No I don't."

Dad carries on, relives the event and recaptures his past once more. The stories roll out like Santa's list as we chase each other down the hill, over and over again.

"One more?" I ask.

"We haven't tried Rolling Thunder," he points up the hill to a run that snakes through the thick forest. It has an aggressive fall-line. We will only do it once.

"Bet it's good." Dad heads to the lift.

I shake my head and call after him, "You are one crazy old man."

He laughs.

From the top of the Goat's Eye chairlift to the bottom of the ski-out, an eight-kilometer run, Dad carves his trademark turns. I cross them to make perfect figure eights, our signature to finish off the year. At the bottom, he looks back up the mountain.

"Wunderbar!" His moustache twitches above a huge grin. He pops out of his bindings. A couple good taps shake the loose spring snow off his skis before he heaves them over his shoulder. His right hand clutches his ski poles and he swings them forward. The momentum propels his ski boots to take a step. He's slower now as he shuffles his way across the parking lot.

A few snowboarders, with snow pants that hang low on their bums, watch him.

"Poor old guy. He can hardly walk." They shake their heads.

~Barbara Wackerle Baker
Calgary, Alberta

30

Winter Dragon

You haven't been bit till a dragon does it.
~Tamora Pierce, Emperor Mage

A late spring storm has swirled in and left behind drifts galore. Sunshine sparkles on the snow and makes for a brilliant day. I'm happy for one last chance to try my luck with the snow blower. So far this season, mastery of the mighty beast has eluded me.

The snow blower is like a winter dragon that lets stinky, flatulent fumes fly from one orifice. From its snout shoots a great sluice of snow. Its roaring never ceases. I'm a small, five-foot-two, one hundred and twenty-five pound woman. The snow blower weighs one hundred and fifty pounds, and is a huge hulk, heavy to maneuver. Still, I'm undaunted—and up to the challenge!

In the garage, I start up the engine then move out onto the driveway. I point the dragon towards the street, grab the "reins," "crack the whip" and we're off, but immediately there's trouble. A mighty wind is blowing and snow is shooting from its gaping gullet back onto me and into the open door of the garage. I'm okay. I have goggles, gloves and really good winter gear. But, the garage now has a dump of snow in it, and I know I'll have to dig it all out later. Sighing, I stop the beast, go into the garage, shut the big main door and try to shake off this unfortunate start to the day. You would think this dragon, with all his mighty blasting force, could blow back against the wind.

We continue to labour up and down the driveway at a solid pace, me hanging on and leaning back, like a plowman in a field pulled along by the oxen. At each turn my heart pounds and I'm sure my blood pressure rises, as I frantically manoeuvre to both turn the huge beast and adjust the spewing snout at the same time. Somehow I manage to complete our driveway, and if that hasn't been challenging enough, I decide to do my neighbour's as well!

As we trot down the sidewalk, I notice clods of black earth and frozen grass flying onto the white snow. Bloody hell! He's edging the lawn as well as plowing the snow! I quickly re-aim the dragon down the middle of the sidewalk. Ever the optimist, I reflect that there will be one less job in spring, until I suddenly I realize he hasn't cut a straight line. Now, I'm thoroughly annoyed. But what can I do? I'll assess the damage in spring. Thank goodness it's our lawn and not the neighbour's.

On my neighbour's driveway, the process continues as wildly as before. Up and down we go until the last pass down. I'm on the home stretch! Suddenly my feet shoot out from under me. I land hard on my bum on solid ice, but that dragon just keeps going like a runaway team.

"Stop! Stop," I yell, but language is useless with this wretched beast. On and on I slide until suddenly I remember, I need to let go. Like all problems, "letting go" quickly solves it. The animal abruptly halts. I get up slowly, with a sore tailbone and bruised pride.

On the way home, the dragon behaves better than he has all day. I finally remember the old axiom about slow and steady. No longer in a rush, we walk easily down the centre of the sidewalk back to the stable. The dragon will sleep now, hibernate for the summer. But I'm sure that next winter with a little tune-up, he'll be rumbling and snorting for action. I'll remember that it's okay to walk on a sunny winter's day.

~Carol Kavanagh
Saskatoon, Saskatchewan

31

Chicken Soup for the Soul

A Winter Moon

... And if we wrapped up against the cold, we wouldn't feel other things, like
the bright tingle of stars, or the music of the Aurora...
~Philip Pullman, The Golden Compass

I am not in the habit of setting my alarm and rousing my family at 2:30 in the morning, but in the early hours of December 21, 2010, I did just that. My sleepy boys, aged thirteen and eleven at the time, put on hats, mittens, coats and boots over their pyjamas while my husband and I collected binoculars and set up the telescope.

Forecasters had said that the moon on this night, just days before Christmas, would be unparalleled. It was the first time in almost four hundred years that the lunar eclipse would occur on the winter solstice. It promised to be a spectacular sight, truly a once-in-a-lifetime event, and I did not intend to miss it.

Special events have taken on a whole new significance since I was diagnosed with a terminal illness in 2008. I carry the word "terminal" like a heavy stone in my pocket, and the question that begins with "Will this be my last...?" hangs in the air like a constant cloud over my head, despite my best efforts to remain positive. As a result, every special occasion has come into sharper focus, and I have found a deep motivation to make these occasions truly special and memorable. I've learned that now is the time to cherish those closest to me and to offer them enough gratitude to last a lifetime; now is the time to do the things I've always wanted to do, and now is the time to give my boys and my husband all the unconditional love my heart can hold.

My goal each morning is to squeeze every last drop of joy out of the day.

And so, there we stood, looking like four Newfoundland mummers on a frosty, winter night, our eyes fixed heavenward. The moon glowed with a copper-orange light, which I read was the reflection of every sunrise and sunset occurring on earth at that moment. Unlike the usual flat disc we are so accustomed to, on this night the moon appeared as a beautiful, luminous ball, a Christmas ornament for all the world to share.

The cold quickly worked its way through our layered clothing, and it wasn't long before we trundled back into our warm house and cozy beds. Christmases have come and gone, each one a blessing filled with traditions and magic. Memories melt into one another like snowflakes. But I will never forget the December of 2010, when just a few days before Christmas, I was moon-struck.

~Joanne Webster
Orillia, Ontario

Boys into Bear Cubs

A friend is a brother who was once a bother.
~Author Unknown

It had been a very long year parenting my two teenage sons. A single mom, I often felt the weight of the day-to-day burden of guiding, helping, disciplining, and raising two boys in a town of 80,000 in central Ontario. In many ways my boys were oil and water, each one's needs seeming to grate upon the very soul of the other. For a number of years I wondered if they would ever be friends the way my siblings and I are. The older one was doing the obnoxious teenage things we all worry about, and the younger one passed up no opportunity to tell his brother what he thought of him.

"This is the only brother you have," I would remind them. "You will have each other for your whole lives. You guys need to be friends."

"No way," one of them would say. "He's a creep."

Then came the Christmas holidays. Eager to try anything that might ease the tension and offer a fresh perspective for our family, I booked us into a resort near Horseshoe Valley. On Boxing Day I loaded the boys and their gear into my car and we drove north to ski country, staying near the slopes. After a day of racing down double-black-diamond hills, the frost between the two brothers had almost begun to thaw.

The next day I said, "Okay, we're going out to play in the snow and take a hike. Put on your snow clothes."

"I'm too tired," complained one.

"I don't want to," whined the other.

So out we went anyway.

Deep snow, sunshine through the trees, rocks to climb, snow piles to dig into surrounded us. Within twenty minutes, my sophisticated, worldly-wise, moody teenage boys became bear cubs: jumping, running, falling, climbing, and digging. One slid down a steep bank, the other found a branch and extended it to pull him back up. My heart melted as I watched my young men playing like they had when they were little. Afraid to break the magic, I did not say a word. I watched them play, and my heart rejoiced. Snowballs, snow caves, playing tag in hip-deep snow. They were having fun with one another!

The miracle had happened. Away from suburban life, away from the distractions of computers and friends, my sons began to relate in a healthy, playful, and loving way again. We stayed out in the snow and cold until the boys were rosy-cheeked and soaked through. Then we headed in for hot chocolate and a roaring fire. Gone were the enemies they had become. The picture of them tromping back to our room through the snow, arms around each other's shoulders, still brings tears to my eyes. Who knew it could be this simple?

My boys are young men now, and still working at their friendship. They don't always see eye to eye, although more and more they enjoy one another's company. But I give thanks for the gift of healing brought by a Canadian winter's day, the romp in the snow that gave my sons back the gift of a brother.

~Deborah Kinsinger
Newmarket, Ontario

Polar Plunge

Winter is not a season, it's an occupation.
~Sinclair Lewis

When we moved onto our acreage just north of Cochrane, Alberta in the spring of 1994, we were enamoured by the 180-degree view of the Rocky Mountains to the west of us and the beauty of nature surrounding us. While planting my first garden and watching my children chase gophers around the yard I thought this had to be the most idyllic lifestyle I could ever imagine.

We spent many evenings that summer sitting on our deck, listening to the yipping of nearby coyotes, and later, when the leaves turned colour in the fall, we took long walks and marveled at the Northern Lights. Having grown up in Calgary, I knew winter was just around the corner, but after having spent those memorable first few months enjoying our new home, I pictured an equally tranquil winter scene, curled up by the hearth, sipping hot chocolate and watching silent snowflakes flutter by our window as we remained cozy inside.

We had just finished the Thanksgiving turkey in October when the north wind blew in strong and fierce. And the list began. The walls around our house were not as well insulated as we thought. As ice started to form on the inside of the windows, my husband added "replacing windows in spring" to the growing list of "to-do's." When the first major snowfall hit in November and the snow blower the previous owners had left us refused to churn through the cement snow drifts, my husband added "buy a bigger snow blower."

As the snow accumulated in front of our house so his tractor couldn't even clear a path, we parked our vehicles at the top of the driveway and trudged through knee-deep snow and minus twenty-degree temperatures to get to our cars. The weatherman called it a Polar Plunge. I had more descriptive terminology for the weather, as I slid on my backside, yet again, carrying groceries from the end of the driveway to our front door. The bruises on my derriere were starting to add up.

A couple days after Christmas, a Chinook blew in from the west. "Snow Eater," as the natives call it, chewed a huge swath of snow down our long driveway and we were finally able to move the cars into a warm garage. The melting snow ran in rivulets around our yard, and the temperature rose to a balmy 2 degrees Celsius. We wrestled the kids into their snowsuits and we built snow forts and snowmen and finally experienced the winter scene I had always imagined in our new home… at least for a few days.

On New Year's Eve the temperature plummeted, the snow fell yet again, and the frigid north wind whistled and whipped the house with ferocity. We watched helplessly as roof shakes blew across the yard. My husband added, "Replace roof in spring" to the now lengthy list. When our son's plastic sandbox blew past, I added, "Buy new sandbox too."

I had never seen six foot drifts before, but on New Year's Day there they were, like mountains in the middle of our driveway. With no snow blower to dig us out, we were in a quandary how to get the cars out of the garage again. My husband bundled up and started to shovel. The kids and I watched him from a window as he struggled with the heavy snow, the wind kicking up whirling vortexes of white twisters all around him. It was a valiant attempt but after breaking one snow shovel… I added that to the list… I thought our only hope would be for another Chinook to blow in or we would be snowed in forever. He pointed a mittened hand and yelled at me through the window, "Add… buy snow fence for next year!" and obediently I wrote that on the list.

My husband managed to find another old snow shovel in the garage and in a fit of insanity I thought I should go out and help the man. I don't know what I was thinking; perhaps it was the fact that he was braving the elements and I was warm inside. I pulled on my coat, toque, mitts and scarf and thought that my presence outside would somehow lift his spirits. We were a team and we would accept this snow-clearing challenge together, even if there was only one snow shovel between us.

No sooner had I stepped out the front door, than a powerful gust of wind blasted me from behind, and catching my winter coat like a sail, picked my body up and blew me head first into a snow bank. Try as I might to regain my footing, the wind kept battering me back until finally I had to crawl on my hands and knees to the front door where I finally collapsed in a heap. It was only my pride that was hurt, but my ears certainly stung by the sound of my husband's hysterical laughter and my kids waving and pointing at me. Still, I like to think that it was my "polar plunge" that was just the comic relief we all needed to get us through that long, cold winter.

~Lynn Dove
Cochrane, Alberta

Chapter
4

O Canada
The Wonders of
Winter

Childhood Memories

In childhood, we press our nose to the pane, looking out. In memories of childhood, we press our nose to the pane, looking in.

~Robert Brault, www.robertbrault.com

34

Oh to Play for the Canadiens

We played because we had nothing better to do. Our heroes were the guys who were ahead of us at the local rink. It was always just about the next step.
~Wendel Clark

Growing up in Sault Ste Marie, Ontario, the city operated outdoor rinks at just about every ballpark and playground. On cold winter days from blocks away you could hear the cracking sound of ricocheting pucks echoing off the boards, and the sharp hiss and schussing of skates cutting into the ice during Saturday morning shinny. Shinny is generally a very democratic sport. Hockey sticks were thrown into a pile in the middle of the rink and the smallest kid dealt them like cards to each side of the imaginary centre ice red line. I was the smallest kid on the ice and still unsteady on skates.

One sunny frosty Saturday morning at the North Street rink, the big guys put me in goal. There was a certain master skater and puck handler on the other team. This true wizard of puck control was visiting a cousin and was new to our rink. All the players on both teams were in awe of him. He was a joy to watch. They called him Philly.

Early in the game on a breakaway, Philly whistled in on me, stick handled left right, left right, left right sending me sprawling in one direction, and my stick in the other. He stopped and tapped the puck against my toe and said, "Nice save, kid."

That gesture gave me the confidence to actually make some real saves later in the game. Philly was a hero to me and to all of the other players. Every boy there, including me, dreamed of being in the NHL.

Every night, the North Street rink scheduled hockey from five till seven, skating till nine, hockey till ten, then lights out. On weekends I skated with friends, then played hockey, and after everyone left, I dipsy-doodled from end to end alone in the dark, stick handling the black puck on the white ice. Laying down on the ice and looking at the stars in the crystal night air I listened to the Algoma Central Railway diesel engines off in the distance straining, pulling the long line of empty ore cars up over the height of land and into the rolling hills en route to Hawk Junction, Wawa, and Michipicoten Harbour. Around midnight I would then walk home in my skates, squeaking sounds amplified in the 20 below temperature. One day I would wear the red white and blue Canadiens sweater worn by the likes of Jacques Plante, Maurice Richard and Boom Boom Geffrion.

Eleven years later Philly was a scoring star for the Chicago Blackhawks. It turned out his full name was Phil Esposito. I, much younger, played for the Crusaders in the Midget League. We wore the Montreal Canadiens' sweater with a big C on the front, standing for our team name. It was the last game of the season in Sault Michigan where our team had just lost a big tournament by one goal. I, the goalie, was sitting in the dressing room mentally replaying my one big mistake when in walked Scotty Bowman, the scout for the Montreal Canadiens. Scotty Bowman… future multiple Stanley Cup winner. The Canadiens! My team! Mon équipe! I sat upright beaming expectantly.

Mr. Bowman walked straight towards me, reached into his wallet and pulled out his card. The beloved red CH image flashed as it went right under my nose. Michel Paquin, our secret import from Quebec, sitting on the bench beside me, gratefully accepted it.

Scotty said to him, "I would like to meet your parents."

Maybe I gave up too early, but sadly, at that moment, a light went on in my head. I wasn't going to make it. I can say though that I did sniff the big time. It was right under my nose.

Twenty-eight years later, I was boarding an Air Canada flight out of Sault Ste. Marie. When I sat down, to my surprise I found myself sitting beside the fast forward, "Philly." I waited until we were airborne, looked at him and said, "Hey. I've played against you."

I could see him wracking his brain through thousands of professional games. I laughed and said, "The North Street outdoor rink."

He shook his head and said, "You know, playing shinny in the Sault was the most fun I had playing hockey."

My secret remorse for not making the NHL evaporated.

I told this same story to my friend Dennis Hull, a former Chicago Blackhawk, brother of Bobby and member of Team Canada in the 1972 Russia series. Dennis in his wisdom added that maybe the reason I didn't make the NHL is that he and his brothers would play on their outdoor rink till 2:00 a.m., not midnight.

"You quit too early," he laughed.

~Lloyd Walton
Port Carling, Ontario

35

The Duck at the Top of the Stairs

I deeply believe that when one seeks and touches and feels the ordinary
things and events in life, they become the extraordinary. Existence itself is
the extraordinary miracle.
~Roy MacDonald

Our worst fears had been realized. Last night the temperature had finally dropped, cold enough to freeze. In the frigid morning air we anxiously made our way to the pond—and found the ducks huddled together in the centre, half-dead with cold. Their feet were trapped in a layer of thick slush, which was slowly freezing to ice.

Our hobby farm lay just north of Toronto in the little community of Sharon, Ontario. The ducks had joined my family early in the summer, a present from my father, bought from the local farmer's market. They were a mating pair, beautiful white ducks with bright yellow legs and orange bills.

The large pond lay in a clearing in the woods behind our house, and the ducks had immediately made it their home. All through the long hot summer, when my sister and I delighted in picking our way through the woods to fish or swim, they were always there. We loved watching them as they entertained themselves paddling in perfect lines from one end to the other, dabbling in the shallows, or preening themselves comfortably on the bank.

But the soft greens of summer had turned to the bright colours of an Ontario fall. Suddenly, winter was upon us and still the ducks hadn't left the woods. Although we tried, it had been impossible to catch them, and now they were trapped and freezing.

That's when my mother stepped in. Like always, she knew exactly what to do. She sent me running back to the house for the antique carriage whip her father had given her. When I brought it back she stretched herself out like a seal on the ice, and then crawled steadily forward until the ice was too thin to support her. By then she could reach the ducks with the whip, and she used it to tap them on the legs. It wasn't gentle, but it did the trick. Slowly, one at a time, my mother prodded the ducks out of the freezing slush. As we watched in relief, they staggered across the ice to the shore.

I was just a child, but I remember distinctly the sight of my mother, wet coat open to the wind with one shivering, miserable duck stuffed under each arm. Once back in the warm house we made a makeshift nest for them in the basement, using newspaper and towels, and brought them food and water.

The ducks huddled together on the towels in the warm basement. Chunks of ice stuck to their wings. They were too cold and exhausted to even quack.

We decided to leave them alone to warm up and recover, while we ate a very late breakfast. We knew they had enough food and water — and were probably frightened out of their wits — so we didn't go down to the basement again that day.

That evening we were reading by the fire in the living room, when we heard a strange sound on the basement stairs. There was kind of a "smacking" noise, then a pause, then the smacking sound again. Over and over.

"Could that be the ducks?" my mother asked my father as they went to investigate.

It was indeed the ducks — at least one of them. The big male duck was standing on the second-highest step, bobbing and flapping his wings for balance. He gathered himself and made the difficult leap to the highest step, the source of the strange "smacking" noise.

When he saw my parents he didn't go back down, but started quacking frantically, beating his wings until he tipped back and forth with the effort. It quickly became obvious that he wanted my parents to follow him.

Once they began moving towards him, the duck turned and immediately began hopping down the stars again, looking over his shoulder from time to time to make sure they were right behind. About halfway down to the basement my parents discovered what had driven him up the stairs.

It seemed we had carelessly left our fishing rods leaning against the wall, quite near where the ducks were bedding. Somehow the female had got herself tangled up in the fishing lines. She was now lying on her back on the floor with her yellow feet completely bound up in the nylon line. Her wings were spread out to help support her, her eyes fixed upon my parents in a pathetic plea for help.

It took a pair of scissors and many minutes to get the line off, and all the while her mate looked on, waiting for us to free her. The instant the female duck could stand again she rushed over to her mate. They spent a while quacking quietly to each other, and touching their beaks as if confirming that the other was indeed all right.

The second rescue of the day accomplished, my family stored the broken rods safely out of the way, and leaving the two ducks to their gentle reunion, we went back to reading by the fire.

Several years have passed since that night. During this time, I've met many people who think animals are stupid, that they don't understand compassion, or kindness; that they can't feel trust, or gratitude, or love.

I know they're wrong and I have all the proof I need. It happened one winter's night when a duck saved his mate by climbing the stairs.

~Leah Silverman
Canadian living in College Station, Texas, USA

The Miracle Coat

The human race has one really effective weapon, and that is laughter.
~Mark Twain

In the autumn of my seventh year, I needed a new winter coat. The coat I had worn to kindergarten—swing-skirted, sapphire blue (and with a dear little grey squirrel collar) no longer fit me.

So, Mother and I made the trip from the Dickie Settlement, as it was called then, across the Grand River and into the town of Galt. When we arrived at the dressmaker in town, Mother instructed them to "Make Dolly a hat and coat set, and make it big enough to be let out later on."

The Great Depression of the 1930s was upon us and Ontario was no different than anywhere else. Clothes were let out, turned, mended, remodelled and handed down several times before they were finally cut up for dusters. The best materials might end up in patchwork quilts or rag rugs. Dollars had to be stretched.

A week later, Father drove to town and returned with my new hat and coat. I put it on, stood before the full-length mirror in my parents' bedroom—and cried buckets. I hated the outfit.

Made of navy blue chinchilla cloth, it was a dull successor indeed to my swing-skirted, sapphire blue (with a dear little grey squirrel collar). Its "reefer" style, worn by both girls and boys, was what I found hardest to accept. I had seen pictures of moustached artists wearing floppy smocks and the same type of idiotic beret that accompanied my new coat. In total contempt, I refused to wear the rig.

Our Bible text on the following Sunday was: "Ask and ye shall receive." Then and there I decided to start a prayer campaign. From then on, each night, after the "Our Father" and the God blesses, I tacked on a postscript: "Please God, send me another coat." Pondering over the matter, I decided that since I was petitioning the highest power, I might as well ask for the best.

The next night, I made a revision. "Dear Lord," I prayed, "Please send me a fur coat."

Only God and I knew about this prayer. Had Mother known, she would have said with a practically born of necessity and experience, "You may as well ask for wings to fly to the moon. There's a depression on."

Then one day, The Miracle happened. Father drove to town, where he went from house to house offering Dooley and Irish Cobbler potatoes for a dollar per hundred-pound bag. At noon he stopped at Grandmother's house for lunch. When he was about to leave for home, Grandmother handed him a large bolster case saying, "There are some things in there for Dolly to play with."

Father brought the bolster case into our warm kitchen and spilled its contents onto the pine floor. High-heeled shoes, fancy dresses, purses and hats (all cast off by my aunts) spilled out and delighted my little girl heart as I looked forward to playing "dress up."

There was still a great lump in the bottom of the bolster case. A mighty tug from Father brought Aunt Charlotte's old raccoon coat into view. At that moment, only God and I knew The Miracle was happening.

It was miles too big of course. As soon as I saw it, I decided to be more specific in future prayers and give all-important details, especially sizes.

As the winter wore on, the coat hung in an upstairs closet and became more of a burden than a pleasure. It haunted me. God had sent what I asked for, and Conscience said it would be only polite to wear it — at least once.

One morning in early March, after a night of wet snow and high winds followed by a blast of arctic air, day dawned on fields covered with a sun-buttered crust. I put on my fur coat, left the house, and slipped and slid across the glossy fields to visit our neighbour. The snow's hard crust supported me, but in order to climb the rise where the two farms joined, I had to punch holes in the surface with my heel, go down on all fours and pull myself forward. At last I made it to the crest, but upon attempting to stand up, I lost my balance and found myself rolling swiftly downward.

As I spiralled downhill, then floundered to get to my feet, a CNR passenger train whistled and roared as it sped past along the rails a few hundred yards in the distance. Astounded passengers were lined up with their noses at the train's windows. They had witnessed my whirling and twirling descent.

The next day, Mother pored over the local *Galt Daily Reporter* and read aloud accounts of the storm. One article told of a startling scene witnessed by passengers and crew of a train travelling through a rural district. They reported seeing "a large animal of unknown species" sliding downhill and then floundering in a field.

The general conclusion was that it was something blown in during the storm from far north.

Farmers kept guns at the ready for several months after, but to everyone's relief, the creature was never seen again.

~Dorothy MacAulay
Cambridge, Ontario

Wonder Mom

Unconsciously, Canadians feel that any people can live where the climate is gentle. It takes a special people to prosper where nature makes it so hard.
~Robert MacNeil

It was a Friday morning in January of 1977. Gigantic snowflakes swirled into drifts across the deck outside our kitchen window. I crunched my Flintstones vitamin and listened to the radio announcer list all the cancelled buses in Prince Edward County in southern Ontario, fingers crossed. At last he said, "6G."

I stopped listening. Craig and I jumped up and down, sloshing milk from our cereal bowls onto the table. Daddy declared he was off to work and later to the Oyster Stag at the Yacht Club in Picton. Mom frowned.

No doubt there would be a crowd of loud men, lots of food and an endless supply of Canadian on tap where Daddy was going. I pictured Fred Flintstone in a tall, furry hat on his way to the Lodge of the Loyal Order of Water Buffaloes, as Mom closed the front door with a bang. She sent Craig and me to the basement. In our pajamas. Without even brushing our teeth!

The morning unfolded in a series of game shows, cartoons and floor hockey downstairs. Bologna sandwiches with mustard in front of the television for lunch. I was over the moon. If only *Wonder Woman* had been on instead of *The Flintstones*.

Wanting to check on the snow, I skipped upstairs. Mom sat at the kitchen table, where I think she had been stationed since Daddy left, with a coffee mug glued to her hand. The windows rattled. Wind howled as it often did from across Lake Ontario and over the Sandbanks toward our house, only louder than I'd ever heard it. This was the best snowstorm ever!

Mom puffed one cigarette to its end and lit another. I leaned against her shoulder. "I thought you quit."

She crushed out the barely-smoked butt, reached for my hand and pulled me closer.

"Mom, is everything okay?" I asked.

She spoke into the top of my head, "Of course it is. How could it not be on a day like this?"

The house creaked as Mom got up and led me to my room. I took *Alligator Pie* from my bookshelf, and then Mom handed Mrs. Beasley to me as though the doll were real. I hugged her to my chest. A great sense of comfort wrapped around me like a blanket, and Mom headed back to the kitchen.

Hot dogs for supper without Daddy seemed wrong. As Mom tucked me into bed that night, she wrinkled her lips and said, "Your father is stranded in town. At the Oyster Stag." She kissed my forehead. "Sweet dreams."

I snuggled in deeper with Mrs. Beasley.

By Saturday morning, Daddy still wasn't home. I knew he'd be back. Nothing could stop him.

From her post, Mom said to my brother and me, "You two can have whatever you want for breakfast, downstairs."

I looked at Craig. Together we sang out, "Froot Loops!"

Mom agreed and reached for the bowls without hesitation. I made a face and she smiled back. "Special treat."

Life couldn't get any better than this.

That afternoon, dressed in Mom's nurse's cape, I sat on the basement floor in a pile of clothes from the dress-up closet. The phone rang and soon Mom called down, "Can you kids come up here, please?"

We clomped up the stairs. "Mom, what is it?" I asked.

She dragged her cross-country skis from the front hall closet. "I have to go out. The neighbours can't get home. They want me to go next door to see if their lights are still on. They're worried about the pipes freezing."

Eagerly I said, "I can go with you!" The scrunched look on her face said "no" before she opened her mouth.

Mom wriggled into her lime green and brown ski pants and jacket. Then she pulled on Daddy's balaclava over her goggle-sized glasses. I laughed. She looked ridiculous! When she opened the outer storm door, a drift as high as the doorknob spilled across the tiles to the edge of the carpet. Climbing up and over it, she shoved her way out into the storm.

There was nothing to see through the front picture window but a shifting wall of white. We waited. And waited. Finally, the front door burst open and Mom reappeared, covered. Snow cascaded across the floor and past the edge of the carpet. Mom leaned her skis in the corner by the door and slapped her hands on her hips, her eyes focused in a serious look. Just like Wonder Woman.

Wonder Mom to the rescue! "Did you see the lights?" I asked.

She rubbed her temples. "No, I got lost. I didn't even get out of our yard." Slowly she grinned.

Sunday arrived and still no Daddy. His phone calls were not enough. Mom seemed frazzled. Snow blocked every window and door in the house. Craig had become annoying and I was bored. Sunday afternoon TV was awful, and the stations didn't come in clearly no matter which way I turned the rotor. Daddy needed to get home before bedtime.

That evening, the sound of skidoos whined outside. The engines stopped. I rushed to the front hallway and waited with Mom and Craig. We opened the inner wooden door and heard the crunch-swish of shovels. At last I saw the tip of a shovel, then a boot, then Daddy's nose smooshed against the glass like a kid. Daddy was home!

A week after the storm hit, Mom held my gloved hand tight as the whole family headed to the end of the laneway. Joining with all our neighbours, we watched the huge snowblowers and plows from

CFB Trenton clear the West Lake Road. As the soldiers worked and waved, above the groans of machinery, came a collective cheer for the heroes who had come to free us from the remnants of the storm.

It wasn't until years later I discovered just how protective Mom had been. For her, the storm of 1977 was a time of immeasurable anxiety and fear. Would the power go out? Or the phones? Did we have enough oil in the tank? And food? Would we stay warm? She had never been so overwhelmed as a mother, or so alone.

Ever since then, Mom makes sure to always have at least a month's worth of supplies and food in the house, no matter what the season. Stocking up in case of emergencies became the norm. It still is. But the real lesson—the true gift she gave to me—came from a mom's love: During that storm, and for decades after, Mom preserved the innocence of the experience for me like a true superhero.

This is the memory I hold dear in my heart.

But do I think Wonder Mom deserves a new cape, and maybe some shiny red boots.

~Susan Blakeney
Toronto, Ontario

Namesake in a Legend

From the time I first saw Barbara Ann Scott, she was everything
I wanted to be. She seemed to be the perfect Canadian girl. She was my
role model, no question about it.
~Marilyn Bell Di Lascio

I t was March 1958 in Banff, Alberta. The headlights faded into the blackness of the mountain night as the 1948 Chevy crept along the highway, its wipers defenseless against the snowflakes plastering the windshield.

John, my soon-to-be father, gripped the smooth steering wheel and maneuvered the heavy car through the thick slush that sucked at the tires. He strained to catch a glimpse of a recognizable landmark, any recognizable landmark. The front right wheel caught in a heavy drift at the edge of the shoulder. The car tilted. Dad held his breath. With white knuckles and muscular arms he cautiously steered the car to the left.

"Ja. Ja." He puffed out stale cigarette breath. His back ached. His eyes burned. He leaned forward and swiped his hand across the fog on the windshield.

"There, the *licht von das* power house." The eerie glow of the transformers floated by the passenger window. "*Wir haben* enough gasoline."

Stretched out in the back seat, his young wife, Ilse, my soon-to-be mother, clutched the bottom of her swollen belly. She too held her breath.

I gave her a gentle kick to ensure she knew I wanted to come out soon.

"Hurry," she moaned. "*Es kommt.*"

Dad stretched his neck forward like a hungry chicken. His left work boot tapped the high-beam button. A sky full of huge snowflakes pelted the windshield blinding him as they plopped and slid down the glass.

He switched back to dims.

The wipers squeaked as they smeared across the pitted window. Dad strained to see.

"*Schnell,*" Mom urged. "Hurry. Hurry."

I was their second child, a boy for sure and obviously quite an impatient one.

And then Dad saw it—the flashing yellow light that signalled the approach to Banff's traffic circle. He steered the sedan towards the exit. Flakes streaked down the windows as the car bounced over the train tracks.

The car inched by the faint lights from the Mount Royal Hotel and the dark shadows of closed storefronts as the tires slid through the heavy slush of Banff Avenue. The car crept across the Bow Bridge and then after a sharp left turn, the rear end fishtailed its way up the hill. It chugged, sputtered and lurched forward as it skidded to a stop at the deserted hospital entrance.

Dad rushed out.

He opened the back door and grasped Mom's hands, pulling her up and out of the seat. He wrapped his arm around her back and steered her inside.

A solemn lady in a starched white nurse's cap and meticulously pressed uniform marched over, took Mom by the elbow and guided her down the fluorescent lit hallway.

Dad left to fill the car up with gas. When he returned he was ushered to the waiting room and handed a *National Geographic.* Hours later the tight-lipped nurse woke him up.

"You have a baby girl." She gave him a polite smile.

"A girl? Are you sure?" Dad asked, as he rubbed a knuckle across his eyes. "It's supposed to be a boy."

"We are sure. It is a girl." The nurse turned and disappeared down the hallway again.

Dad shook his head as he got up to follow her. "How could it be a girl?" The disinfectant scent in the air tickled his nostrils. He swiped the back of his hand across his nose. They were so sure it would be a Hans or a Johann, possibly Johann Wilhelm. But another daughter, how could that be?

The nurse tightened the faded pink blanket around me. "What's her name?"

"*Ich weiß nicht.* I thought a boy it would be." Mom pulled the blanket away from my cherub face. "Do you know? A name?"

"How about," the nurse tipped her head, put a finger to her chin as she glanced around the room. "How about Barbara, Barbara Ann? Like Barbara Ann Scott," her voice got excited. "You know? The famous Olympic figure skater, the one that won the gold medal for Canada. She's so beautiful."

"Barbara," Mom whispered. "Barbara Ann. *Ja, das ist schön.* Barbara Ann." Mom and Dad nodded...

And that's how I got my name.

In 2010 I turned fifty-two, and decided to contact Barbara Ann Scott.

Why you ask? After all these years?

I knew she was running a segment of the 2010 Winter Olympic Torch Relay in her hometown in Ontario. I was running the flame from that same torch in Alberta. What better time to tell her the story of how I got to share her name and, of course, the excitement of our torch relays.

Right off the bat I knew I couldn't send an e-mail or a typed letter. This had to be a sit-down-at-the-desk-and-write-a-proper-letter. With my favourite pen in hand, I used my best cursive writing skills. In no time, a number of squished paper balls lay on my office floor.

This letter had to be perfect.

A few hours later, with a numb middle finger and a cramped thumb, I finished my story. I thanked her for listening, folded it with a ruler into three equal parts and sealed it away with a stamp stuck square in the corner.

Neat. Proper. Appropriate.

Weeks later the red light was blinking on my answering machine. I tapped the button and a lively, clear voice filled the room.

I recognized it immediately. It was her, Barbara Ann Scott. She said she hoped she had the correct number to leave a message for Barbara Baker.

"Yes, you do! Yes, you do!" I danced a jig right in front of the phone while I listened.

She thanked me for the letter and told me she too was thrilled to run the Olympic Torch. She closed off with well wishes for my torch run, then paused before she said goodbye.

I played the message a hundred times. I phoned and e-mailed all my friends to share the news. Then, so as not to lose her voice, I copied the message and filed it away for safekeeping.

Wow! How exciting was that?

Sometimes I still can't believe it. I have this connection with a Canadian legend. And what a gracious lady she was to take the time to call.

Truly Barbara Ann Scott was a genuine sweetheart.

And despite my parent's initial disappointment, aren't I lucky I wasn't a boy? That boy, my brother, showed up three years later. And what a nuisance he turned out to be.

~Barbara Wackerle Baker
Calgary, Alberta

The Skating Rink

Grandfathers are just antique little boys.
~Author Unknown

In the darkness of night, his back and shoulders rounded to protect him from the full brunt of winter, my grandfather stood
alone creating a skating rink for my sister and me. The only
illumination, aside from the moon and stars, was a single light from
the back porch.

My grandparents took on the responsibility of raising two little
girls, my sister and me, after the failed marriage of their son. It must
have been an enormous decision. Adding to the weight of his responsibility, my grandfather had to cope with a history of depression and
tuberculosis along with other modern day illnesses. But there he was,
in the cold of the winter night, making our dreams come true.

The process of building a skating rink was a labour of love. First,
he created the boundaries of the rink by defining the shape with
piled up snow. Next, he methodically compacted the base of the rink
with a yard roller. Grandpa then began spraying the water, lightly at
first, until the first layer of ice was established. He would then flood
it each night until the rink was open for business.

My sister, Dona, is eighteen months my junior. Due to the
changes we experienced in our young lives, we were inseparable.
We fought like cats and dogs, and at the same time we looked after
each other. Beneath the growing pains we truly enjoyed each other's

company. From the kitchen window we watched Grandpa with great expectations.

"Is it ready yet?" we would ask as he came in from the rink, icicles hanging from his winter hat.

"Come on girls, let's let Grandpa have his tea and warm up," admonished Grandma, always there with a cup of tea.

The rink was taking forever to finish. Eventually the day came when we were allowed to put our skate blades to the ice. Dona and I put on our layers of snow pants, coats, scarves and mittens to protect us not only from the cold but the inevitable falls. Wearing all that winter garb I'm surprised we could skate at all! As I recall, falling down was easy, but getting back up was a challenge. We would start laughing so hard we would lie back on the ice and stare up at the sky until we regained our composure.

We would skate in the evenings after our chores and our home-work were completed. With only that single porch light to illuminate the surface of the rink, we skated in the cold for what felt like hours, creating memories that have lasted a lifetime.

Grandpa always looked proud of what he had accomplished and, I think, happy to see us having so much fun. Throughout the winter he would defrost the hose in the kitchen sink, and the outside tap with boiling water. He missed very few nights of shovelling and spraying.

There was something magical about skating at night. The moon and the stars and the deep silence became our companions. The only sounds came from our blades cutting into the ice. Faster and faster we circled the oval surface. I became more daring and even learned to skate backwards, often ending up on my back on the ice. I won-dered, then, if the stars I was seeing were in the sky or in my head. That didn't stop me. I tried doing some jumps I'd seen Barbara Ann Scott do on television. But my favourite trick was to spin around and around until I staggered off the rink dizzy and dazed.

Every so often I'd see Grandpa watching from the window. I can't imagine what he thought about my skating.

Frequently, the laughter of our neighbourhood friends resounded from our back yard. We spent countless hours twirling, jumping and whipping each other around the ice rink with careless abandon. What fun we had!

When we were finished, we enjoyed Grandma's hot chocolate. Happy, tired and warm, we sat at the window and watched while Grandpa worked his magic once again.

When I got older, the task of flooding the ice rink fell to me. It was now me standing in the freezing night with the hose, the spray sometimes being thrown back at me by the wind. As I lost the feeling in my fingers and toes I would remember my grandpa with his shoulders bent against the cold, and felt a sense of sharing. My grandparents were not able to give Dona and me a lot of material things in life, but they gave us all they could. We will always remember those many winters of terrific fun in our own back yard as a very special gift.

~Dian Bowers
Alliston, Ontario

Somebody's Kid

I'll tell you what Canadians do better than anyone else in the world—that's produce hockey games. Hockey Night in Canada does a hockey game better than ABC, NBC, or CBS ever could.

~Dan Matheson

"When you get to the door, pretend you're with the guy in front. Look like you belong. Be confident. The door guard will think you're somebody's kid and should be here." With those last words of advice, my erstwhile accomplice, Karl, and I quickly fell into step behind two important looking customers and entered the Hot Stove Lounge. The uniformed sentry barely noticed us as he welcomed the club members on their arrival. Once inside the hallowed chamber we quickly made ourselves scarce, not wanting to arouse suspicion.

It was May 2, 1967 and of course, this exercise had been accomplished many times previously, but the fact that this was Stanley Cup Finals heightened our anxiety. Once again, we were sneaking into Maple Leaf Gardens to watch our venerable heroes do battle with the Montreal Canadiens. This was the final game of the series and it would be the last time the Leafs won the Championship.

Merely getting into the Hot Stove Lounge was not getting into the Gardens. One substantial hurdle remained, but we were undaunted, as experience had taught us well. Just before the opening face-off the patrons of the Club hustled down to the door leading into the east hall of the Red Seats. A Gardens' employee ripped ducats as the season ticket holders filed by. These were Toronto blue-bloods so very little was scrutinized, especially two well-dressed fifteen-year-olds in ties and blazers. After all, they must be somebody's kids.

Now, standing at the gateway, staring the gentleman in the eye, I pointed my thumb behind me and stepped briskly into the crowded hallway. Karl, behind me did the same. We had long vanished by the time the man behind Karl handed over his tickets. "Kids, what kids? Never saw them before," might have been his reply.

To an awestruck teenager, the inside of the Gardens was a glory to behold, a veritable shrine and we knew it well. Unexpected staircases and tiny closets long lost to memory were all known to us. No usher ever caught us in a chase, and more than once they'd lock the place up knowing that intruders still ran through the bowels of that great arena. Once we knew they'd given up, the excitement of the game was over so we'd find our way out and go home.

On hockey night, a map of the place firmly imprinted on our young minds, we'd work our way up to the Greens above centre ice. It was here we'd watch the first period before finding plusher accommodation below. The ushers in the Greens would stand at the top of the steep stairs directing patrons to their seats. At the bottom, the stairs separated right and left out of the usher's view and that's where we'd sit for the first period. No one bothered the two well-dressed lads who sought no attention. We acted like we belonged and were well gone by the time the puck was dropped for the second.

From this vantage point we'd choose three empty pairs of Reds on the other side of the rink. Normally the owners of seats not arrived by the end of the first were unlikely to show up for the remainder of the game. If they did arrive, while we occupied them, we'd act confused and then move along to our back-up seats. This Stanley Cup final proved no different from the other games.

I remember screaming myself hoarse that game. It was a close battle, with fabulous goaltending. Wasn't it the Chief's last hurrah as well? George Armstrong was a wonderful captain and worked so hard, and on this night he scored the final goal, an empty-netter, which iced the game and the championship for our fantastic boys in blue!

The hero that night however, was Dave Keon. He did a Trojan's service to bring home the Cup and it was I that night who led the Gardens' masses in paying homage to him. At the end of the game, standing on the arms of the seat, I began to chant "we want Keon." One diminutive voice was soon taken up by thousands... and Dave came back out onto the ice and took a final bow.

It was so exhilarating! This was my team in my city and we were champions. That's the great thing about being a fan—because you live and die with your team, you feel a part of their victory. I didn't want the celebration to end and it seemed that it had moved into the Leaf dressing room. Obviously that was the next logical place Karl and I had to go.

As a whirlwind of photographers, journalists, and media assaulted the dressing room, the single doorman was clearly over-whelmed. I fell into the deluge and mumbling platitudes, was swept right past the guard. Before I knew it the inner sanctum was mine.

There they were, right before my eyes: my Leafs, my heroes. They were shouting and screaming and shooting champagne over everyone. The media milled about thrusting microphones in faces looking for quotes. Cameras whirred, wires tripped the unwary and one teenager stood in the middle of the frenzy and confusion, alone and in awe.

The room was bursting with greatness. There was Terry Sawchuk, Ron Ellis, and Allan Stanley, Tim Horton and Bobby Baun, Frank Mahovlich,—and then I saw Dave. Surrounded by the throng, he looked somewhat uncomfortable with all the attention.

Later, when the hubbub moved along, I approached my hero. I needed something for him to autograph, and lacking paper, I grabbed one of the empty champagne bottles and asked him to sign the label. He obliged me, accepted my praise, and shook my hand. I almost fainted. I actually had a Stanley Cup champagne bottle with Dave Keon's signature on it! Later, several of my other heroes added their signatures, leaving me with a sacred reminder of a great adventure, cherished to this day.

On my way out I was collared by a journalist who thrust a microphone in my face and asked, "What'd ya think of the game, son?"

"Absolutely fantastic," came my reply.

"Who's your favorite player?" he continued.

"Dave Keon, the most under-rated player in the NHL."

"Is that so?"

"Without a doubt. Look what he did tonight."

"Can't argue with you there. Did you have good seats?"

"Oh, yes sir, the best... five rows behind the penalty box."

"Five rows, eh?" He seemed to think about that. "What's your name, son?"

I told him. "Pardon me?" he blinked.

I told him again. He sort of furled his brows, obviously trying to remember, but it was no good. He drew a blank. Thanking me for my time, he turned his back and immediately began to rewind the tape.

As I headed for the door with my bounty safely in hand, I overheard one of his fellow reporters inquire as to my identity. My interviewer said he didn't know — never heard of me before in his life.

Looking back over my shoulder, I saw the other guy shrug. "Must be somebody's kid," he said.

~Randall Crickmore
Niagara Falls, Ontario

41

My Guardian Angels

I would rather walk with a friend in the dark, than alone in the light.
~Helen Keller

"Star light. Star bright. First star I see tonight." When I was pre-school age that was the way I began my nightly prayers. While kneeling beside my bed I would choose the brightest star I could see and make my wish. Then I would pray that God would bless and care for my loved ones.

When I was five years old we lived in an older home that had been inherited from my grandparents, in the Allandale section of Barrie, Ontario. That Christmas Eve the house was full of company so at bedtime I had to surrender my spot to sleep on a cot upstairs all alone. This part of the house was rarely used, and it was frightening for me to be up there by myself. My mother knew that I was both nervous and excited so she came up to get me settled in. She got down on her knees with me, and when I began the ritual she listened closely to hear my wish, which was to be safe and unafraid in the dark. Just as I started my prayers, Mom told me to look again at the star I had just wished on. I had already been told about heaven and angels and where my grandma, grandpa and baba went when they died, but that night Mom told me about a very special angel. She told me that from now on when I looked to the stars, I should direct my wishes to Robert. Robert? I had a guardian angel named Robert?

My mother explained that before she married my father, she

had been married to a wonderful man named Duncan McKenzie. She and Duncan had a baby boy they named Robert. He was born in December, but tragically died Christmas Eve. Then the very next New Year's Eve, Duncan was killed instantly in a head-on train crash in Sudbury. She told me how lonely and frightened she was feeling that night too, and still did on every Christmas Eve no matter how many years passed. We cried, grieved and prayed together. I fell sound asleep that night feeling safe and comforted knowing about my special guardian angel.

The year I turned seven, another Robert came into my life. He was a Down syndrome child about eleven years old, placed in my grade two classroom experimentally. We bonded instantly. Robert sat in the seat in front of me so I could help him with his work. He became very reliant on me and would make a fuss if he couldn't stand next to me in line, or keep me in sight at recess.

One day I fell in the schoolyard before the morning bell rang. My knees were skinned and bleeding badly and I was weeping. Out of nowhere, Robert scooped me up into his arms and carried me off. The teachers were slightly alarmed and yelled at him to put me down, but I couldn't see what they were concerned about. I felt quite safe. He was much bigger than the other kids and able to push past everyone as he marched me into the school directly to the main office. There, Robert walked right into the principal's office where he laid me down on the desk and announced, "Fix her. She's my friend!"

That Christmas, King Edward School put on a pageant and invited the parents to come on the afternoon of Christmas Eve to watch. Our class did the nativity scene with Mary, Joseph, shepherds, wise men and an angel that stood out front to narrate the story. I was a pretty good reader and had long, blond curls so our teacher, Miss Shepstone, chose me to play the angel. I was ecstatic!

My mother made me a beautiful costume with delicate wings and a golden halo. While she fitted and sewed the costume, we talked more about my guardian angel. I told her my theory that her baby Robert had not died. I felt sure there had to have been a mistake at the hospital, and that the Robert in my classroom was really her child, all grown up. I tried to reassure her that although he was different than the other kids, and lived in a special place, he was still being my guardian angel and I loved him.

She reminded me that we had often visited the baby's grave, but told me that I should be very grateful to have two Roberts watching out for me. Later that week I was able to prove just how thankful I was.

Every day before the pageant we rehearsed our nativity. I was beaming with joy over my duties and loved every minute of it. Except for one disturbing thing. Robert wasn't able to have a speaking part in the play. He would play a shepherd seated on the floor with a scratchy, grey, woollen blanket pulled over his head and body, with only his face revealed. He didn't mind that at all. In fact he took his role very seriously. He knew when he must stand up and sit down, but he desperately wanted to be closer to me.

During the course of every rehearsal he would creep up and play his part seated on the floor near me. Miss Shepstone explained over and over to him how important his part was and that it must be played in the proper spot. He said he understood, and he continued to be a wonderful shepherd, but only when he scooted forward on his blanketed behind and stayed front and centre with me.

I would take him back to his spot and sit with him a while, but to no avail. He was just too nervous on that crowded stage without me in his sight.

Two days before Christmas Eve Miss Shepstone paid a visit to our house after school. What on earth had I done wrong? I'd never heard of a teacher coming to someone's house before. My mom and Miss Shepstone had such serious faces when they told me I had a big decision to make. They said they would understand and stick by me whatever I decided.

They wanted to know what I thought we should do about Robert. The choice I had was this. I could still be the Christmas Angel and be out front to narrate the play, but Robert would have to be kept out of the production completely because he refused to stay in his shepherd's position. Or I could give up my part and the costume of the angel to someone else, and sit in the back under one of those heavy blankets playing the part of a shepherd with Robert so he could remain in the play. What a weight to place on the shoulders of a seven-year-old!

Time has passed and I still have a fascination with the stars. I gaze at the brightest ones and think of all the loved ones I have lost—including my dear mother who died suddenly at Christmas time too. My wish every Christmas Eve is that they all know how grateful I am to have known them and for their outstanding guidance. I also hope that Robert knew how thankful I was for his unequivocal friendship when we held hands under our scratchy, grey, woollen blankets many Christmas Eves ago.

~Lea Ellen Yarmill Reburn
Central Ontario

42

Winter Dog

What counts is not necessarily the size of the dog in the fight;
it's the size of the fight in the dog.
~Dwight D. Eisenhower

The dog found us late in February, that trough of winter after the valentines have been sent, when there's little left in the world to love, when the first peeping violets seem an eternity away. As if rising from a drift of snow, it suddenly appeared to us, ragged and yellow, shivering, rib-worn and gaunt, yet wagging its tail frosted like fern. Its floppy ears looked frozen at their tips, its scraggly Terrier-like-beard grizzled with frost. It was no dog we knew, and living in rural Ontario, the dogs of our township were familiar, part of the neighborhood fabric. This unknown one stood scratching at the door of our house, lifting one paw at a time as if to offer each a brief respite from the cold. Wagging its frosted fern-tail.

"Don't let it in!" my mother called out to me from the kitchen. "You let it in, it's game over. Besides, we already *have* a dog—and he eats too much."

This was a fact. Ed was our big, lumbering part-something, part-something else mutt. He had a huge appetite and slept away much of the day beside the stove. He was supposed to have been a fierce farm-guard. That had been our plan for him. He was not scary at all, could have been a stand-in for a cartoon dog quite popular at the time, Marmaduke. Ed didn't even bark when the strange yellow dog scratched for help that day.

I opened the door a crack, enough to see the poor mutt's system of raising and lowering its paws. It whimpered and still Ed did not hear, or hearing did not care. I compared Ed's warm, padded cushion by the stove with the plight of the winter dog, with its frostbitten ears, outside.

"Mom—it's cold—please?"

My mother emerged from the kitchen, her hands covered in flour. She was trying to give me the evil eye or, as we called it then, the hairy eyeball.

"You want to let it in," she said to me, in flat tones.

I bobbed my head energetically. "It's cute."

"Cute? Can it shovel snow?" she asked.

I shrugged.

"Can it clean stables?"

An even weaker shrug from me.

"Then what use is it?"

• • •

The yellow dog, of course, came to live with us. The truth was, it was not uncommon for pets to be driven to the country in a car, then dumped out and abandoned. Drifter, I named the stray, because he looked, when he appeared to us, like he had risen from a drift of snow. There were many storms in those days, and in fact our road had been closed for two days when Drifter came scrabbling at the door. If someone had dropped him off, he had been alone in the howling wind and blizzard for at least a couple of days. Winters were more severe in the years of my youth.

The yellow dog loved us for taking him in—he rolled about in a bliss of gratitude meant to be entertaining, we supposed, until my mother would say, "Yes, all right, all *right*, Drifter, you are here, now, you can stay."

Ed regarded Drifter with a benign indifference. As long as Ed's food bowl wasn't affected, Ed was cool.

•••

Drifter was frightened of cars. If it was true that he had been abandoned and pushed out of a car, as we speculated, perhaps he feared a car would open its door and snatch him away from us. Ed, on the other hand, loved riding in the car.

One day, two winters after Drifter was brought into our house, my mother took Ed to town with her, grocery store run, taxes to pay. I didn't want to go to town, I needed to work on my 4-H project: a pair of pajamas I was sewing. Leopard pattern, the latest thing. I was old enough to stay home alone, had done so before. Besides, I *wasn't* alone. Drifter was there. I whirred the machine into a pleasant frenzy. I didn't hear the car engine idle in the yard, but Drifter heard it. At first I thought it was my mother and Ed, back from town. She had promised to buy puffed wheat cereal and marshmallows; we would make squares. I'd been thinking of those squares the whole time I sewed, so I ran to meet her.

It was not my mother. It was a frowning man in a dirty overcoat and sloppy galoshes. Already out of his car, beating his way over the snowy path to the front door.

Drifter sent out a wail of volleying barks, guttural, alarmed. Growls I'd never heard issue from his throat before. He stood on his hind legs and watched, through the window, his nose poking through between the drapes, the man approach our house. The man knocked on the door, spiraling Drifter's growls and barks into an even more crazed, intense pitch.

"No one is home!" I called nervously through the door.

"Doesn't sound like that to *me*," the man snapped.

I started to blubber that my mother would be back any minute. Then man paid no heed.

In those days, no one locked their houses. The concept of a

locked door was foreign to us, for city people. The man pushed the door open enough to stick his ugly face into the kitchen.

Drifter went berserk. He leapt and lunged at the man, and sank his teeth into his dirty overcoat, ripping a segment off the lower sleeve. Whatever kind of dog Drifter was, there must have been some wolf in his line. His eyes lit like two red-orange, searing flames.

The man swore at Drifter, but could not shake him off his sleeve, though he kept cursing and shaking his arm. It was like Drifter's teeth were permanently stuck in the man's coat. I cried harder.

Suddenly my mother appeared at the doorstep. And Ed. Like I said, Ed was the biggest, sleepiest, laziest dog, but something about seeing Drifter clinging, growling, at the man's sleeve, lit dynamite under him. He became, at that moment, the guard dog we had envisioned. Ed grabbed the back of the intruder's overcoat and it was clear to all of us that his next move would be sinking his teeth into the man's backside.

My mother told me to phone the police. By the time they arrived from town to our farm, the man had retreated back into his car and, throwing out a long spray of snow from his spinning tires, he tore out of our laneway and down the road in a white cloud. When the officer arrived, we were able to describe the man and his car in detail. Not long after, the police caught him. They had been looking for him for a while.

After that day, Ed and Drifter guarded us with their lives. They became a tag team, a duo-security force. I got these neat gold badges from prizes in cereal boxes and I attached one to each of their collars.

Though my mother and I never spoke about that first day Drifter came to us, I knew from the start she would let him in; country people have an unspoken custom about any desperate, hungry creature shivering outside in the wild, freezing elements—it is bad luck not to help them—moreover, they will repay your kindness someday when your thoughts are far as they can be from any economy of generosity, when you've embarked on an errand of absolute ordinariness, like making a run to town for milk and bread and cereal and paying the tax office.

~Jeanette Lynes
Saskatoon, Saskatchewan

Shoe Shoe Train

My father didn't tell me how to live; he lived, and let me watch him do it.
~Clarence Budington Kelland

If I close my eyes I can relive tobogganing on a glorious sunny afternoon as if it were happening now, even though it was forty years ago. It was nothing planned. Just a group of teenagers with nothing to do but have fun on that winter day.

Without thinking I said, "Why don't we go back to my house for hot chocolate and get warm?"

I instantly regretted it. A typical teenager, I was full of insecurities. What if the house was a mess? What if my mom asked stupid questions? Or, what if my dad was taking a nap on the couch?

All the way home I prayed that all would be "normal" at the homestead. I sighed with relief when I entered the house. My parents appeared sane.

Dad stayed in the background while Mom got busy making hot chocolate, as we kids hurriedly left our boots and coats in the entrance hall and went downstairs to the rec room.

Lots of laughter, board games and hours quickly passed. Finally it was time for everyone to go. We swarmed upstairs. Last in the group, as I hit the last stair I could hear laughter coming from the entrance hall. That horrible teenage-angst surfaced. What had my parents done now?

I peered around the corner. My father had taken the dozen or so pair of boots and shoes and lined them up in a line going through the living room, dining room and kitchen. In the first shoe was a sign saying "shoe shoe train." In the last boot the sign said "caboots."

I was mortified.

Once I got over the initial shock and embarrassment I noticed that my friends were absolutely delighted with my dad's project. They thought he was cool!

As they scrambled to retrieve their boots and shoes they all commented how this never happened at their homes and how lucky I was to have a fun dad. I suddenly saw my dad in a new light, well kind of—he was a fun dad? Yes, he was a fun dad!

The "shoe shoe" train story has become a family legend. Grandchildren born after my father's death enjoy hearing about the funny grandfather they wish they had known. I realize now how that one carefree winter's day has come to symbolize my childhood.

The story could end there, but it doesn't. A childhood friend recently passed away. I made a promise to her son to find newspaper articles and pictures of her in happier days and make an album for him.

For years my mother periodically brought me documents and pictures she thought might interest me. I was usually too busy to give them more than a glance before I threw them in an old trunk. Now, this trunk proved to be a treasure trove of just what was needed for that album. There were newspaper articles and pictures about my friend. There was also a sign that I figured had been thrown away long ago that read "Shoe Shoe train." The stress of losing my friend disappeared and I was transported back to a day when my biggest problem was trying not to be embarrassed by two loving, nurturing people. Suddenly I could feel my dad with me, making me laugh, just as he had that winter day.

I now have the sign framed and in my kitchen. It's a wonderful reminder of the day I discovered just how lucky I was to have such a wonderful family.

~Cindy Armeland Clemens
Lambton Shores, Ontario

O Canada
The Wonders of
Winter

On the Ice

Then there's the incredible feeling of skating itself,
of getting on this shiny, slippery surface and moving faster
than your feet would otherwise move, of feeling the breeze
that you've created yourself in the act of skating.

~Ken Dryden

44

The Good Old Hockey Game

Crosby scores! Sidney Crosby! The golden goal!
And Canada has once-in-a-lifetime Olympic gold!
~Chris Cuthbert, February 28, 2010

February 28, 2010:
I remember the day vividly. Having beaten the Slovaks in a well-fought battle to advance, to our collective relief Canada had made it. Once again, just as it had been in Salt Lake City, it would be Team Canada against Team USA—a fight to the death for the coveted Olympic Gold in hockey.

It had been a tough tournament for Canada, and the once boisterous atmosphere in my home city of Vancouver had been replaced with insecurity as our entire nation held its breath. I was in no mood to subject myself to any of the four-hour pub line-ups that snaked through the downtown streets, so I opted to watch this final game at home alone.

The lead up to this moment had been memorable and awe-inspiring. With the world watching during those two weeks of the 2010 Vancouver Winter Olympics, my city had been transformed into a veritable sea of red and white, generously peppered with high fives and hugs between strangers united in a collective jubilation rarely seen.

Despite the intoxicating essence of it all, as I wandered the streets

I felt the air now somehow hung thick with an unspoken tension. We waited for hockey.

A squad of honoured hockey gods was assembled. I stared in awe as they announced the starting Olympic roster on TSN. It was the team I'd hoped for, one infused with the un-equaled puck-handling prowess that Team Canada has become both feared and revered for.

With a "Lucky Loonie" embedded at centre ice — just as in Salt Lake in 2002, I watched breathlessly as hockey nations great and small laced up to do battle. When the Swiss had beaten us 3-2 in a preliminary round I was shocked, and somehow hurt. But when we lost to the Americans 3-5, my heart sank.

At the end of that preliminary round Canada had ranked 6th out of 12, while the United States, Sweden and Russia ranked 1 through 3, respectively. "Not again," I thought as I remembered our dismal show-ing at the 2006 Torino Winter Games. "And especially not here."

Our hopes had risen when we defeated Germany 8-2 to advance to the semifinals. But next up was the undeniable Russian powerhouse.

I sat frozen during that game, but when it was all over, Team Canada had defeated the Russians by an astounding 7-3. With that staggering performance, my optimism returned in force.

Now, as I sat watching this final game alone, time stood still as titans clashed, our guys knowing that, as they fought tooth-and-nail for gold on home ice, as much as they fought for themselves, they fought for us. And fight they did. We took the lead early thanks to Winnipeg's Jon Toews, and when Corey Perry put us up 2-0 in the second I allowed myself a moment of elation. Kesler's goal for the U.S. on his NHL home ice late in the second drew some hasty boos from the crowd, but didn't upset me enough to cause any doubt.

Then, with one minute and twenty-seven seconds left, the Americans pulled their goalie. Alone in my living room I stood gnaw-ing on a clenched fist. Why on earth had I felt it necessary to watch this alone? The die was cast. I knew it was over. We had done it!

Then, like in some horror movie, with twenty-five seconds remaining in the third period, Team USA scored to tie the game, thrusting us into overtime. Darkness overtook me. As the Americans celebrated it seemed as if all 17,700 fans in attendance, along with the estimated twenty-two million Canadians watching on live TV— had been punched in the gut.

I had to take a walk. I realized my entire incredible Olympic experience now hinged on this single turning point, and there was nothing I could do about it. When I got home I set the beer aside, poured myself a Scotch and, taking a deep breath, sat down to watch the finish.

Overtime passed as if in a dream. If the house had caught fire, I'm not sure I would have noticed. I was caught in a strange combination of optimism and melancholy as the outside world slipped away.

Suddenly, the red lamp lit—and as I watched in total shock, Ryan Miller—the American goalie—slid forward and hung his head. Sidney Crosby then leapt into the corner glass, delirious! What? Was it over?

Crosby! Sid the Kid—had scored for Canada!

The fans went wild and hockey-gods dog-piled like ten-year-old-boys. I couldn't believe it! Canada had won and I fell to my knees in that living room.

It was nothing short of surreal. In sheer jubilation I donned my best red and white, fastened a flag to an old Sherwood lefty hockey stick, and took to the streets. It was as if a dam had burst in my heart—pride and pure, un-filtered joy washed over and through me. The only thing in my mind was an overwhelming desire to share it with other Canadians.

Approaching a bus stop I was surprised and delighted to find several similarly dressed guys who hooted excitedly at my arrival, offering me a cold beer and hugs. All around us hockey fans continued to crawl out of the woodwork. When a BMW pulled over, the driver eagerly offered anyone who wanted one a ride towards downtown. With The Tragically Hip blaring loudly and the maple leaf flapping proudly, he and his new friends sped off.

"No charge," announced the grinning bus driver as we boarded and were bombarded with hugs and high fives by everyone on board. Every stop we made brought more of the same—every one of us were family. Rousing renditions of "O Canada," Stompin' Tom Connor's "The Good Old Hockey Game" and The Hip's "Fireworks" were repeatedly sung en masse. Soon, with the bus filled to capacity, we were compelled to hang our flags out the windows as a salute to our comrades left behind as they shouted encouraging words and praised us in our noble cause.

I was lucky enough to kiss at least three beautiful women on that bus ride—all of us lost together in a haze of bliss like nothing I've ever experienced. The bus sagged low under our weight as we crossed the Burrard Street Bridge and headed downtown, where the magnitude of this mass celebration became quickly apparent. The streets were flooded with revellers. After descending from our impromptu patriot chariot, it took over an hour to walk a distance ordinarily covered in ten minutes; that was all this jubilant, pulsing, throbbing, screaming red and white organism that occupied downtown Vancouver would allow.

I will remember that day for the rest of my life. Not for the perseverance of our team, our victory as a nation, or our glory as a people, but for the subsequent and spontaneous outburst of joyous camaraderie the gold medal inspired. Gone were the blinders we wear every day on our way to and from work. Gone were the insecurities that cripple us and keep us to ourselves. Gone were regrets from the past, and doubts for the future. Gone was a city of strangers, replaced by a family bound to each other if only in spirit, and if only for a few magical hours.

I will remember that day for the rest of my life for it was the most Canadian scene I can hope to ever see.

~Matty Hughes
Edmonton, Ontario

Winning the Gold
for Canada

Not once, in everything I've done, have I ever felt the same wonder and
humanity as when I'm playing the game of curling.
~Paul Gross, John Krizanc, and Paul Quarrington, Men with Brooms

The reflection in the hotel mirror revealed the truth. I leaned closer, to see if the dark circles under my eyes were just a shadow or really mine. I was so tired. There was no mistake; the grueling season of intense competition was taking its toll. It was championship day, and the expectation on us to win a gold medal for Canada was beginning to show.

Later, at breakfast, I could see the pressure was starting to weigh amongst the team. We all brought different moods to the table, and this morning we were unusually quiet. There was very little eye contact, and it was clear we needed a change of routine.

We decided at the last minute to walk down to Hamilton's Copps Coliseum, hoping some fresh air would blow away the emotional mist that was beginning to engulf us.

It was near the end of March and the softness of the annual thaw was in the wind. The sun was pouring out springtime energy and our team needed some of it. With our curling bags slung over our shoulders and the bright red maple leafs riding proudly on the backs of our team jackets, we started out the front door of the hotel like a small train leaving the station.

I was leading these magnificent women and when I looked back, I could see the mist evaporating. Everyone was smiling.

I decided to pick up the pace a bit. My team loved the challenge of walking faster and let me know with a few small cheers.

As we waited at the first stoplight, we were startled by a car horn. The driver and passengers leaned out the windows, waving and shouting, "Go, Canada, Go!"

As the light turned green, everybody was cheering, yelling and screaming at us, causing a chain reaction. We saw people with red maple leafs painted on their cheeks. Some even ripped open their shirts to bare flaming red Canadian flags on their chests. We stood there waving back and laughing with excitement at being surrounded by our fans, who we knew had come to watch us play.

As we turned to cross the street, the autograph seekers swarmed us. We quickly scribbled our names on scraps of paper being pushed our way, but our focus was blurring again. It was our coach who asked the fans to step back and let us get to the game.

Our small train now quickly transformed into a faster moving locomotive. We began sprinting up the boulevard, waving madly to the honking cars passing by.

We steamed through a mall entrance that we knew would lead to Copps. Inside, the locker room would be our sanctum for the next forty-five minutes before practice time.

Like usual, we gathered around in a tight circle for our team meeting. I felt a very powerful unity amongst the squad. Our faith and belief in one another gave us the courage to rise above and be the best we could be. We just had to go out onto the ice and do it.

My mind was crystal clear, focused on the task at hand. Except for my pounding heart, there was no sound. Twelve thousand people sat breathlessly on the edge of their seats waiting for my final shot. I needed to breathe. I needed to breathe deeply. I was here at Copps Coliseum ready to win the 1996 World Curling Championships for my second title.

An air of déjà vu permeated the moment. Time seemed to pass in slow motion. I had practiced this shot so many times at my home rink, the St. Catharines Curling Club. When nobody was looking, I would pretend this was the shot that was going to win the Worlds. In my mind, I had seen myself here. Over and over again I'd imagined the feeling of victory.

Releasing the rock with ease and a direction of exact aim, I watched it slide perfectly down the ice and knock the opposition's stone out of play. I held myself expectantly for a few seconds, waiting for that sound I'd longed to hear. The crowd exploded with a roar as my teammates jumped for joy.

Cameras immediately zoomed in on our celebration, clicking and whirring as they captured the team's elation for posterity. Reporters quickly swarmed around us for our first responses.

"How does it feel?" was the question of the day.

My heart was overwhelmed with gratitude and pride. I wanted to embrace these few seconds of utter joy peacefully by myself.

"Unbelievable and magical" came my response. I had rehearsed this moment and was determined not to let others hurry us in our time of celebration. I thanked my coach. My team members put their arms around me in a tight circle. We were bonded for seconds and no one else could touch us. I looked each of them in the eye and said exultantly, "Enjoy the moment!"

As I stood on the platform waiting for the announcer to call Team Canada to the highest podium, I was aware of every detail. I could see all the faces in the crowd smiling and waving Canadian flags wildly. My eyes rested on the beaming faces of my family. By this time, both arms were high above my head waving back, saying thank you to the fans who had supported us all week. It was their constant clapping, cheering and loyalty that gave me inspiration when I needed it most.

Shivers ran up my spine as I saw our gold medals coming toward us in the hands of our presenters. I will never forget the feeling of gratitude as I bowed for the president of the World Curling Federation to hang the medal around my neck.

As I sang the words to "O Canada" a kind of humility engulfed my spirit. Tears stung my eyes as I watched our Canadian flag rise higher and higher, highlighting forever in my heart that treasured moment.

~Marilyn C. Bodogh
St. Catharines, Ontario

Fulford's Rink

The best thing we get out of it is seeing the kids smile.
~Bobby Orr

The clatter of Harry Wood's diesel engine drew me to the living room window. The owner of Wood's Paving, father of our daughter Jennifer's best friend, was running his grader up and down the vacant lot next to ours. He was preparing the ground for the flooding of Fulford's Rink, a project that would occupy much of my husband's spare time for the rest of the winter.

It was early in December, and Don Fulford decided to present the neighbourhood children with a skating rink, a splendid outdoor rink — the kind that had never before been seen in the town of Dryden, Ontario. First he obtained permission from the town engineer. The weather co-operated. Although there was still no snow, it was soon cold enough for water to freeze outside. With the help of a neighbour, Jerry Smith, my husband began to flood the now smooth lot. Every evening, all weekend, and into the next week they worked. At that time, in the late 1950s, we still had long winters with stretches of 30 and 40 degrees below zero Fahrenheit. Sometimes it was so cold they could not flood with a hose; the water froze too quickly and would not spread evenly across the rink.

"Let's use a barrel," Jerry suggested. "I have one in my back yard." They filled the barrel, dumped it completely on one section of the lot, refilled it and moved quickly to dump it on another section. This method worked. After they had a base they were able, on a warmer evening, to use the hose to spray water on the new ice surface.

Fulford's Rink was ready for use by Christmas and it was an instant hit. Our own daughters, Judy and Jennifer, enjoyed it. Having it so close by meant there was no urgent need for them to lace on their skates at every opportunity. But it was not so with others. As soon as school closed for the day, children flocked to the ice, not only from our immediate neighbourhood, but also from streets so far away that those skaters could not get home to use the bathroom without sacrificing serious skating time.

One Saturday afternoon our back door flew open and Bobby, an eight-year-old with desperation in his eyes and covered in snow from a recent tumble, clumped hastily into my kitchen and cried, "Where's the bathroom?" There was obviously no time for a polite exchange (nor to take off his skates) so I led the way across the kitchen and through a corner of the living room. Bobby followed, shedding snow and still lurching on his skates. He was only the first.

When he left, I said, "Please, Bobby. Tell your friends to come in sooner, while they still have time to remove their skates."

I was somewhat annoyed that day, but pretty soon I began to enjoy the frequent contact with these young visitors. When winsome Sally, golden curls fringing her purple toque, stood shivering at my door, I drew her into the house, rubbed her cold hands and gave her a cookie. This too became a pattern—with the smaller children.

Meanwhile, Don was frequently out giving a fresh flood to the tired ice surface that had recently gotten chopped up by our happy band of skaters. Sometimes he was able to fill in cracks just by spraying on the water.

And then there was trouble in Paradise. One Friday night, actually in the wee hours of Saturday morning, Don and I returned from an evening of dancing at the Fireman's Ball. We planned a long morning sleep-in. Our two daughters were good about quietly reading or doing jigsaw puzzles until we awoke. However, at 8:30 on this Saturday morning, there came a loud knocking that abruptly roused us both.

"Mom," said Judy apologetically, "there's a whole bunch of girls at the door and they want to see you!"

The leader, a chubby redhead whose face was flushed with righteous anger, said, "Mrs. Fulford, the boys are playing hockey and we can't skate!" So, Don got up and went out to settle that dispute. Eventually he established a couple of hours on one weekday evening for hockey, and the boys had to be content with that.

One day a local hockey coach telephoned with a request. There was only one other rink in town large enough for hockey practice. The coach requested rink time for his team. But there were no boards around our rink, so Don had to refuse.

Snowfalls were a continuing challenge. If Don was not quick enough with his shovel, an ambassador was sent to inform us that the rink was covered in snow. As the winter progressed, these little people developed quite a strong sense of entitlement. Shoveling a lot-sized rink was no small task, but Jerry often came over to lend a hand, and his generous support shortened the long hours of labour. Still, after a hard day's work, Don sometimes had to drag himself to the rink. Once he said, with a rueful smile, "I think I've got a tiger by the tail here."

All that winter my husband shoveled the rink, sprayed the rink, and settled disputes. He was spurred on by the satisfaction of bestowing a unique gift. The other large rink was used primarily for hockey, with only a couple of hours here and there set aside for pleasure skating. Our rink had free access, was open to all children, and was used to the hilt.

I welcomed the youngsters who came to pee, to get warm, and sometimes to phone home for a ride. And guess what? It was fun! After school and on evenings and weekends, there was never a dull moment that winter. I learned that a neat, perfectly clean house did not yield the same satisfaction that came from interacting with the kids and meeting their needs. Life is messy, and that winter our house and Fulford's Rink fairly teemed with life!

We have lived in Thunder Bay now for forty years. Whenever I think of Dryden in the wintertime, I remember the year my husband devoted so much of his time to creating and maintaining Fulford's Rink. That time before the PC, before video games and before the smartphone. That vanished way of life is now like a winter scene captured in a glass ball. Whenever we choose, we can view in memory that wonderful kaleidoscope of brightly coloured toques, mittens and snowsuits as they were, steadily gliding past the window of our home in Dryden, on Fulford's Rink.

~Hazel Fulford
Thunder Bay, Ontario

47

The Angels of Hockey

Stress is nothing more than a socially acceptable form of mental illness.
~Richard Carlson

I shall not soon forget the Great Hockey Weekend of 2012: three kids, three minor hockey tournaments, one weekend. Not just three kids, three goalies.

To say I was stressed about this weekend would be an understatement. The disaster was foretold months before when my husband announced he was going golfing in Florida on the first weekend in February.

During hockey season?" I screeched, "Who goes golfing during hockey season?" Handling one hockey tournament weekend alongside sibling league hockey is challenging enough. Here I was staring down the trifecta of manic hockey weekends.

"It's so much cheaper to go in February than in May," was his reasoning.

"Oh no," I thought, "not cheaper. Somehow, some way, this will cost you!"

I was in serious need of hockey angels that weekend. The Christmas just prior to the Great Hockey Weekend of 2012, my mother-in-law bemoaned the fact that none of my kids had a hockey tournament near their home in Collingwood. Living in Ottawa, how we managed an entire year without a tournament in or around Toronto was beyond me.

"I sure would love to see them play!" she said.

Well Lordy, Lordy, the Angel of Hockey mercy hath rested her wings in your goal crease, lady! I called my mother-in-law from our home in Ottawa and said, "Have I got the weekend for you!"

I, of course, was thinking only of my in-laws' chauffeur and canteen service, and less of their relationship with their grandchildren, but they didn't need to know that. Because we had three games on Friday, I really needed them to arrive in Ottawa on Thursday, even though doing so posed some inconveniences to them. Whether it was due to my tears or my bribes, they planned their arrival for Thursday evening, those hockey angels of mine.

The wrath of the hockey gods treaded lightly at first, and Game #1 Jersey #1 took place Thursday evening at the arena around the corner from our house, meaning my son could walk home, as he was not willing to keep me company during the first of my two tours of volunteer duty that weekend.

Following my stint as Canteen Queen I quickly headed home to welcome my in-laws, after their six-hour drive, with open arms and cold pizza. Too tired to strategize the weekend events with them, convening in the Situation Room would have to wait until the morning.

Early Friday morning saw me quietly slip the empty wine glass that seemed to have followed me to bed into the dishwasher, fill my tank with gas and head off to Cornwall for Game #2 Jersey #35. Jersey #1 was beyond disappointed that, unlike his two siblings, his schedule for the Great Hockey Weekend of 2012 did not permit him a day off school.

"The hockey gods hath no mercy," I told him. "I should know."

As a consolation prize, I passed him $10 for a rare cafeteria lunch, without admitting the real reason: I had forgotten to make his lunch. I then left a quick note next to the half-empty coffee machine reminding my sleeping in-laws that my friend, and hockey angel, Karen would pick up my daughter for Game #2 Jersey #31 for her late morning game in Nepean. I also left a map and directions, and quickly texted Karen to tell her I was going to collect my daughter… whenever. She understood.

After having lunch in Cornwall with my oldest, I left him in the care of yet another hockey angel for Game #6 Jersey #35, and quickly returned home to Game #4 Jersey #31. I retrieved my daughter from Karen's care, but not before printing off the directions for my in-laws for Game #5 Jersey #1 in Osgoode.

"Hope you're having a nice day!" I said, as I came in the front door and headed out the back door.

Sadly, the game scores barely registered with me throughout this weekend, for I secretly prayed that none of our teams advanced beyond the round robin games. I ignored my husband's texts from Florida looking for updates. I knew my daughter had lost one game and tied another as we headed to the local sports bar for a team dinner. I wasn't sure what my in-laws were eating that night.

When taking my drink order the waitress asked, "Would that be a six-ounce glass or a nine-ounce glass of chardonnay?"

The hockey dad next to me answered on my behalf, "I think she'll just take the bottle," taking the words right out of my mouth!

Oh yes, she too was a hockey angel, that waitress!

At some point, hockey angel Nancy returned my firstborn to me, Jersey #35, and offered to take him to their afternoon game in Cornwall on Saturday. I mentioned that my in-laws might like to see Game #7 Jersey #35 for they had not yet seen him play, but I soon reconsidered that statement and took her up on her offer. I quickly printed off another map for the in-laws, and offered them the job of spectators, but not chauffeur.

Saturday morning came and I felt I was being pulled to the white light. Only it wasn't the white light, it was another gas station, and I was off to Game #8 Jersey #31 in Nepean. My second tour of volunteer duty followed soon thereafter, for which I dragged my daughter along for the ride. I was happy to share the quiet of late Saturday afternoon raffle table sales with several other hockey moms and our daughters running around the arena selling 50/50 tickets to a slowly emptying arena. We were both soon off to Osgoode to take in Game #9 Jersey #1, who sadly (or thankfully) lost all three games in their tournament.

At this point in the weekend, I'd lost track of my in-laws and my firstborn, Jersey #35, but he had the foresight to text me that they were together somewhere along the 401 between Cornwall and Ottawa, and would be home for dinner.

Oh right. Dinner.

He also confirmed that his team had advanced to the quarter-finals Sunday morning, and we were on for Game #10 Jersey #35.

Now officially out of clean travel mugs, I knew the weekend must be drawing to an end. Game #10 Jersey #35 saw a loss for my firstborn's team, and therein ended the Great Hockey Weekend of 2012. My in-laws, who had been treated to a rare grandkid hockey-fest, were able to catch at least one game of each grandchild, even though all were regrettably in one stretch of thirty-six-hours.

Hockey moms know full well that the hockey community stretches beyond the immediate family, and often grandparents, aunts and uncles are among the spectators (or are called upon for angel duty).

With post-hockey latte in one hand and a basket of dirty laundry in the other, I felt as relaxed as I could with ninety percent of my weekend "to-do" list still to do.

I looked at the dogs and shared a happy thought out loud with them: "We made it!" This thought was quickly followed by another, not-so-happy thought....

"Oh no! Did anyone feed you guys this weekend?"

~Astra Groskaufmanis
Ottawa, Ontario

48

Playing with Your Whole Heart!

Dream Your Dream, Make it a Great Dream, and Dream it Greatly!
~Plato, and Father Athol Murray

When I was a kid growing up in Kincardine, Ontario, we were all big Toronto Maple Leaf fans. I loved playing hockey but, like in most small towns in Canada, at the time, girls' hockey wasn't available. So, I entered the minor hockey system and played with the boys. I loved it. This worked well enough through the lower levels, but I knew at a certain point I'd need to find a team where I could play with girls.

My older brother, Caleb, decided to go to a private sports school in Saskatchewan where he could play hockey and when I was in grade six, my family visited him there. I fell in love with the place.

When I was fifteen and it was time for me to stop playing hockey with the boys, I wrote a letter to Notre Dame asking if I could come. They called and said, "Yes! Come! We're starting a hockey team for girls; we'd love to have you!"

So at age fifteen I attended this great school where I got to play hockey every day as part of the school program. I played lots of other sports too, but for me, it was always about hockey. I learned a lot about discipline, and my skating really improved from playing on their big Olympic sized ice surface.

It turned out that Notre Dame was about more than just hockey; it also gave me a whole lot of valuable wisdom about life. I'd always worked hard because I loved to play hockey, but there I learned to work even harder, manage my time better, how to be a leader, and how to keep balance in my life between sports and academics.

I also learned how to set goals — how to dream a dream — and go for it. I knew I wanted to get a teaching degree, but my dream was to play hockey as long as I could, and now I could see how my dream might actually happen.

When I graduated in 1992, my hard work had paid off. I was accepted at Dartmouth College, an Ivy League school in New Hampshire, to play collegiate hockey. I was able to continue to play hockey, along with competing in track and field, while I completed my degree. I was pretty pumped.

After I graduated from Dartmouth in 1996 I did a two-year degree program in Education at the University of Regina and earned my B.Ed — the first part of my dream fulfilled. Then, in 1998, the university presented me with an unexpected opportunity. When I arrived they'd had a women's club hockey team. The Athletic Department decided to start a Varsity Hockey team and play in the CIAU. I applied for the position of coach. By now I'd realized that I might have to modify my hockey dream — and what better way than to coach. When they offered me the job on an honorarium basis while I completed my Master's in Education, I didn't know where it would lead but I knew this was what I wanted. I accepted the position.

Financially it was quite challenging but I loved the job. After the third season the university made it a full-time salaried position, so I stayed!

A few years later I was approached by Hockey Canada and they invited me to become part of their team coaching pool, which was an amazing honour. In 2011 I was named head coach of the Canadian National Under-Eighteen Women's Hockey team.

When we went to Sweden in 2011 to compete I finally got my first experience at a World Hockey Championship. After an exciting tournament we advanced to the final game against the Americans, and brought home the silver medal for Canada!

Getting to hear our anthem after every win was an incredible experience; I was so proud of those girls and their achievement! I've also coached the Women's Under-Twenty-two National Team, both as assistant coach and as head coach.

I love working with my girls. I enjoy helping them learn to find the balance between sports, athletics and giving back to the community. I take pride in being able to see what their demands are, and being able to manage them and help them find balance.

Back when I was a kid in Kincardine, I dreamed my dream, and set my goals. I wanted to play hockey at the highest level I could for as long as I could, and while I wasn't quite good enough to play on a national team, I've fulfilled that ambition by becoming an elite-level coach. I couldn't have guessed I'd be involved as a coach with Canada's national teams, but I'm very happy. I started out wanting to be a teacher and work with kids, but it turns out that what I really love is coaching. I've been able to build a career I really love out of my passion for hockey!

Today I'm the mother of an active little girl, which brings my life additional balance and great happiness. So I'm a working mom. I'm very satisfied with my life and I take immense pride in what I do. I really love watching the girls grow and develop, and knowing I'm part of that is just a great feeling. I'm also very proud of developing the women's hockey program here at the University of Regina into an excellent one, a place where I'd send my own kids.

I'm inspired by kids who still play sports with their friends, road hockey or whatever—just because they love to play, and not because of where they think it can get them. I think we all need to do things that bring us happiness, and I'm lucky to be doing that on a daily basis.

When I do something, I go all out—and whatever I do, I think it's important to play with my whole heart! I really am living my dream!

~Sarah Hodges
Regina, Saskatchewan

49

Blue Line Blues

The game is bigger now, but it will never be bigger than a small boy's dreams.
~Bobby Hull

I almost spit out my Cap'n Crunch at the breakfast table when my dad told me he'd signed me up. From that moment on I thought of almost nothing else. For an eight-year-old boy growing up in Toronto in the fall of 1967, it was understandable.

I'd been tearing up the rink at our school for a couple of years already. On our street I thought I was road hockey's answer to Bobby Orr. The garage door looked like it had been used to stop cannon balls. Most vertical surfaces in our house bore the scars of a hockey-mad kid. Of course, Saturday nights were spent in the den with my dad watching the Toronto Maple Leafs on *Hockey Night in Canada*. But all of that was a mere prelude to the glory to come.

I was going to play house league hockey!

That's where men suited up and clashed just like titans on frozen oceans. Well, not quite... but it was where future stars were born. I wanted to be Bobby Orr. I wanted to be Dave Keon. They were my heroes long before the Great One and Sidney Crosby came along. But they all had to start somewhere and, in hockey, that's house league.

Unlike titans, nobody had to try out for house league. If you could put one skate in front of the other you'd have a good chance of being a star. The kids who could barely stand on skates played goal.

House league also had dressing rooms, benches, nets, blue lines, red lines, referees, penalties and fans. Just like the Leafs. But more important than all of those things, the key to a boy's happiness, fulfillment and self-esteem: team sweaters with matching socks! Putting them on for the first time would be a thrill I'd never forget. However, that moment didn't come off quite the way I'd hoped.

Saturday morning my dad drove us to the sports store to buy hockey gear. Seeing all those shelves full of helmets and pads was exciting to say the least. I walked out of there with all the stuff I needed: a helmet, gloves, shoulder pads, elbow pads, kneepads and hockey pants. Actual Maple Leaf Blue hockey pants! My dad explained to me why the jockstrap was a must. I couldn't wait to add my new team sweater and show my stuff to the world.

I had only one month to practice before the season began. Would the school rink be ready in time? Then one morning there it was. They'd put up the boards and flooded it overnight. The ice was so clear you could see the frozen grass underneath.

Shortly after my first day on the ice kids started showing up to play every morning. We'd go at it and then it was off to class. The school day took forever; much of it was spent in a trance staring out the windows at the rink. Getting through the day without a detention would get you back on the ice by 3:35 p.m. On the weekends, we'd spend all day on the ice, tossing our sticks in the centre, choosing teams and playing every game for the Stanley Cup. I'd be late for dinner, trudging home in my skates on feet that were numb from being tied up in those skates for eight hours in sub-zero temperatures.

The never-ending month finally passed.

I woke up during the night before my opening game—my big day—feeling funny. I had a strange taste in my mouth. I spent the next few hours throwing up with guttural cries my mom later described as "quite a performance." She nursed me through it. At some point, I fell asleep.

By the time I got up, the night was a vague memory. It was early and no one was awake yet. I felt just fine, excited as heck despite my overnight stand at the toilet bowl. I took my equipment out of the closet, put on my pads, stepped into my hockey pants and went downstairs to the den. (In a couple of hours, I'd be playing my first game in my brand new uniform.)

All I remember about the next few minutes are two things: Mom saying something like "Don't worry Sport, You'll be all set for next week." That and crushing disappointment.

She said I had the flu and I was too sick to play. There'd be no house league this day. No referees' whistles or cheers from the crowd. And no new sweater. Not for another week at least.

Over the years I'd often remind my dad about what he did for me that day, how he made sure at least part of my dream came true.

I spent the day in bed and was sick one more time. At some point I drifted off to sleep. When I awoke, on the end of my bed sat a bag. Inside I found a brand new hockey sweater and socks! They were white with blue stripes. Leaf colours! The team logo read "Simpson's Cartage." On the back was number 14. My dad had not only gone to the arena to get my new uniform, but he made sure it had the number of my hockey hero on the back!

The following week I finally made my debut. I even scored a goal in my very first house league game. It was a great season and we ended up league champs.

I continued playing organized hockey for many years, and have lots of great memories. But none will ever compare to that first season when I got to live my dream, had a dad around to make things happen, and wore the coolest team sweater I ever had.

~Gregory Ryan
Toronto, Ontario

Riverside Ritual

The thinner the ice, the more anxious is everyone to see whether it will bear.
~Josh Billings

The rumours began circulating at afternoon recess. A brisk November breeze was deepening the already bitter cold temperatures on the school playground and battering the seventh and eighth graders, who huddled in small groups speculating excitedly.

Winter had arrived in the form of light snow and sub zero temperatures on Remembrance Day and the frigid weather had stayed with us for more than a week. I was new to Riverside Public School, which, true to its name, was situated hard on the bank of the Credit River near where it emptied into Lake Ontario. Our family had moved to Port Credit during the summer and I had enjoyed my first few months at Riverside. My teacher was cool, my classmates were friendly and I had already earned a position on the village's peewee ice-hockey team. But I was still getting used to the customs and traditions of the school and I was about to discover a new one.

As a sixth grader, I was able to wander close enough to the seniors to overhear the words, "tonight, after school" and "at the river." Something was up.

The recess bell rang. We lined up to enter but the teacher had to quiet the buzz of conversation before admitting us. Once seated things settled down until one of my classmates entered late from a visit to the washroom. He brought with him important news. A hastily scribbled note began to make the rounds. I noted the interest and smiles as the message made its way toward me. My friend Bill received it, read it and then passed it to me, whispering "Great news!"

I opened the note. "After school, at the river, hares, ice. Be there." I had no idea what it meant. I started to pass the note on when a voice of authority brought me up short.

"John, you know my rule. If you pass notes everyone gets to know the contents. Please read your note to the class." There was no escape.

"Yes sir. It says: 'After school... at the river... hares... ice... be there.'"

"Really?" said my teacher. "That's terrific and about time! I think I'll go myself to watch the fun. Now let's get down to work."

I still had no idea what was up, perhaps a fight, but I doubted a teacher would want to watch or permit it. I looked to Bill for more information but he mouthed, "Meet me after class." I would have to wait.

Dismissal came. Bill had already crossed the street that ran between the school and the river and called for me to join him on the bank. Many other kids followed, and everyone's attention began to focus on a group below us, near a large boathouse and dock at the edge of the frozen river.

"Okay Bill, what's going on?"

He pointed, "See those kids? That's the Hare family. They're getting ready to test the ice. It looks good, but there is a pretty strong current here and you can never be sure when it is safe. The Hares own that boathouse and are experts on testing the ice, but it's their way of doing it that attracts all the attention."

Standing on the dock, the group of kids was dominated by a very large teenager. I knew one of them; a seventh grader, Don (Duckie) Hare, and the others were his brothers. The big guy was Albert (Albie) the oldest, and he had a coil of rope slung over his shoulder. The ritual began with Albie tying the rope around the waist of his little brother Billie, a first grader, and then lowering him onto the ice.

Billie did not seem reluctant and, with the rope trailing behind, he began inching his way out onto the ice. A hush fell and conversation ceased as little Billie made his way toward the centre of the river. About twenty yards off shore he stepped on some crunchy shell ice, stopped and looked back. But his brothers encouraged him until he reached the middle of the river. Turning, he then scuttled quickly back to shore to cries of, "Way to go Billie!" and mitten muffled applause from the watchers.

Next up was Duckie. Secured to the rope, he too began carefully, mincing his way gingerly away from shore, one tentative step at a time, until he was well out onto the ice. His return to shore was a tad more dramatic. After making a running start he then slid back to the dock, finishing with a flourish, grasping a piling with one hand and waving to the crowd with the other. He also was heralded by the gathering.

Then the crowd began to chant, "Albie, Albie!"

Albert Hare responded by tying the rope to his own waist and securing the other end to the dock. He stepped down to the ice and, like his brothers, his first few steps were tentative.

Then he stopped suddenly. A loud "crack," like a pistol shot, sounded and a sudden fissure appeared in the ice.

The crowd gasped. After pausing briefly to assess the situation, Albie carried on. Once he reached the centre of the river he turned to face the shore and began to jump up and down. The ice held. Suddenly a mighty cheer went up from the onlookers; the test was complete. The ice was safe. Let a winter of fun begin!

Before I graduated from elementary school I witnessed this ritual three times. Not once did a Hare fall through the ice, and their validation of safety was the signal for hundreds of us to begin enjoying winter on our booted blades of steel.

Years later I moved north to begin my teaching career. I pleasure skated, played hockey and coached my children's hockey teams indoors, on artificial ice.

To this day, when winter descends and the lake near my home freezes, I dig out my skates and hockey stick and take a trip back in time on natural ice. And when I make those first tentative strokes, along with the snick snick of my blades carving the ice, I hear chanting—"Albie, Albie"—and remember the simple joy of knowing the ice was safe and my winter fun could begin.

~John Forrest
Orillia, Ontario

Chicken Soup for the Soul

The Puck Whisperer

People would say, "Girls don't play hockey. Girls don't skate."
I would say, "Watch this."
~Hayley Wickenheiser

For as long as I could remember, I wanted to play hockey. But girls growing up in rural, northern Ontario in the 1970s and 80s didn't play hockey, they figure skated. It wasn't until shortly after my thirtieth birthday when I approached a woman leaving my local rink with a hockey bag slung over her shoulder and a hockey stick in her hand that I discovered a beginner, recreational, hockey league for men and women.

The next season, I joined the league, bought and borrowed some equipment, and couldn't wait for my first game. I was placed on the "teal team," one of four teams in the league, and was one of only two females on the team.

I could barely skate that first season, and often grabbed one of my fellow players to help me stop. While all the players were new to the sport, I definitely was the weakest player on the team. But I was lucky to play with a group of guys (and Samantha) who didn't mind me using them as a wall to help me stop; they encouraged me and tried to help me accomplish my big dream: to score a goal.

As the season wore on, every player on my team had scored a goal except me. Even our goalie had an assist—something else I hadn't accomplished. I played left wing and my right wing man was always Lance, who could have been a stand-up comedian. He knew (as did all my teammates) about my desperate desire to score. Whenever we were on the bench, he'd have me in stitches as he'd strategize ways to help me score.

"I've got an idea, Sandi," Lance deadpanned. "You skate to the net and yell to the goalie, 'Your fly's down!' Then, I'll pass you the puck, and while the goalie's looking down at his fly, you pop the puck in the net. What do you think?"

I giggled. "I think the goalie's too smart to fall for that one, especially since hockey pants don't have flies."

"Here's another strategy next time we're on," Lance explained two weeks later. "You could point to the stands and yell, 'Look, someone brought the Stanley Cup!' Every hockey player wants to see the Cup. While the goalie is looking at the stands trying to see the Cup, I'll pass you the puck and you zing that baby behind the crease."

In spite of Lance's support (and crazy ideas), our team had one game left against the maroon team, and I had yet to score.

During the warm-up, Lance and I stretched in front of our bench.

"See that goalie in the maroon jersey, shoot on him. But see that player in the teal jersey," Lance pointed to our goalie. "Don't shoot on him. He's our guy."

I laughed, "I can't even score on the opposing team's goalie, so I think our goalie's safe."

"Hey, don't get discouraged. I'm going to whisper a message to the puck to let you score." The ref had put the game puck at centre ice and as we stretched, Lance stared at the puck, with buggy eyes, and began whispering. I was chuckling so hard that I couldn't hear what he was saying.

Lance's puck whispering didn't help me in the first or second period, but it did help two of my teammates who scored. Unfortunately the other team must have had a puck whisperer on their side because they scored one goal in the second and another early in the third making the score 2-2 with a minute left in the game.

Lance and I were on for this last shift of the game and as we skated to the face-off circle, Lance winked and with a twinkle in his eyes said, "Don't worry, Sandi, I've whispered to the puck, and mark my words some hockey magic will happen before this game is over."

With fifty seconds to go in the game, their goalie almost stood on his head making a remarkable save, stopping an amazing shot from the point by our right defenseman.

Then, with thirty seconds left, the other team's centre got a breakaway and fired the puck on our goalie. The puck rebounded and was caught by our left defenseman who hammered it down the ice for an icing call.

The clock showed twenty-five seconds left in the period. I was proud of myself for finally learning how to play hockey, and figured with such little time left I'd have to wait until next season to score.

The face off was in our end. Our centre won the face-off and passed the puck to one of the defensemen. And then the hockey magic happened...

The defenseman passed the puck up to me, and in a miraculous moment I caught the pass. Suddenly I tore up the ice with Lance skating a little ahead of me. Even though he was supposed to be on the other side of the ice from me, for some reason he was only a few feet away. As soon as he hit the blue line, he performed a dramatic slow plow stop to avoid an offside call. I popped the puck through Lance's legs, darted around him, and caught the puck on the other side. Next, I made a marvellous pass to our centre, who then shot the puck on the net. He missed. Somehow I anticipated this, had my stick firmly planted on the ice, and got the rebound.

The goalie, who was still facing our centre on the other side, didn't manage to turn in time to stop me as I trickled the puck into the net. It wasn't a pretty goal, but it was a goal nonetheless.

The guys on the ice swarmed me and my teammates on the bench cheered so loudly that they could have woken sleeping babies across the country. We won the final game of the season 3-2 and I scored my first goal—the winning goal of the game!

After the game, the ref presented me with the game puck, something I keep in my hockey bag to this day.

That moment happened ten years ago. I still play hockey, although now I play in a women's league, so I no longer have Lance whispering to the puck for me. I'm still not the greatest player on the team, but I have scored many goals since that first one.

A few years ago a woman named Sarah joined our team having never played hockey before. Halfway through the season, she hadn't scored yet and shared her frustration with me during the warm-up. I told her about Lance and my first goal, and I whispered to the puck for her. Do you know what happened? She scored that game. Perhaps the puck sometimes does listen to the puck whisperer.

~Sandra McTavish
Toronto, Ontario

Hockey Bells

Ice hockey is a form of disorderly conduct in which the score is kept.
~Doug Larson

In my small Ontario town, hockey is king. We don't have a shopping mall or a fancy restaurant, but in the centre of town we do have a large two-pad arena, and our very own hockey team — the Sugar Kings, named after maple syrup, another thing our town is famous for.

My husband's favorite hockey team is our twelve-year-old son's Pee Wee team, and he cheers them on wildly. One day, a friend lent him a large metal cowbell that he started bringing to games, to supplement his enthusiastic cheering. I hated that bell. The ringing embarrassed me to no end. It was loud and clangy, and he seemed to ring it throughout the game with any good pass or save. I tried to hide the bell, and began sitting as far away as possible from him, cringing as that bell sounded out across the ice.

Then, during a home game when the enthusiastic crowd was raising the roof with their shouts, a fan brought an especially loud horn called a vuvuzela. It was so loud it disturbed local residents, who began to make official noise complaints. This resulted in the township passing a new noise bylaw. Making any noise louder than a quiet cheer was now banned at all hockey games in town.

The fans were outraged. How could they possibly sit quietly as their team scored, saved a puck from the net, or made a great pass? "This is not a library!" they loudly objected.

For a few weeks, my husband complied and put his beloved bell away. Then he got an idea. At a local iron shop he had a number of specially designed bells made, painted them in our hockey town colours. Then, bells in hand, he went to visit the mayor. "These hockey bells are to encourage good, healthy cheering," he explained, and then gave him his own special bell. The mayor was impressed, and put a personally signed seal of approval on each bell.

The mayor also made some amendments to the noise bylaw, and the bells were allowed. The only stipulation was they could only be rung for a few seconds at a time. "But for those five seconds we will ring them as loud as we can!" my husband grinned.

By the end of the first week my husband had sold all the bells he had made. Then people started coming to the door looking to buy more. The boys on my son's team loved hearing the bells as they played, knowing it was their fans cheering them on.

At the next game, a reporter from the local newspaper came to the arena and did a front-page story about the hockey bells. Accompanying it was a photo of all the parents of the players on my son's hockey team - proudly holding their bells high.

The season continued, the bells rang, and as the last playoff game ended, I looked around the arena. That single bell I had wanted to silence had instead multiplied, and with it, brought people together. I surrendered, and raising my hockey bell high—I let it ring!

~Lori Zenker
Elmira, Ontario

Pond-Skating Season

Winter came down to our home one night
Quietly pirouetting in on silvery-toed slippers of snow,
And we, we were children once again.
~Bill Morgan, Jr.

When we boarded the plane for Toronto, all of our essential possessions (including two pairs of skates) were packed into two hockey bags. I'd wanted to bring more books, but my boyfriend, Craig, had insisted on the skates.

"What's the point in going to a place where there's real winter if you don't have skates?" he'd said.

It was the mid 1980s, and we were leaving behind an economic slump in BC, no job prospects, and looming student loan payments to return to school to earn a master's degree at York University.

Settling into North York and the university, everything felt new and exciting. Then, as the leaves fell from the trees and an icy wind (which we hadn't expected) pierced through our Cowichan sweaters and blew black grit several stories up the sides of apartment buildings, the differences between Toronto and the west coast became glaring. No mountains. No ocean. We'd ask for brown bread in a restaurant, and the waitresses thought we meant toast. There were no neighbourhood pubs. People talked about American football, and going to Florida for spring break. No one recycled. Worse, there was no coverage of Vancouver Canucks hockey.

"It's all Toronto," was Craig's repeated complaint as he riffled through the sports section of the *Toronto Sun*, a look of disgust on his face.

"Look." He tossed the open newspaper onto the grad residence-issue coffee table, a slightly more "skookum" version of a basic wood Ikea table. "Back page. Vancouver 5. Los Angeles 3. That's it."

The feeling of isolation and desolation grew as the winter progressed and the days grew shorter. I'd sit alone in my study cubicle on campus, watching darkness settle on the grey spindly trees of the "woodlot" north of the building, and feel homesick for big, mossy, Wild west coast trees, for my friends and for my family. The discordant calls of starlings seeking shelter for the night seemed amplified, as if echoing through an empty space. There was no sign of the beautiful Ontario winter we'd expected.

Then it snowed. We woke up one morning to find the campus transformed. All the grey, grimy ugliness was hidden under a clean, white blanket. Between classes, people who had never spoken to each other before gathered together at windows. The international students from Africa, who were seeing snow for the first time, chattered excitedly.

Craig and I walked out into the woodlot. The branches were now laden with snow, and a hush among the trees seemed full and expectant. As we stood for a moment, bird songs started up again, and the red wings of a cardinal flickered ahead of us through the trees. We walked deeper into the woodlot, making our way to the pond at its centre.

On the west coast, winters are mild, and areas of water seldom freeze hard enough to skate on. My boyfriend and his friends were always the first out testing local lakes and ponds, ready to skate the moment the ice could hold their weight. So, of course, we'd already been out to test the woodlot pond. The last time we'd checked, the ice still wasn't nearly thick enough, and we were beginning to wonder if it had been a mistake to pack our skates from BC to Ontario after all. This time, we approached the pond holding our breaths, and Craig cautiously took a step onto the frozen surface. It held. Laughing, we slid through the snow, grabbing onto each other as our feet slipped out from under us.

Back in our faculty building, the Ontario students scoffed when we told them the ice was thick enough to skate on.

"It's not even Christmas yet," they said. "The ice won't be thick enough until January."

Back home, ice (on the rare occasions it formed) could be thawed by the next day, and there was no guarantee it would freeze again that winter. We did not believe in missing opportunities. I hurried back to the student apartments to get our skates, and Craig recruited a French Canadian student (a Montreal Canadiens fan, equally enthusiastic about hockey and the prospect of skating), to help him clear the snow from the ice with a piece of plywood salvaged from the faculty storage room.

By the time classes finished that day, there was a buzz of excitement throughout the building. An impromptu Christmas party started. When Craig and Jean-Marc announced the ice was ready, the party spilled outside into the woodlot. Once they'd demonstrated the solidity of the ice, skepticism quickly gave way. Skates were donned, hockey sticks and a puck materialized, and voices and laughter filled the woodlot. I took off my skates and lent them to a student from Nairobi, who had never stood on ice before. She laughed with the unrepressed delight of a child as two other students took hold of her arms and pulled her across the pond.

As the sounds of laughter and skates scraping across ice wove through the trees and drifted out across the snow-covered campus, I knew we'd packed the right "essentials" for our move to Toronto. Pond-skating season had begun.

~Jacqueline Pearce
Vancouver, British Columbia

54

No Taste for Skating

*If you can't laugh at yourself, then how can you laugh at anybody else? I
think people see the human side of you when you do that.*
~Payne Stewart

I never learned to skate. Do you realize how tough that is for a
Canadian to admit? To this day when I tell people I can't skate,
I feel like I'm confessing to some cold case crime. Sometimes I
think that's exactly how they react to the confession.

It wasn't for a lack of effort. I tried to learn, and one winter I
almost made it.

First you need to understand a little about the town I grew up
in. It sits almost in the middle of the great Canadian prairie. Wakaw,
Saskatchewan; the name derived from the nearby lake. Wakaw itself
is Cree for crooked. In later years I would describe my childhood
there as *Stand by Me* without the dead body. There were many pleasant summers spent at the crooked lake, many summer adventures
of comrades left together to their own devices. Winter was another
story. Winter was about hockey and skating.

Two large landmarks distinguished our thriving town from
smaller villages and hamlets nearby. One was the looming pale green
water tower, and the other right beside it, a large aluminum granary-
like structure; the local hockey arena. As a child I had assumed one
was built near the other so they had easy access to enough water to
form a sheet of ice. I'm not sure it wasn't so.

By the time they were eleven most of my friends and school-mates were quite proficient at skating. The boys played hockey, the girls were into figure skating. That's just the way it was. I would often hear my dad comment about a local little hockey star, "That kid could skate before he could walk."

How was that possible? I would wonder. I spent a lot of time contemplating such life mysteries. That, along with hobbies, comic books, et al, was probably why I never bothered learning to skate. There always seemed to be something more interesting happening in my room.

But then one day Marnie Madsen happened. Marnie was about as sweet a vision as one could imagine, and imagine I did. At that age I wasn't even sure why I was interested, but I was. Marnie sat next to me in class, and one day she asked why I never came out to the rink Saturday and Sunday afternoons for public skating. I think I told her I had "stuff." I think I *did* have stuff. I wouldn't dare tell her I didn't skate.

I actually had been at the rink upon occasion during those after-noons and, unnoticed, I had observed the clockwise rhythm of public skating. Many of the boys and girls I knew skated together as couples, holding hands. Aha, so *that's* what she meant. Suddenly, "not skating" became a huge void in my life. I had to learn. How tough could it really be? I had seen people do it, and that one kid apparently could do it before he could walk. I already had the walking. I could just walk... on ice... with blades on my feet. No problem.

I talked my parents into a pair of skates for Christmas, never letting on the reason for my newfound desire. Near the beginning and end of public skating times, when my friends were least likely to be there, I went and began practicing, making sure Marnie would never see me. (One could imagine there would have been a series of homemade rinks and frozen ponds on the prairie where I could learn on my own. But if they existed I was unaware of them. And one *never* went to the lake in the winter.)

After several weeks I was good enough to give it a go. I arrived early and was skating at a pretty good clip when Marnie stepped onto the ice. Surprised to see me she called out as I passed. I can hear her voice to this day. "Larry!" she said, because what else would you say? I turned quickly to say hi, and suddenly my whole body turned. I was now skating backwards. Just one thing, I didn't know how to skate backwards. I started to lose my balance. My arms flailed trying not to fall and crack the back of my head open. It worked. Instead I fell forward, and literally, flat on my face.

I don't remember much of the next few seconds, including why I didn't use my hands to break my fall. I assume my arms had been flailing all the way to impact. Some older boys picked me up off the ice and said my face was full of blood. My tongue hurt, and when I stuck it out I heard a gigantic "Ewww" from the crowd, including Marnie. I had bitten a piece off the end of my tongue, and it was now hanging by a thread from the rest of my tongue. I can't explain why my tongue would've been between my teeth at the exact split second I hit the ice. It just was.

The older kids drove me to the hospital and called my parents. I had three stitches on my tongue, and I got to live on milkshakes for the next two weeks. More importantly I also, and finally, had a skating story to tell at school. My skating career ended that day. I never went back.

Years later we moved, and I lost touch with Marnie.

I never forgot the experience, but the story didn't really surface again until many years later when my own young son expressed an interest in learning to skate. Obviously I had not thought about him skating or playing hockey, because of what had happened to me.

Luckily, Santa brought him skates that Christmas and I took him to a local rink to learn, me wearing slip proof winter boots. I told him that Dad couldn't help him much because I didn't skate. He assured me that he already knew how, even though this was his very first time. He had seen people do it. "It was like walking with skates on," he thought.

I never held Marnie's hand, but I held his tightly and walked him out onto the ice. He told me he was okay on his own, and off he went. You know what? That kid could skate. He *did* know how.

"Don't bite the end of your tongue off!" I yelled, and as he turned to me he was skating backwards. But it was all right. He could do that too. The kid was a natural. I was in awe.

The salty and sweet taste buds are in the tip of your tongue. For a while they worried that I might lose those, or at least some sensitivity to those tastes. I never did.

Over the years I have tasted many salty tears, some from very sweet memories, like those of Marnie and of my son skating for the first time, ensuring that at least someone in the family wouldn't have to make that embarrassing Canadian confession. I can't skate.

~Larry Fedoruk
Toronto, Ontario

55

A Hockey Grandma's Jacket

Nobody can do for little children what grandparents do.
Grandparents sort of sprinkle stardust over the lives of little children.
~Alex Haley

"Oh! Thank you so much," I said as I pulled the lovely black jacket from the box, noticing it had the name of my grandson's hockey team printed on the front. "What a perfect birthday gift. It is just what I wanted."

My daughter promptly informed me that, if it fit correctly, they would have "Hockey Grandma" printed on the back.

"I will wear it with pride," I proudly announced as I held it up for all to see. "What a meaningful gift." They also announced they would print "Hockey Grandpa" on the jacket my husband received for his birthday, as well.

As the party continued, I smiled as I watched my eleven-year-old grandson devouring his chocolate cake with his sister and cousins by his side.

"I'm glad you like it, Grandma!" he said when he had swallowed his mouthful of cake and ice cream. I was fortunate that all four of my grandchildren enjoyed their own individual interests. It made being a grandma very interesting, indeed. It also helped me discover and learn a lot of new things about myself.

While my husband has always been a serious hockey lover, I have to admit that up until my grandson started to play, I had little or no time for the game. I had convinced myself that I had no interest in sports at all.

As I sipped on my coffee, I thought back to the first few times my grandson was on skates at the age of three. He definitely rebelled against the idea of having to stand up and move around on such a cold slippery surface. After numerous attempts that only resulted in more downers, my little guy chose the only other way he could think of to handle this dilemma. He lay down flat on his back on the ice, arms and legs spread eagled, and with the most pitiful, helpless look he could muster, he turned his face towards his grandma and cried as loud as he could.

Thankfully, the skating lessons continued and the more my grandson practiced and learned, the more he grew to love the game. The more he loved the game the better he played. Hockey became the highlight of his winter months.

My husband and I started to attend his games on Saturdays, and I started to develop a genuine interest in the sport. I even began taking an interest in the Saturday night hockey game.

"So you are watching the game with me tonight?" my husband would ask with a smile on his face. As we all watched the game during dinner, it brought us closer together.

At work I found myself asking, "Did you watch the game last night?" Even at the hospital, I found that the patients who suffered from dementia would sometimes perk up if we talked about hockey.

"You know, I never thought I would look forward to reading the sports page before I go to work," I told my husband one day.

"I never thought you would either," he laughed as we drove to my grandson's game.

As I tried on my hockey jacket, I thought about how important it is for me to try on different coats in life, even those that did not fit that well before.

"Look! It fits great!" I declared.

"Way to go!" my grandson, Liam, declared.

~Elizabeth Smayda
Burnaby, British Columbia

Chapter 6

O Canada The Wonders of Winter

Love in the Snow

The Inuit has fifty-two names for snow because it is important to them; there ought to be as many for love.

~Margaret Atwood

Ski You Later

*You will find as you look back upon your life that the moments
when you have really lived are the moments when you have
done things in the spirit of love.*

~Henry Drummond

When I first spotted Kris, she was driving a canary-yellow Ford Mustang two-door sports coupe with six cylinders under the hood and a four-speed manual transmission. Years later I would joke that I fell in love with the car before I fell in love with the tall, blond driver.

Kris and her girlfriend—both teachers—were moving into the same Toronto apartment building where I lived with my long-time buddy. The year was 1972 and all four of us were recent university graduates and starting our careers.

I was an eligible, twenty-four-year-old bachelor and Kris was a stunning bachelorette. We both loved sports and soon became good friends. Very quickly we discovered that downhill skiing was our passion.

For the next year, as we progressed from companionship to love, we found that the relationship was quickly "going downhill"—that is, we were downhill skiing often at the Blue Mountain ski area in Collingwood, Ontario. Once, on a mountain outside of Calgary, Alberta, I hinted to Kris that one day I would propose to her on top of a mountain.

For years, I'd had an abiding desire to move to Australia. The more I learned about it, the more I fell in love with it. I liked the Aussie's love of sport and the temperate climate, with 340 sunny days a year in the city of Sydney. That appealed to me since Canada sometimes seems like ten months of winter, and two months of bad skiing!

Best of all, I would not have to give up my love of downhill skiing because Aussies ski in the snow-clad Australian Alps—in July and August.

I decided I would quit my job, give up my apartment and move Down Under. That was the easy part.

The hard part would be telling Kris.

She knew of my desire to live in a country 9,670 miles from Toronto, and had made it clear she would never leave the country of her birth, her family and friends, or her teaching career.

I knew that in order to realize my dream I'd have to break up with Kris.

I chose a warm summer evening to break the news to her. I invited her to go for a walk with me in the neighborhood, and brought along some tissues because I knew there would be tears from both of us.

As we sauntered along Talara Drive, near our building, I broached the subject slowly. "You know how I've always wanted to move to Australia?"

She slowed her pace. "Yes," she replied somewhat hesitantly and expectedly, as though she knew what was coming.

"Well, I'm going to move there at the end of the summer. I wish you would come with me."

Kris stopped and looked deep into my eyes. I saw a tear roll down her cheek. I prepared for the waterworks that I knew were coming, but I was taken off guard.

"Dennis," she said in a voice as kind as could be. "I just want you to be happy, and if this will make you happy, I think you should go."

Whoa! That's not the reaction I was expecting!

Was this a test to see how much I loved her? No. I realized she was speaking one of the fundamental truths of the universe: that love isn't owned and it can't be taken, only given. She knew if you really love someone, you have to give him the freedom to choose.

I mumbled something like, "Oh, okay, um, well, we'll see."

We continued on our way but I was deep in thought about this wonderful woman walking next to me. If she was willing to sacrifice her happiness so I could live my dream, she was a very special lady.

In the coming weeks my life's priorities changed. My desire to emigrate to Australia weakened as my love for Kris strengthened. A year after that fateful walk, Kris and I were skiing at Mont Sainte-Anne near Quebec City. I knew the time had finally come, so during one ascent up the mountain in the chairlift, I proposed to her. She accepted immediately, and not because I had threatened to throw her off the chair and into the snow if she refused!

We were married on August 22, 1975 and thirty-eight years later our love is as deep as the mountain snow we have skied on together, in places like Whistler, British Columbia; Sunshine in Banff, Alberta; Steamboat Springs, Colorado; Jay Peak, Vermont; and many areas of Quebec, including Mont-Tremblant in the Laurentians, Mont-Orford in the Eastern Townships, and of course, Mont-Sainte Anne.

Kris and I have travelled together to dozens of countries since our first date and we still enjoy downhill skiing as much as we did when we first met. We've still not visited Australia, but it's on our "Bucket List" and when we do, you can be sure we'll be skiing together in the Australian Alps, and we'll think of what might have been.

We may even exchange an Australian greeting for the decisions we made so very long ago: "Good on ya, mate!"

~Dennis McCloskey
Richmond Hill, Ontario

Snow Man

My old grandmother always used to say, "Summer friends will melt away like summer snows, but winter friends are friends forever."
~George R.R. Martin

I fell in love with a man holding a snow shovel. It wasn't very convenient, in fact, I already had an ardent admirer—a fellow who was very good at math, and things were going along very smoothly with him. I was doing well in calculus, and even physics. I knew this man was destined to do great things, much greater things than ensuring that I passed my exams. But there he was, this snow man, standing outside my door, shovel in hand, a little frozen drip hanging off his reddened nose and snow clinging to his corduroy bomber jacket and toque. I shouldn't have opened the door, but I needed to know if he was the one who had been shovelling my walkway and driveway all winter long. And if he was, then why?

When I opened the door that was the end of it. Love at first sight, even with the drip. His brilliant blue eyes pierced through me and I was done for. That was it. Truth be known, we had met before, many times, but during those previous introductions there had been no love at first sight. I will even admit that he was, in fact, my physics lab partner. But there had been no snow in the physics lab. I couldn't possibly have seen there what I could see so clearly on my doorstep on a brutally cold February evening, after a huge snowfall. Or, perhaps I had just not raised my eyes.

In my heart I know it was the snow that did it. The blast of cold air that met me when the door opened, the steamy breath loosened from his own mouth as he turned and looked up to meet my eyes, just the shadow of a beard under his scarf, the drip—and those eyes. How had I not noticed those eyes before? Was it some kind of a trick? Trick eyes that brighten in extreme cold, lit from the warmth inside—that must be it. Very likely he knew about this trick and had used it before. A snow man trick.

My mother had warned me about various tricks and sudden true love. It had been the one piece of advice she had given me when I was packing my things to make my way to university—how to avoid it. Keep focused, but keep your eyes down. I had not understood about keeping the eyes down until that very moment. My mother had said nothing about snow and its ability to make blue eyes penetrate deeply to the heart. Blue-eyed herself, she probably knew about this, but I suspect if there was a shovel involved she had not been the one holding it. It was very disconcerting to have fallen in love in a split second just by opening a door. I could not lose focus. I felt a little angry.

He claimed he needed the exercise. His hockey coach had suggested shovelling snow between practices.

"I've been shovelling everyone's walkway on your street," he said.

"What about driveways?" I asked still a bit perturbed.

"Well, I just do yours, but it's such a little one, it seems silly to shovel your walkway and not do your driveway as well."

"But I don't have a car."

He seemed a little embarrassed then, but less so than I thought he should be. There were so many questions I wanted to ask him with the door wide open and the heat escaping and the cold entering. The stillness and quiet of the frigid February air peripherally sealed it. I thought I might launch myself at him and kiss him on the spot within that vortex. But, I needed more proof that my heart's piercing was a reasonable result when opening a door to a man covered in snow. The drip and driveway weren't enough. Perhaps like all snowmen, he really just liked the cold.

Weren't all the hours of ice time exercise enough, for instance? I knew enough about hockey to know he endured grueling workouts every single day, and an A on his burgundy corduroy bomber jacket told me he didn't sit on the bench much.

Didn't he have midterms to study for? I had been doing nothing else for days.

Were his eyes really that blue? Could he explain the physics behind the effects of snow on a pair of blue eyes? Could he help me with calculus? Did he want a tissue? But what I asked was if he'd like to come in for some hot chocolate.

That was our first date, I guess you could say. On our second, we built a snowman. I pressed two large blue button eyes into its dear face after he'd left. I didn't care much that I had ruined my favourite sweater to do so. I heard him say over and over again, in my brain full of the cool detachment of calculus and physics, that my eyes were the colour of hot chocolate. My reluctant heart had melted. I didn't need any further evidence. Love at first sight is a reasonable conclusion to opening the door to a snow man carrying a shovel, even if that was not your objective.

Now when there is enough snow, we build a family of six snow-men ranging from very small to very large. Half of them have brilliant icy blue eyes and half have eyes of hot chocolate.

~Carol Margaret
Fenwick, Ontario

Police Report

*'Tis sweet to know there is an eye that will mark our coming,
and look brighter when we come.*

~Lord Byron

"Gee, what a hunk!" I thought, as the blue-eyed RCMP officer strode towards me from behind the police counter.

"How can I help you, Miss?" he asked, very formally.

"My father's missing," I said without preamble. "He's overdue from driving back from a job in Edmonton, and we haven't heard from him. My mother's frantic. She thinks he's gone off the road somewhere."

"I'm acting, here, for my mom," I made sure to stress, even as I felt myself shrinking to the size of a six-year-old. "She's the one who wants to file the report."

The dashing Mountie asked me a few questions, and then filled out a missing persons report.

"I'll pass the report on to the CNR Police in Edmonton," he said. "I'm not on duty tomorrow so someone else will call you as soon as we hear something."

I repeated my phone number for him—twice, seared his nametag into my memory, thanked him, and left.

It was an exceptionally cold winter. The snow, both in town and on the highways, was above average, making for dangerously icy conditions. It certainly was out of character for my dad to not call my mom along the route from Edmonton to our hometown in north-western British Columbia — a driving distance of over 800 miles.

When I walked into the house I shared with my twin sister, I blurted out, "I've just met the most wonderful guy on the face of the earth. And… I got his name!"

"You'd better phone Mom," she said, rolling her eyes.

The next day someone, not Blue Eyes, called from the RCMP detachment to announce that my father had been located, safe and sound.

"Your dad was a little embarrassed at being pulled over by a police cruiser," the officer added. I relayed the good news to Mom and the family breathed a collective sigh of relief.

Days later, after Dad had arrived safely home, he confronted me. "Do you know how embarrassing that was? I've never been pulled over by a cop in my life."

"But Dad," I retorted in self defence. "Mom made me do it!"

Crisis passed, I searched for Blue Eyes in the phone book but he wasn't listed. Darn it, I thought, I'll never see him again.

From then on, every police car I saw took on new meaning. No longer trying to avoid them, I was now aiming for them, hoping to catch a glimpse of Blue Eyes' face. But no face was his, and a few Mountie faces even scowled at me as I nearly drove into them! After a few weeks of near misses with every police car in town, Blue Eyes was still nowhere to be seen.

Several months passed before I saw him again. As fate would have it, we crossed in the doorway of a local pharmacy. He was dressed in civilian clothes, wearing a suede leather jacket that was quite becoming. After saying an initial "Hi," I thanked him for his assistance three months earlier, we engaged in light conversation, and then slowly retreated from the doorway to get out of people's way.

Then, under the stares of other shoppers, he said the magic words: "Do you want to go somewhere for coffee?" Inside I was jumping up and down. We went to a restaurant a block away where we drank hot chocolates and talked about ourselves and our families, including my no-longer elusive dad. Before parting, we exchanged phone numbers.

"You know that wonderful policeman I told you about?" I enthused to my sister, "Well, I just had hot chocolate with him at a restaurant!"

As of this writing, we've been married thirty-eight years, and two of our four children have followed in their father's law-enforcement footsteps. I've always had an aversion to ice and snow, but when those exact winter conditions forge warm hearts, as they did with us, there's no complaint from me.

~Chantal Meijer
Terrace, British Columbia

Catching Snowflakes

Falling in love consists merely in uncorking the imagination and
bottling the common sense.
~Helen Rowland

I was twenty-seven years old. I don't know why I did it, but I turned down a dream job in Vancouver, and flew home to Toronto two weeks before Christmas.

As I unpacked at my parents' country estate, Dad endured -15 Celsius whipping winds while barbecuing steaks for us outside. We chatted over dinner at the pine table, and it was over butter tarts that my mom sprang the news. My dad had fixed the rusty red sedan I'd left behind in his shed. My insides jumped—I had wheels! I immediately called my friend Steph and made dinner plans at her house for the next day.

Waking early, I baked a loaf of bread and popped it into a gift bag to take with me. I styled my long blond hair and dressed in a black velvet skirt and black high heels.

"Aren't you dressed a bit fancy?" Mom queried. "There's a snowstorm coming. Those are not exactly sensible winter shoes."

I scowled. "I'll be inside."

"Still," said Mom, retreating to the laundry room.

"I'll be home late," I called, as I headed out.

Snowstorm, eh? Despite my bravado, as I began the forty-minute drive I decided I'd better stick to the main roads. Halfway there it started to snow like mad. Cars slowed. I strained to see even with the wipers on high.

The sound of a siren announced the approach of an ambulance and I pulled aside to let it pass. As I inched back into my lane, the traffic light ahead turned red. I stopped. My stomach grumbled. The bread made the car smell like a bakery. I realized I was starving.

The light turned green. I pressed on the gas, and then that old car sputtered and died.

I tried to start it. One click, then nothing. Before I could do anything else, two scruffy guys raced over from the nearby sidewalk. I rolled down my window a crack.

"Give us a sec," one of them said. "We'll get ya outta here." Before I could reply, they had started to push. While they pushed and guided me, I steered into a parking spot in a strip mall beside a fast food chicken joint.

"You'll be fine now," they said, and before I could even thank them, they took off into a dark lot behind the plaza.

The snow fell faster. I rolled up my window and called Steph on my cell phone to cancel. Next, I called my parents to come get me. I was parked in front of a brew-your-own-wine shop. Luckily it was open, so I went inside and explained to the well-dressed, older couple behind the counter that my car had died, and I hoped to stay in their parking spot and eat chicken while I waited for my folks.

"Certainly!" they said.

I was very hungry. But there I was in my high heels, with soaked feet. I walked to the fast food restaurant and back. My mother was right. I sighed, wondering why I'd gotten dressed up in the first place.

I feasted on chicken thighs from a cardboard box inside my frigid car. The steam rose and fogged up the windows. I wiped off a spot and looked out. There was a man coming toward my car, approaching from the dark lot where the scruffy men had gone. He was alone. As he drew near, I saw he wasn't scruffy.

Nervous and confused, I locked my car doors and sized him up. He was about my age, clean-shaven with wavy, blond hair to his shoulders, dressed in jeans and hiking boots. He looked kind of rugged.

I cracked the window.

"Hello," he said.

"Hi," I said, wiping my greasy mouth with a napkin.

"This is my dad and his wife's store," he explained. "I just took the garbage out. They said to invite you in to warm up."

"Thanks," I said, "but my parents are coming, plus I'm eating chicken."

"You can bring your food inside," he said with a smile that was very nice.

"That's nice, but I'm good," I said.

I wasn't about to pig out in front of a handsome stranger.

"But it's snowing—really, really hard," he said, tipping his head toward the black sky.

The flakes were now huge, more like goose feathers than snow. Opening his mouth, he tried to catch them on his tongue. He stepped back and dodged a little to the left, then a little to the right, and back. In that split second, I changed my mind.

"Actually, I will," I said.

"Great," he said, "'cause it's really snowing."

I smiled. "I'll just finish my chicken first."

"Sure," he said, and went inside.

Shortly after, I entered the store to a warm welcome. We all sat on high stools in the shop's rear, and chatted about the storm and holiday plans. The young man, whose name was Ian, was quiet, shy even, but he asked questions, grinned a lot, and brought me a glass of fruity red wine. My parents arrived not long after and jumpstarted my battery. After saying my thanks and goodbyes, I left the store.

"Let's go before the roads get worse," my dad said, heading for his truck. "We'll follow you in case you have trouble."

As my mom went to join my dad in the truck, I suddenly yelled, "Wait! I need to go back in."

"What for?" she asked. "You heard Dad. He wants to get home."

"Yes, I know, but… the wine store guy, Ian, I have to see him again."

"Oh for Pete's sake, don't be boy-crazy."

"No, this is different," I said.

"Sure," she said, shaking her head.

"No, it is," I insisted. "I have to go back in."

"Be fast!" instructed Mom.

I grabbed the bag of bread from my car and ran inside. Ian was not in sight, so I gave the bag to his parents, took a business card and left.

The next day, I mailed a thank-you card to the wine storeowners. In a P.S., I invited their son to join me snowboarding sometime, "as friends," and included my phone number.

The months passed and I didn't hear from him. I figured that was it. Then, in March, the night before St. Patrick's Day, my phone rang—and it was him. The next day, over green drinks, I learned his parents had sent my bread home with him the night we met, and he enjoyed it. But they had wisely kept my thank-you card—the one with my phone number, until he split from his then-girlfriend.

It turned out I was right—this was different. Eight months later Ian asked me to marry him—and I said yes! Not long after we took a trip to Vancouver, and I taught him to snowboard on Cypress Mountain. We married October 3, 1998.

This past March, we stood as giant snowflakes fell and watched our seven-year-old daughter Gracie, and our ten-year-old son Reece enjoy their first snowboard lesson in Calabogie, Ontario, proof positive that sometimes during a snowstorm in Canada you can catch more than snowflakes on your tongue—you can catch true love!

~Patricia Miller
Bradford, Ontario

Annie and the Fish Pond

*Being deeply loved by someone gives you strength, while loving someone
deeply gives you courage.*

~Lao Tzu

The minister agreed to marry us in my mother's living room so Steve wouldn't have to stand up in front of "all those people." We dressed up for the occasion, went out to dinner, and spent the night at a small country inn. One year later, with a new life and Annie making us a family, it was time to celebrate again.

The sun was warm but the hills and fields were still deeply blanketed with snow. We were moving into the little house set well back from the road and barns at the farm in the Laurentians where we would manage a flock of sheep, several chickens, and a trout pond. It was the country life we'd sought — two suburban kids escaping "real" jobs, the hustle and bustle of city life, and the noise.

In our new oasis of peace and quiet, there was no need to talk as we unpacked. The windows were open and the breeze that blew in would have flapped the curtains had there been any. A candle, scrounged from one of the many boxes strewn about the kitchen, graced the table for later. We had gathered large, brown eggs from the hen house to scramble for our anniversary supper. Everything was ready when the precious silence was shattered.

The sound soared like a soprano solo and then stalled at the point of a scream.

Sudden silence again. Steve and I looked at each other, questioning… then knowing. We recognized the voice. It was Annie. Something was wrong.

More falsetto notes drifted in through the open window.

Only Annie, our pride and joy, had a voice like that. She sang in ecstasy at the sight of you. She howled in agony at your leaving. She yodelled for the fun of it and she had the best nose for trouble of any dog I ever knew.

Her cry for help was unmistakable. Then it stopped. The silence taunted us. We were ready to run as thoughts of leg-hold traps and wild animal attacks caused us to gasp in anguish. Then high-pitched yelps rose again, this time from the direction of the fish pond.

We ploughed down the hill, up to our knees in snow softened by the April sun. The wailing continued like a siren, guiding us. When it paused, we paused, confused, hating the silence. We struggled on, now following dog tracks that circled the pond and then disappeared.

The trout pond lay in a depression between snow-covered banks and was half covered with ice. The open water in the middle was black. It was quiet. We waited, not knowing where to look next. The silence flowed around us, toying with our nerves.

Then a small brown head bobbed into view and a pitiful, water-choked cry reached us.

Annie hated water. We didn't even know she could swim. We watched as she paddled to the edge of the ice and pawed at it. She knew we were there and made no more sounds except for an exhausted wheeze. Her eyes were wide with panic and pleading. She strained to pull herself out of the water but the ice splintered under her weight. She slid backwards and her head vanished again under the cold water.

I was frantic. Annie was drowning while I stood with my hand over my mouth, unable to think.

A boot hit me on the shin. A second boot landed beside the first. Steve's jeans lay in the snow, coins and keys spilling from the pockets. His heavy flannel shirt settled in a heap. I watched him hop on one foot, then the other, as he tore off his socks. He glanced around, not meeting my eyes, and shed his underwear.

He high-stepped through the rotting ice at the pond's edge, fists clenched and shoulders hunched against the cold. He hesitated as pond muck engulfed him to the ankles. He paused, I think, to calculate the potential appetite of hibernating trout before plunging in. With water up to his neck, preserving his modesty for the moment, he reached the dog's collar and towed her to safety.

On shore, Annie yapped and cavorted. Her voice echoed around the hollow where the pond lay. Heart hammering with relief, I shushed her.

In the silence that folded around us once more, I stared as Steve retreated, bare-backed and bare-footed, through the snow to our little house, and the warmth of an anniversary candle and scrambled eggs.

~Joanne Darlington
Wentworth, Quebec

61

Children in the Snow

A grown-up is a child with layers on.
~Woody Harrelson

My husband Eric and I awoke to the loud sound of a howling dog. "Nanook wants to go outside to do his business," yawned Eric, stretching his arms into the air. "I'll take him." Eric rolled the covers back and slowly made his way out of bed.

A minute later I heard, "No way! I can't believe it."

I opened my eyes again. "What is it?"

"Shawna, the entire front door has been snowed in. We can't get out!" Eric's voice carried through the house.

Eric had opened the inside door and was staring at the glass window of the outside aluminum door. The door that was usually transparent was completely white.

"We'll have to use the back door," I said.

Eric shook his head. "It's also snowed in."

"What are we going to do?"

Nanook the Husky let out a howl as he paced the floor. He needed to go outside to do his morning business.

"I know," said Eric. "I'll try going out the window."

We walked into the living room and opened the drapes to expose our wide window. "The snow is just below the window frame," he said. "I'll get my coat and boots on and jump down first. If it's safe for the dog to come out you can guide him through."

A moment later, Eric stood on a living room chair and turned the window handle. A rush of cold fresh air flowed into the room as it opened outward, leaving a space large enough for an adult to fit through.

He put one foot up on the window ledge and then the other. The ice beneath him made crackling sounds.

"Be careful," I admonished.

Eric crouched down so he could sit on the ledge. He pushed his bottom to the edge of the windowsill until his right foot lightly touched the snow just two feet below. Grabbing onto the edge of the windowsill he tested the stability of the snow under foot.

"It feels solid." He slid his second foot down. "Okay," he said, "you can send Nanook out."

I clipped the leash onto Nanook's collar and tapped on the chair below the window with my free hand. He looked at me and then looked in the direction of the door. He had never gone out the window before and couldn't understand what I wanted. I had to lift his front legs onto the chair and then his rear end quickly followed. Outside the open window Eric kept repeating, "Come on Nanook, this way."

"Go with Eric." I encouraged. "Go outside." As Nanook leaped out the window I let go of his leash. Jumping around in the snow and wagging his tail while Eric patted him on the head, he was finally free to do his business.

"Come out and join us, Shawna," Eric said with a big smile on his face.

I quickly put on my boots and coat. Standing on the living room chair I climbed onto the ledge of the open windowsill. Never in my wildest dreams had I imagined I would be leaving my house through the living room window. It made me feel the way I did on my first trip to the playground as a child—nervous, but excited. I let go and jumped down into the snow below me. Once my feet were firm beneath me, I joyfully jumped around with Eric and Nanook. I looked up at the white snowdrifts and glistening ice that covered the walls and doors of our house. It looked like a house made of snow from a children's storybook.

That day the child inside of me let loose. My husband and I romped around in the snow with our dog for hours.

"Nanook probably thinks he is back in the Arctic," I said, as we watched him roll around on his back. And then we both laughed at our dog. It took us a few days, but we did eventually clear paths to both our doors.

Nineteen years later, we don't usually get the same snowfall amounts on the southwest corner of the island of Newfoundland as we did back then. But every winter my husband and I find ourselves reminiscing about the day we had to use the living room window as a door, and the fun we had playing like children in the snow with our dog. That winter storm left us with truly precious memories.

~Shawna Troke-Leukert
Doyles, Newfoundland

62

Skating into Winter

We have hot summers and resplendent autumns, but it is winter that estab-
lishes the character of our country and our psychology, the Canadian Mood.
~Robertson Davies

It had been a long time since my fingers had awkwardly pulled on the laces of these figure skates, a Christmas gift from my parents when I was twelve. Now twenty-nine, I was enjoying a delayed honeymoon with my new husband, in Quebec City at the Carnaval de Quebec, the Quebec Winter Carnival, a huge annual celebration of all things winter.

My husband and I did not usually celebrate winter at all. Instead, we usually clung to the safety and comfort of the couch and stayed indoors all winter. Winters left us feeling a little blue and sluggish, both mentally and physically. In our home in Fredericton, New Brunswick, winters typically lasted from November until the end of April. We were not fans of this long and dreary period of the year, and it was an odd choice for us to spend our honeymoon in cold weather. However, we were attempting to try some new activities that might help us to, if not embrace winter, at least tolerate it a little better.

Now, as we sat side by side on a wooden bench at the outdoor skating arena, we were surrounded by a crowd of rosy-cheeked smiling people. They seemed to almost hover over the frozen surface as they glided smoothly across the ice in their skates.

"There is no way that I can do that!" exclaimed my husband,

looking down at his borrowed hockey skates. "If I fall, there's no way I'll be able to get up again!"

"Well, I'll try it first," I offered, even though my own thoughts echoed his fears.

I stood up unsteadily, holding tightly to the wall surrounding the rink. I cautiously placed one skate blade onto the ice and kept both hands on the wall, holding on with a grip that kept my knuckles white. As I moved my feet against the ice, pretty soon it started to come back. After all, I had done this before. Before long I was moving in laps around the edge of the rink, carefully staying within reach of the wall so I could catch myself if necessary.

Inspired by my foolish performance, my husband gathered his courage and joined me in my clumsy movements across the ice. Holding onto each other, we were soon red-cheeked and smiling ourselves, just like the people we had watched with envy only a short time earlier.

To our amazement, it was the greatest and most inspiring afternoon of our trip! We discovered that we loved to skate!

As soon as we arrived back in Fredericton my husband did some research and discovered four arenas in our city offering recreational skating time. Suddenly, we were enthusiastic about the remaining winter ahead. We became preoccupied with how to fit the skating time slots into our weekly schedule.

My husband was skating almost every noon hour and we both eagerly anticipated the evening and weekend skates. Before we knew it, April had arrived, and skating season was over.

One sunny afternoon this past winter, we were skating around an outdoor rink at a local park enjoying the fresh, cold February air. We both had hockey sticks in hand, and laughed as we attempted to pass a puck back and forth across the ice. Looking around at the snow covered fields that sparkled in the bright afternoon light, I realized all we had been missing by dreading winter. Staying hidden inside and complaining about another long Maritime winter was no way to spend nearly five months of the year. By just trying something new, and perhaps looking a little foolish on that winter afternoon in

Quebec City, we had opened a door to a new, more fun, and much healthier lifestyle.

We were no longer sitting on the sidelines, waiting for another season to pass us by. We're enjoying every day of every season, and all the possibilities that each of those days holds!

~Kimberley Campbell
Lincoln, New Brunswick

63

Winter Roses

The color of springtime is in the flowers;
the color of winter is in the imagination.
~Terri Guillemets

There have been times, I confess, when I have struggled to see the good in winter. I do not skate. I do not snowboard. I don't careen down ski hills or leave parallel tracks across country trails. I couldn't tell you who won the Stanley Cup for many years. I am a regular Scrooge of winter; once the strings of twinkling lights festooned through trees or along verandas in December are snuffed out, only the long months of darkness lie ahead, or so I once believed. I have even Googled: *Winter—Why?*

Winter is a turning away, it seems, the earth's axis rotating away from the sun. Our planet tilts 23.3 degrees in its axis of rotation and that's why we have winter. According to science. Why were these facts not more satisfying, I mused gruffly, on those mornings when I scraped ice from the car windshield, or my weary arms and back lifted shovel after shovel of snow from the driveway? While sprinkling salt on the sidewalk, I thought about the earth turning its back on the sun; perhaps it was like two people who needed a break from each other.

This is Canada. I am supposed to embrace winter, not turn away.

Scrooge had thin blue lips. One day, after scraping the ice off the car's rearview mirror, I caught my own reflection in the round silver. My own lips were set in a tight straight line and looked suspiciously—well, blue. I was cold. I'd been scraping ice for a long time. A large stone of silence had wedged itself inside my house and neither hot ginseng drinks nor reality television shows that ended well, in weight loss or romance, could dislodge it. Since I have already confessed I was a blue-lipped curmudgeon in a toque, snow shovel or ice scraper or salt bag in hand, I will tell you these were dark days. He and I had been growing apart, and the fact that this was happening gradually, over a period of time, a winter of its own, a long, unwinding heartbreak, did not make it less difficult.

One morning, though, after an ice storm had raged for hours, sunlight flooded the old maple in the front yard until it resembled a diamond tree from a storybook and hundreds of little ice-chimes tinkled at the tips of its long graceful branches. That same morning, the seed catalogue from Prince Edward Island arrived in the mail. It was a Saturday, a holiday from scraping. I spent the day with that catalogue, growing excited while making notes and mapping the garden I would plant. I would need to start the seeds indoors and not so very long from then, either. Winter's days sped ahead as I waited for the seeds and plants to arrive. Mostly I had chosen familiar things, like tomato plants and giant marigolds. But then an inner restlessness overtook me; I went out on a limb and ordered hellebores. *Hellebores*? What an unpleasant name! How could something with that name be beautiful? But these evergreen plants, early bloomers, according to the catalogue, were also called Lenten roses or winter roses, which reassured me as I wrote the cheque to the mail order company.

The winter roses were the loveliest green bouquet against their white backdrop, their blooms brazenly early and fresh as apple blossoms. The first time I saw them I thought I was hallucinating, but they were there, those winter roses.

Winter taught me to *see*. My garden was not, after all, a withered white wasteland during the cold months. The dappled light boogied like a disco ball over the chickadees flicking around the birdfeeder. The flowerpots I'd left outside for something to look at wore adorable domed snowy caps. Then there was the fence with its long white brow, the arbor latticed in frosting, occasionally a rare red flash of cardinal, and soon, very soon, roses would rise from the snow.

Scrooge did not stay Scrooge; if he had, it would have been a terrible story. And I do not live there anymore. Difficult as it is to leave behind a garden we love, we carry with us the knowledge that we created beauty in that place. I no longer turn away. Each year the earth rotates slowly away from the sun. It brings a new patience and makes me a believer; for if roses can spring from the snow, what else might be possible?

~Jeanette Lynes
Saskatoon, Saskatchewan

64

All Hearts Lead to Niagara Falls

Our wounds are often the openings into the best and most beautiful part of us.
~David Richo

A few years ago, autumn left me with a broken heart. When the love of your life falls in love with someone that isn't you, it leaves you with cracks and bruises within the soul. The advancing of a harsh Canadian winter left me with little hope that those scars would be healed any time soon. But as much as my heart was broken, I had the desire to be surrounded by love.

Niagara Falls fit the bill. As a popular destination for honeymooners, Niagara Falls has a way to create the most intimate moments and revive the deepest loves. As much as it can help you fall in love, I thought, maybe it could help heal me from love as well.

With a few clicks of the mouse I booked myself into the Tower Hotel for a late November weekend at "The Falls." Although the nights leading up to my departure were chilly, I was already feeling a new warmth in my heart.

Using Greyhound as my personal chauffeur, I stared out the window for most of the two-hour bus ride. Light snow had started to fall, making for a beautiful view as we rolled closer to our destination.

As we pulled into town I was reminded again how, time after time, the place had always taken my breath away. There is a serene beauty about it that's hard to describe, and during the winter months it's even more captivating. Once I heard the first rush of the falls, I was confident I had retreated to the right place to start the process of healing my broken heart.

After checking in, I decided the night was too gorgeous to keep myself locked up indoors. Bundling up, I made my way down the hill towards the falls. Instantly, the continuous sound of the falls made me forget the numbness that was setting into my fingertips. There truly is something about the sound of rushing water that makes me skip a breath or two. After getting as close as I could, I closed my eyes for a moment and just took it all in. I wanted to allow the sound a moment to soothe my aching soul and weary heart.

Then, I saw them.

Whether they were young or old, newlyweds or veterans, the weather didn't deter these couples from enjoying their slow, loving stroll past the falls. Some were holding hands; others had their arms linked. The wounded romantic in me even assisted a few couples with pictures in front of the falls, with the gentle mist and snowflakes framing their love. It felt to me like this experience held a special place within their relationship. Whether it was their first long week-end away, or a return to where they had enjoyed their honeymoon, I knew they were there to rekindle their love.

The quietness of the city during the winter months is truly something special. After walking around for a couple of hours in the mist, enjoying the magic of the lights on the rocks, and of course the sound, I retreated back to my hotel for the night. I left the lights off, opened my drapes and watched the scene from the privacy of my room. I let the silent tears fall, and knew this was what I truly needed to start putting my broken heart back together.

My full day at the falls was filled with walking through snow-dusted streets and finding my own inner warmth within the frosty temperatures. I visited all the attractions, and enjoyed myself the way a tourist is supposed to. The fullness of the day allowed me no time to sit and wallow. Niagara Falls was my heart's companion and within those moments, she took great care of me.

The last night of my weekend escape was a moment I've cherished to this day. I walked down the hill and made my way to a bench that gave me a complete view of all the people strolling past nature's beauty. Seated there, for the next couple of hours I allowed the sounds of the falls to comfort my soul. As I watched the couples from a distance, I realized that a broken heart wasn't meant to stay broken forever. This moment I was going through was going to get better, and the love that I saw between those couples was something I knew I would experience again. I truly believe that no other place and no other time of year would have allowed me to come to this realization. The bitter cold of the falls brought some kind of inner strength to the surface and allowed it to shine through, and I was grateful for that experience.

It was a different me that boarded my Greyhound chauffeur for the trip home. The bitterness and deep aching hurt within me had vanished, to be replaced with a calmness that allowed me to know I would get through this. Later, during times when my heart would want to hurt, the sound of the rushing currents would come back to me and I could feel yet another broken piece inside me was mended. The memory of that weekend stays with me always, and reminds me of why Niagara Falls holds a special place in my heart.

Since that unforgettable weekend, every November I have treated myself to an escape from the hustle and bustle of the city, and returned to the serene and slow moments that Niagara Falls offers during the winter months. As soon as I arrive I spend a few hours looking at the falls and being forever grateful that their frigid and frosty beauty helped to restore the warmth and fullness within my heart.

~Deon Toban
Ajax, Ontario

Chapter
7

O Canada
The Wonders of Winter

That Famous
Canadian Kindness

So many gods, so many creeds,
So many paths that wind and wind
While just the art of being kind
Is all the sad world needs.

~Ella Wheeler Wilcox

Pay It Forward

The little unremembered acts of kindness and love are the
best parts of a person's life.
~William Wordsworth

Every fast-food employee knows that the drive-through window is the worst position. Perching at the frost-covered glass, a fierce wind spits mercilessly in your face. You press the headset closer to your ear and repeat the order perfectly only to be greeted with a harsh "What? Isn't this Timmies?"

I glared at my Starbucks supervisor every time she handed me the headset. On the early morning shift, the headlights of pick-up trucks blinded me as rig workers sped through in a rush to their well-paying jobs. I frothed milk and ground espresso for minimum wage.

I wasn't bitter. I loved my job. But I hated that drive-through window.

It was a freezing Tuesday afternoon when everything changed.

Every once in a while, the sub-zero temperatures of northern Alberta seal a vehicle's windows shut. Drivers don't exactly enjoy having to stand outside in the cold, screaming their orders into a speaker box, when they had expected to cruise through on their heated leather seats. In such cases, most customers tend to take out their frustration on the employees.

This woman was different.

"I'll get the next car's order as well," she said as she came up to the window to pay. She stood outside, gathering snowflakes on her hair and eyelashes. Though she was obviously freezing, her bright smile lit up her face like a fire.

"You can't take their drinks," I said, confused and fatigued. My breath evaporated into a dense fog around my face.

The lady laughed, her chubby cheeks turning crimson with cold. "No, but I'll buy them," she said. "Pay it forward and all that."

Completely dumbfounded, I charged her as requested, and when the next customer arrived at the window I explained what had just happened. I watched as his expression changed like a succession of photographs on a choppy slideshow—first enraged to be out in the cold, then surprised at the random act of kindness, and finally, delighted by his luck.

"I suppose I'll pay for the next order then," he replied, nodding and waving at the impatient driver behind him. He handed over the cash and received his pre-paid beverage.

The trend continued throughout the entire rush. Customers arrived annoyed and hasty, only to leave humbled and calm. No one had any idea how many beverages they would have to purchase. Some customers were shocked to spend much more than they had anticipated, while others ended up receiving their order for less than half the price.

Five cars passed, then ten, then twenty. No one refused to pay. Customers stood at my window emptying a fist-full of change to buy coffee for a complete stranger. Cars rounded the bend as they drove off, honking and waving their anonymous gratitude, knowing they would likely never see each other again.

Every fast-food employee knows that the drive-through window is the worst position. The window sticks with constant ice, the roar of engines injures your ears; your words are lost in the howling wind.

It only takes one customer, one person, to change the entire flow of traffic. It only takes one moment, one smile, to warm up even the coldest of days.

~Alison Karlene Hodgins
Grande Prairie, Alberta

Loquacious Larry

In Canada, the colder the winter is, the warmer the people are.
~Jean Charest

My wife and I are preparing to load onto a chairlift at the base of Red Mountain in British Columbia. The ski hill is covered with almost two feet of fresh, light powder. It's a glorious site to behold after a winter of scant snow in our more southern latitudes. And we're very lucky to be here — last night we slogged through a howling storm and limped into the town of Rossland. We almost didn't make it and seriously thought we might spend the evening sleeping in our car on the empty road up from Northport. Twelve hours later it's still snowing, which is fine with us.

The chair swings behind us. At the last minute, a guy slips in at our side. The three of us drop onto the chair and start riding up the hill in silence. A moment later the guy looks over at me.

"Larry," he says. He stares at me and smiles underneath a bushy mustache.

I pause for a moment, unused to such an exchange with strangers, and then say, "Tom." I'm hoping his utterance was an introduction, not a case of mistaking me for someone named Larry.

Larry asks if we're from out of town. We are — and tell him we arrived last night from Seattle. Larry mentions that he's a Mountain

Guide. His job is to introduce visitors to the mountain. He offers to take my wife and me around the hill.

We gladly accept, excited that our day has just gotten infinitely better. We know nothing about the area, this being our first visit to Red Mountain. My wife and I are advanced skiers and want to ski in the woods, away from the main trails. But one of our main goals is to not ski off a cliff (you never want to die while on vacation). Having a guide solves this problem. It's a very nice touch not offered by the ski areas where we're from.

Larry takes us down an intermediate trail. The three of us fly downhill through thigh-deep powder. We hoot and holler, having a blast. Ten minutes later we're back on the chair.

"Okay," Larry says as we start our ascent, "now we can do some real skiing. I saw those skis of yours and thought 'uh oh, this must be this guy's first time out… in years.'"

Larry laughs and points at my skis. They're ancient, narrow things, fifteen years old. They look like something you'd nail to the wall in a rustic ski lodge. Kids on the lift often tell me that their dads have skis like mine. I've gotten used to it by now.

"But you're both good," Larry continues, "so we'll hit the woods."

Larry starts telling us the ins and outs of being a mountain guide. He's still telling stories when we exit the chair. Unbeknownst to us at the moment, Larry won't stop talking for the rest of the day.

The three of us spend the next two hours bouncing through the woods like happy little rabbits. Everywhere Larry takes us is fresh, untouched by other skiers. Around noon it stops snowing. The sun comes out, filling our playground with a glorious light that sparkles off the snow. At the end of each run we giggle like little kids. It feels like Larry is an old friend we've been skiing with for years. We've never had a day where the conditions are this good.

We're riding the lift once again when I look over at Larry. I catch him as he pauses in telling a story about the funniest wipeout he ever saw on the hill.

"Hey Larry," I say, "we don't want to hog you all day. This has been fantastic. But if you need to show some other people around, feel free."

This is true. Larry is an amazing guide. We'd hate to lose him, but we don't want to be greedy.

Larry smiles and says, "Oh, I'm not working today. I just wear this coat because it's warmer than my other one. No, let's keep going."

I sit in stunned silence for a moment. I've heard that Canadians are friendly, but this is unreal. It's hard to fathom, coming from the States. And it's beautiful.

Larry points down at a guy skiing under the chair.

"That's Rick, another mountain guide. You don't wanna get stuck with him. He never stops talking."

Three hours later we're coming down the hill. It's another glorious run through a clean field of untouched snow, our last run of the day. Larry arcs next to my wife and I and comes to a stop. Then he slouches over and drops onto his side. He lies back in the powder and waves his arms like a kid making a snow angel.

"Whew," he says, "my legs are tucked."

I grin down and say, "You need to get rid of those fat skis and get some real ones like mine."

Larry laughs and smiles. The three of us look around in silence, taking in the beauty as we catch our breath. I think about Larry. He's sixty-five years old and just spent five hours skiing without interruption. He connected to a pair of strangers with utter ease and then showed them the time of their lives. And so what if he's a non-stop talker—he's full of passion for what he's doing. I want to be just like Larry when I'm his age.

I vow silently to be this nice and friendly at age sixty-five, regardless of what might happen between now and then.

~Thomas Sullivan
American visiting Canada living in Seattle, Washington, USA

Highway Angel

A fellow who does things that count, doesn't usually stop to count them.
~Variation of a saying by Albert Einstein

It was December 1976, and Ian and I had been married for all of two years. My parents had rented a two-bedroom condo in Florida and invited us down for the Christmas vacation. With airfare being out of the question, we decided to drive. At the time, we had a lemon yellow Honda Civic CVCC, which Ian sentimentally referred to as, our "pregnant roller skate." I just called it The Lemon... Oh, how I hated that car!

The weather forecast called for a snowstorm but, at twenty-two years old we were young and fearless. So we loaded up The Lemon and headed west on Hwy 401 to cross the border at Windsor. From there we would head south for the second Jewish "promised land"—Florida.

It was still quite early in the morning and, as predicted, the snowstorm had hit with a vengeance. Just a few hours into our drive, as we were approaching a Puslinch exit, our "trusty" lemon sputtered, coughed and died. Ian managed to coast us safely off to the side of the highway where we gently came to rest, buried in two feet of freshly fallen snow.

Undaunted, my gallant knight popped the hood, got out, and proceeded to poke and prod at the engine in the remote hope that, magically, it just might re-start; he had seen this done numerous times on TV shows, and it often worked. Not this time. Opening his door did however let out all the remaining warm air left inside the car.

So there we sat, shivering in the dark and the cold. There was no cell phone. In the wee hours of that early morning, as the wind howled, as the snow blew and our teeth chattered, we looked at each other in horror. We had no idea what to do.

After sitting in silence for what seemed like an eternity, a set of headlights emerged from out of the snowy haze. Behind the lights appeared an enormous dark blue Ford LTD, its massive snow tires belching out great wads of crushed snow as it approached our little yellow car. It slowly pulled up beside us and stopped. The driver's door swung open, and out stepped a large man, dressed in what looked like ex-lumberjack rags. Ian and I exchanged a fleeting look; I grabbed his hand and squeezed hard.

Ian tentatively opened his window. "Looks like you folks need some help," the big man said, in a deep voice that matched his size. He was certainly friendly enough… for a young couple who had lived all their lives in Toronto, maybe a bit too friendly. But with no sane alternatives, we climbed out of our disabled lemon and joined him in his car. I crawled into the cavernous back seat, Ian got into the front passenger seat, and we quickly exchanged a silent glance saying, "Good-bye. I love you."

Flustered, uncomfortable, and more than a little apprehensive, we drove off into the darkness, to places unknown, with this large stranger. We tried to break the disquiet with inane conversation. As for the man, he chatted away quite comfortably… perhaps a bit too comfortably.

Eventually we pulled up to a modest, old, two-story home situated in, what we would still refer to as "the sticks." Like condemned prisoners, we trod silently, following the big man towards his lair. Then, in the window, we noticed a disproportionately large, elaborately decorated Christmas tree sitting in the corner of an equally festively decorated living room. I whispered to Ian, "Let's not tell him we're Jewish!" In response, Ian threw me his "what-am-I-an-idiot?" look.

In the house, quickly embraced in the warm light of the Christmas spirit, which permeated throughout, we were cheerfully greeted by the man's wife and young daughter. After taking off his lumberjack coat, boots and hat, the man, who we now call Jim, kissed his wife, picked up the little girl and gave her a hug, and then picked up the phone. As he dialed an obviously familiar number, Jim told us he was having his good buddy, who owned the local gas station, tow our car to his station to have a look at it.

Our hosts then invited us to sit down to a delicious homemade breakfast. Breakfast was made even more enjoyable given the fact that, contrary to our initial fears, it looked like our remains would not be found years later, dismembered, in some remote field.

After breakfast, our rescuer drove us to the gas station. By the time we got there our little lemon had already been looked over. Parts, the mechanic told us, wouldn't be in until the late afternoon, and we weren't going anywhere until the next day. Without a moment's hesitation, Jim invited us to stay the night with him and his family. Having been raised in the indifference of big city life, we were flabbergasted at this continued "country" kindness.

We spent the remainder of the snowy day with this Norman Rockwellian family in their pre-Christmas wonderland, well fed and well rested. In the evening, we climbed the musty, creaking wooden stairs to the second floor where a comfy spare room awaited us. In the morning, after another hearty breakfast, we said our goodbyes and expressed our thanks to his wife and daughter, and then Jim chauffeured us back to the gas station. We paid our bill, gave our very sincere thanks to everyone for their extraordinary kindness and Christmas spirit, and puttered away in our little lemon. We never did tell them we were Jewish.

Perhaps overwhelmed by the entire incident, we didn't think to write down their contact information. Sadly, all these years later, neither Ian nor I recall his real name. Perhaps, if by some strange coincidental twist of fate, he or his family might read this, they might recognize themselves and finally know how truly grateful we were, and remain, to this very day.

~Arlene Kochberg
Richmond Hill, Ontario

Above and Beyond

Carry out a random act of kindness, with no expectation of reward, safe in
the knowledge that one day someone might do the same for you.
~Diana, Princess of Wales

It was April 12 but the weather didn't feel like spring. At -24 C we were experiencing the lowest recorded temperatures in Manitoba in 118 years. I had spent the day at a workshop for elementary school teachers in a hotel conference room. The speaker provided ideas for interesting projects to try with students. One idea was to make an Acts of Kindness book where the children recorded in words and pictures the helpful things they saw people in their homes and neighborhoods doing for others.

After the workshop I left the hotel and walked to my van, which had been parked outside all day. When I tried to open the door I discovered all the locks were frozen.

I went back into the hotel and asked for help. The manager offered me a cigarette lighter to warm my key before sticking it into the lock. It proved to be completely ineffective.

Next door to the hotel was a car dealership. They didn't sell my model van, but I went inside anyway and Kerry, one of the salesmen, listened to my story sympathetically.

"Let me just grab some de-icing fluid," he said before putting on his parka and trotting out to my van with me. Twenty minutes and a whole can of de-icing fluid later, my lock still stubbornly refused to give way to the key.

"We'd better go back in," I said to Kerry. "Your fingers are turning blue and your ears are beginning to look frostbitten."

Back inside, Kerry spoke to one of the mechanics.

"We'll let him give it a try," Kerry said. I waited while the mechanic used a variety of tools to try to pry my door open. No luck, the locks and doors remained frozen.

"Maybe I should call my husband," I said to Kerry. "We live forty kilometers away, but he might be able to borrow a car from someone and pick me up."

"Don't worry," said Kerry. With the help of a tractor, chains, a car jack, the muscles of four other employees and another half hour of his time, Kerry managed to get my van towed into the dealership's heated garage. After about fifteen minutes inside, the ice melted and the key slipped easily into the lock.

I am still amazed at how Kerry handled the entire situation. As I watched, he dealt with parts delivery people, impatient customers and took phone calls in between supervising my crisis. Through it all he maintained a polite and positive manner.

"How much do I owe you?" I asked Kerry before I left.

"No charge. I was happy to help," he replied.

I hugged him and thanked him again before heading home.

Later I wrote a letter to the editor of the *Winnipeg Free Press* describing Kerry's exemplary actions. Kerry responded by sending me a card thanking me for recognizing him so publicly.

I did make the Acts of Kindness book with my grade four students, the one I'd learned about at the education workshop that freezing April day. And boy did I ever have a great story to tell them as an example of what it meant to be kind.

~MaryLou Driedger
Winnipeg, Manitoba

The Sally Ann
Christmas Kettle

We make a living by what we get, we make a life by what we give.
~Winston Churchill

The Friday afternoon before Christmas my art group has volunteered to take turns manning the Salvation Army Christmas Kettle inside the Orillia Square Mall. Having been raised Jewish, this is all new to me.

The kettle is strategically positioned inside the mall entrance, next to the donut shop. Repeated wafts of sweet apple turnovers and hot black coffee entice me as I attempt to focus on my task. I'm ringing brass bells to the beat of Christmas music and trying to catch the attention of passers-by as they dash by me.

My friend who preceded me estimated that she collected about seventy dollars in donations during the lunch hour. For the first few minutes I'm stymied. I can't figure out how to inspire shoppers to glance in my direction, let alone reach into the depths of their pockets for loose change.

The clock is ticking and only one toonie and one loonie have been dropped into the kettle slot. At the fifteen-minute mark, I reach into my pocket and extricate my last cash—two five-dollar bills and four loonies. I make a big show of dropping them into the kettle while jingling the bells and smiling.

Finally, I make eye contact and receive a welcoming smile from a young man who appears to be in his late thirties. He settles on the bench beside me.

"You're pretty," he says. "My name is Mark. Do you have a husband?"

My head twirls in shock. I blush, nod, and smile coyly in response. Perhaps I look younger in my runners, jeans and red sweater. Truthfully, I am more than a decade past the half-century mark. On closer examination, I realize that my new admirer is intellectually challenged. Mark's sincerity and warmth have made my day.

"I walk here every day," he continues, as he bends to tighten his shoelaces. "Do you have a sister who's as pretty as you?"

"No sisters—only brothers. Anyway, I'm old enough to be your mother. I have a son your age."

"Really?" He looks surprised.

"How about a daughter?" he asks hopefully.

"Sorry, she's married." I laugh. He smiles. I smile again. I'm in love with my new friend.

A woman in a blue coat stops and searches her pockets for coins. Overhearing our conversation she leans forward and says, "You really do look very young!"

I radiate with pleasure.

By the end of my assigned hour, I have met and chatted with dozens of kind and generous people, including: an elderly couple wearing matching jogging suits who drop in five dollars; three teenagers munching donuts who smile and drop in their change; a young mother, with preschoolers in tow, who empties her change into the kettle and then tells me how grateful she is for the help she received from the Salvation Army the previous Christmas.

"Every penny helps," I say as I thank them.

My shift ends at 2:00 p.m. As I hand over the bells to my friend, Ralph, who is sporting fuzzy reindeer antlers and a colourful Christmas sweater, I notice that somehow the coin level in the kettle has increased significantly.

I hum "Jingle Bells" and then switch tunes to "Fiddler on the

Roof" as I climb into my car on this cold December evening and head home to make Friday night Sabbath dinner for my family.

I can already taste the warm challah, chicken soup and brisket, and I smell the aroma of hot apple strudel.

~Evelyn N. Pollock
Horseshoe Valley, Ontario

A Saltspring Christmas

Christmas is a season for kindling the fire for hospitality in the hall, the genial flame of charity in the heart.
~Washington Irving

I needed a break... from everything. I'd just quit my job, my girlfriend of five years and I had split a few months earlier, and I was discovering the true meaning of stress. So I packed up a suitcase with clothes and books, loaded my computer and printer into the trunk of my car and drove off to the least stressful place I could think of — Saltspring Island.

I told everyone I would be staying with friends and that they didn't have a phone. I lied. I checked into the Saltspring Hotel.

I'd heard a few stories about the place. This was the second version of the hotel, built right where the first one had burned down. My friend Kevin told me his family used to own the old one and the new one was haunted. No such luck. There were no ghosts and hardly any guests either. It was Christmas-time and not a whole lot of tourists show up on Saltspring for Christmas. There was a man at the other end of the hall who was staying at the hotel because his mother was ill and he wanted to be nearby, and there was me with my corner room overlooking the harbour and the parking lot.

I vowed not to make any phone calls to anyone, and I came awfully close (this was back in the dark ages before e-mail). I made three calls one day, but that was it. Otherwise I wrote letters.

Geographically, I was a ferry ride away from home, but I decided that in my imagination I was somewhere far away, somewhere unreachable. So I wrote lots of letters, read lots of books and watched plenty of bad TV.

On Christmas Eve I didn't feel like working. I could only find one open restaurant and it was open just long enough for the staff to serve me dinner as quickly as they possibly could before turning off the lights and heading home for the holidays. The TV was offering non-stop Christmas specials about love and family and togetherness and I was tired of reading so I went downstairs to the pub. There were only a handful of hardy stragglers there. The bartender came up to me after I'd finished my cider and offered me a special coffee.

"Thank you," I said, "but I don't drink coffee."

"You'll still like this," he said, and handed me a swirling concoction in a toddy mug with a rim of fresh whipped cream slithering down the side.

If there was coffee in there I certainly didn't taste it. The drink was sweet, smooth and potent. The bartender and I started talking about life. He was about the same age as me, twenty-five. I learned he was up for a job managing a new restaurant. He liked working at the bar though, except that he'd drawn the Christmas shift. We talked about some other stuff, and then I went to pay my tab.

"The coffee's on the house," he said. "Merry Christmas."

I accepted his Christmas present and went back to my room where I slept till about 10 a.m. Christmas day. Then I switched on the TV, where my choices were *Scrooge*, Christmas services and evangelists. I finally found some non-holiday fare and settled in for my holiday feast—an apple and some cookies I'd bought because I knew everything would be closed for Christmas day.

It was then that for the only time during my self-imposed exile, I started to feel lonely. I thought of calling someone, but long distance wasn't what I wanted. It was just the kind of loneliness that comes from not seeing anyone you know for two weeks. I took a shower, wrote a couple of contemplative letters, and then the room phone rang.

"Hi, this is Stephen," said the voice on the other end. I didn't know any Stephens. This had to be a wrong number.

"My mother just brought a whole Christmas dinner for me. There's turkey and stuffing and mashed potatoes and vegetables. The works. Do you want to come down to the bar and share it with me?"

The bar. Stephen was the bartender. "Are you sure it's okay?"

"Sure," said Stephen. "That's why I'm asking. It's Christmas."

So I put on some clothes, went downstairs, and there was Stephen serving up the kind of Christmas feast that Scrooge delivered to the Cratchit household after his change of heart. Stephen's mother had brought him all the things he'd mentioned on the phone — and more. There were a half-dozen metal bowls with crisp tin-foil covers. Every time Stephen peeled back another bit of foil something else new and tasty was revealed.

After he saw that I was shy about taking too much, he scolded me. "There's plenty," he said. And there was too — until we finished it. And we finished a lovely bottle of red wine. Then we started on another bottle.

He had a TV in the bar too, so we watched a cheesy cop show neither of us had ever seen and both of us said, two minutes into it, "This must be Canadian." We laughed when it turned out we were right.

Top Gun came on after our first bottle of wine. After watching a high-flying Tom Cruise, Stephen's girlfriend showed up. When they started snuggling I got up to leave and Stephen stopped me.

"You're not going anywhere. This is Christmas and you're my guest," he said as if, just maybe, he was kind of proud to have a guest for Christmas.

Then his brother arrived and Stephen introduced me like we were long-lost school buddies. When their sister (who they hadn't seen in months) appeared and hugged her two brothers, Stephen turned to her and said, "Give Mark a hug, today he's a member of our family." She did too. And I probably blushed.

It was well after two a.m. and I'd met a whole collection of Stephen's friends and relatives before I finally made my way back upstairs to my room—fuller than I'd ever been, and smiling like I'd just opened the present I'd waited all year for. It was the most beautiful Christmas I've ever had, and I never did get up the heart to tell Stephen I was Jewish. That day though, I don't think it would have mattered.

~Mark Leiren-Young
Vancouver, British Columbia

Namesake

Miracles are not contrary to nature, but only contrary to
what we know about nature.
~Saint Augustine

Our dogs announced the doorbell before it rang. But I had a hot water bottle against my newly injured rotator cuff and, therefore, no interest in getting up.

When my husband, Harry, answered the door, I heard him say, "What's that?"

Our neighbour's voice was strained. "Our dog found him in a snow bank. I don't know if he's still alive." With curiosity now overpowering the pain, I went to investigate and found Lee Anne heavily gloved and holding a lifeless, three-month-old kitten. I took him from her, but quickly realized he bordered on being frozen. It was December 18th; it had been a very cold Canadian winter, and no one knew how long the kitten had been out in the snow.

"Thanks, Lee Anne, I'll take care of him," I said, not at all convincingly. I laid him across my hot water bottle and searched for signs of life. His eyes and nose were clear and his coat fine, but as my hands tried to coax him back to our world they found skin stretched across bone. The emaciation was almost total; there was so little muscle it was a mystery how he could have moved at all.

I checked for reflexes: my finger produced no gagging when extended down his throat. I tapped the inside corner of his eye: there was no blink. The kitten was much closer to dead than alive. He had no visible respiration but occasionally a ghastly rattle emanated from his throat so I knew he had one tiny toe still on Earth.

"Harry," I sighed to my long-suffering husband, who'd only tolerated animals until he fell in love with me, "if this kitten has any hope of survival, it's at the vet clinic with a warm IV installed."

He didn't miss a beat. "I'll start the truck."

On the way, I stretched the kitten over the hot water bottle, rotating him periodically in a desperate attempt to warm his little body. Always the realist, I wondered about the cost since he was a feral kitten who probably would never tame down anyway, even if he lived.

The clinic receptionist was one I didn't recognize. "I need a vet; now!" I insisted.

"They're all gone," she said, looking upset.

"What about a technician?" I pushed, knowing that without help, this kitten had very little time and certainly none to spare.

"They're gone, too," she admitted.

The next ten minutes seemed an eternity. Finally two of the technicians, Kate and Katy, returned.

"Come on, Diane," they said, motioning me into the back, "let's see what we can do."

An oxygen mask was quickly fitted over his little face. Then we discovered that he was so cold the thermometer wouldn't even register. He wasn't receiving enough oxygen because whatever respirations he had were too shallow. So the techs installed a tube and started bagging oxygen into his lungs.

Still, there was no change. We surrounded him with hot water bottles and took his temperature again. He remained the same.

"Can we get a warm IV going?" I asked.

The "Kates" looked at me. "Are you sure you want to?" they asked. I knew what they were thinking; the charges were really going to run up and he wasn't even my cat.

"Yeah," I grimaced. "It's Christmas. We have to do what we can."

Three consecutively smaller needles later, a vein was finally mined. The IV bag was heated and the frozen kitten started receiving the fluids.

And still, nothing changed.

Eventually, having done all they could, the Kates had to resume their work, leaving me with the comatose kitten. In spite of continually looking for signs of returning life, I found none. It certainly seemed hopeless.

Two hours after we'd arrived one of the vets returned to the clinic. Once she understood the situation she grabbed a stethoscope, and after listening carefully, she sadly shook her head.

"I'm afraid he doesn't have a chance," she concluded. "His heart isn't even beating; it's fluttering. And it's barely doing that."

I remained silent; *but it's Christmas*....

It had been two and a half hours with no improvement and it was now clear to me that human effort was not going to be enough to revive this kitten. Although I'd always had a spiritual focus and was interested in its many aspects, I'd never seriously contemplated the reality of angels. However, I'd just begun reading Doreen Virtue's teachings regarding angels and had been consciously living with them in a new way.

"Well," I thought, "here's a good test!"

I found my eyes searching the ceiling. "Raphael (the Archangel of healing)," I whispered. "I need your help, please. This kitten needs saving and while you're at it, this needs to be paid for because he's *not* my cat!" I then glanced around to make sure no one had heard me.

Within seconds, the little chest rose deeply and fell, rose and fell again.

"Hey, look at this!" I shrieked.

Kate, Katy and the vet quickly rushed over. The kitten was now chewing on the intubation tube so they quickly removed it. Weakly and with much shaking, the little guy lifted his head. Kate opened a can of food and popped it under his nose to stimulate him. As we watched in amazement, our tiny patient reached out and began to eat. In stunned silence, big smiles grew on every face.

"Thanks, Raphael," I whispered.

"I guess I can take him home, eh?"

I tucked him under my jacket and summoned my husband to retrieve us. Not even a little surprised, Harry simply grinned. He was used to my little miracles with animals.

I paid the bill; it was only $107 because the techs alone were involved. The clinic very generously charged me only for the supplies used.

The kitten was indeed wild and hissed often. So I kept him under my warm sweater for the rest of the day, taking him out occasionally to scratch his head and help him to understand I wasn't a threat.

"This little guy needs a name," I said to Harry.

He raised an eyebrow, wondering why I had not yet seen the obvious. "Raphael," he shrugged, not bothering to add, "of course!"

After having dragged this young life back from the other side, it was an obvious decision that Raphi join our family.

A few days later, Lee Anne came over and gave me $55 to help with the vet bill. And then I received a Christmas card from my older brother and his wife. Enclosed was a $50 check made out to "The Nicholson Rescue Team." $105 of the $107 had now been paid.

Raphi ate ravenously until he filled out into a beautiful, healthy tabby. Although definitely feral, he is playful and loving and seems to show only one major scar from his early life. All our cats are "inside-only," but they are allowed out on our deck. Raphi is happy enough to go out in the warm weather, but the moment the temperature dips in the later fall, he cannot be enticed outside. He'd much rather coil into a tight ball, safe and secure and close to the warm fireplace.

~Diane C. Nicholson
Armstrong, British Columbia

Clint's Gift

*Animals can love unconditionally. This is divine love in action, a love that's
there no matter what you say or how bad you feel that day…. We are all
Soul dwelling here in the world of nature.*
~Harold Klemp, *Animals are Soul too!*

Shorty after I had established the Donkey Sanctuary of Canada,
Clint came into our lives. Prior to that evening we had taken
in eighteen other donkeys in need of a home, but Clint's
arrival marked a turning point of sorts. Twenty years later I can see
that from that day my desire to help these gentle creatures became,
without doubt, a lifelong commitment.

On that snowy, grey December morning, which happened to be
the day of our annual family holiday party, the call had come into our
farm from a concerned resident who lived two hours away.

"For several days now at the farm next door," he told us, "an old
donkey has been lying in the field. He never gets up. The owner says
he wants to get rid of him. He really needs your help." Soon thereafter, Karen, our barn manager, was on her way to investigate, while my
husband, David, and I remained at home preparing for our guests.

The hours passed. Our siblings, nieces and nephews arrived and
it was soon time for dinner and the sharing of gifts. Everyone was in
a festive mood, although at the back of my mind concern for the little
donkey was ever present.

Finally, just after 6 p.m., the headlamps of our truck and trailer appeared in the gloom. As I looked out from the kitchen window, the lights in the barnyard came on and I saw Karen moving towards the back of the trailer. Hurrying outside I was just in time to see a frail, elderly, mud-covered white donkey try to hobble down the ramp and into the snow-covered yard. We rushed to support him, and then more or less carried him to the drive shed where he virtually collapsed.

Those were my first, unforgettable moments with Clint.

We were, in those days, very new at the practice of animal rescue and care. Our nineteenth century barn had a selection of falling down stalls, all of which were currently occupied by other animals. The temperature forecast was to stay well below freezing during the coming days. We sensed that this latest arrival, weakened as he was and showing a fever, would not survive the cold temperatures in an open part of our old barn.

A solution had to be found. Without thinking twice we looked over at the semi-heated garage attached to the farmhouse. We quickly realized its above-freezing indoor environment provided our only option.

In great haste family members were commandeered to bring bales of hay, straw, blankets, and pails for water up from the barn. Three nephews worked quickly to cart up and then assemble the portable stall. This Christmas party would not soon be forgotten!

Before too much time had passed, and just in time to mark our veterinarian's arrival, we supported the exhausted donkey as he hobbled across the yard only to sink down gratefully into the fresh thick straw bed in the portable stall. Clint had suffered from the ravages of repeated exposure to freezing temperatures while he lay in the field, day after day, with hooves so overgrown he could barely stand. We knew his recovery would be painfully slow.

In those first moments with Clint in the garage we did not imagine that our emergency solution would turn into an extended residency, one during which two people and a donkey would share living quarters for weeks on end while one of them gained enough strength to cope with the demands of our Ontario winter.

At first, Clint lay down most of the time. His damaged hooves caused him too much pain whenever he tried to put his weight on them. Our veterinarian cautioned us that improvement would be gradual, and most likely minimal. Clint would probably have to take pain medication for the rest of his life since the founder in his hooves had caused the pedal bones to rotate. Slowly, though, day by day, his condition improved and he was able to stand for longer and longer periods.

And the healthier Clint became the more vocal he became. As it happened, our bedroom was above the garage and Clint learned very quickly to recognize the sound of our feet in the morning when David and I got up to begin our day. His clarion call became a daily feature of our morning routine. Clint was hungry and he wanted us to know it.

Now, as you may know, taking care of equines requires the carrying out of many chores that never come to an end. Since his stall was virtually in the house, separated only by a single wall, it had to be cleaned out completely every day. Manure and urine had to be removed and the floor washed, while bales of hay and straw were toted up from the barn on an ongoing basis. Then there were the pails of water that needed frequent replenishing. As his recuperation continued, we got to know Clint very well. He looked forward to receiving our attention, and loved it: scratching his long beautiful ears always soothed him, while a good brushing of his coat could occasion grunts of contentment.

Improving health had its downside, however, which came in the form of Clint's increasing restlessness. His vocalizations began to noticeably increase. He would bray first thing in the morning as well as every time he heard people approaching the garage. Then, in spite of his hooves, he began to determinedly pace back and forth, albeit slowly. Eventually, the day arrived when all three of us reached the limit. The donkey was getting bored in his solitary stall, and David and I were certainly ready to have a little more peace and quiet.

Five weeks after his arrival, on a sunny winter's morning, Clint walked carefully down to the barn. In no time at all, he settled in most comfortably with his other donkey companions and was much more content, we knew, to be once again a part of the equine world.

Clint went on to live at the Sanctuary for five more years. Although we monitored his condition carefully, as the vet had predicted, he never really returned to completely good health. Running in our fields was never an option for him. But his spirit was indomitably strong and he thrived on the loving attention that Sanctuary visitors gave him. He knew what he wanted at all times and he knew how to communicate his needs. During those years, Clint's distinctive bray became a familiar part of the chorus of sounds in our lives. To this day, I can still feel the softness of the touch of his nose whenever he would nuzzle against my side, looking for a pat and a hug.

Our experiences with Clint will never be forgotten, and they taught us that Christmas presents can take many forms, but the best one of all is the opportunity to give assistance to a helpless creature in need.

~Sandra J. Pady
Guelph, Ontario

The Angel Project

As an additional safeguard against self-pity in our home, Mama kept several charity boxes that were marked "For the poor." We gave regularly. It made us feel rich.

~Sam Levenson

I held onto the hand of my shivering granddaughter as we waited our turn to enter the huge barn-like building. The length of the line-up meant we couldn't see inside, so we passed the time watching the outside line-ups.

At the head of one line, volunteers were busily placing frozen turkeys into bags, and in the other, families and individuals were receiving milk.

On the street outside the already full parking lot, a line of cars and trucks were waiting to enter. Strangely, though vehicles were blocked, no one honked or seemed impatient. It all seemed a bit surreal, as if we were in a parallel universe.

Finally our line had moved enough that we could see into the building. I was overcome with emotion when I noticed hundreds of overflowing boxes. Some were filled with food for empty stomachs. Others contained brand new toys for children who might otherwise go without. Each box, filled with loving care, represented not only hours of time on the part of volunteers, but the generosity and caring of hundreds of anonymous individuals from throughout the town and area. This was the "Angel Project" in action.

Touched by this enormous expression of kindness I was I suddenly aware of tears flowing freely down my cheeks. Feeling a bit self-conscious I turned away from the crowds of people to wipe them away, and as I did I saw everything through a mist, causing the area to take on a kind of glowing appearance. "How fitting," I thought, "to see the Angel Project in this way."

It was four days before Christmas and today marked the climax of the Angel Project, an annual event in Calgary. This was the day that families in need could pick up food hampers and toys. Everything here had been donated through the generosity of strangers.

The people in this room had dropped everything in order to sort, label and number boxes, and then hand out delivery addresses to other volunteers so they could deliver boxes to those who had no transportation.

When it was finally our turn at the table, I found it difficult to speak past the lump in my throat. I was overwhelmed by all that was happening around me. Every box in that massive room represented the love of others. Every toy had been carefully selected to be given away, yet the receiver and the sender would never meet.

I felt something extraordinary there in that building. It wasn't quite definable but there was something special—a love that went beyond friendliness. I felt very privileged to be there and be part of it all. You see, my granddaughter and I were on the delivery crew! Jani was visiting me, and earlier that day, when I had suggested that we participate as volunteers, she grinned and said, "Yes, let's do it."

People helped us pack the trunk and back seat of my car with food and toys. I was given two addresses and we set off to make our delivery to the first family. I felt blessed to have a tank full of gas and the opportunity to be doing this.

Whatever it was I expected, I was simply not prepared for the greeting we received when we arrived at the first drop-off location. I found a basement suite and rang the bell, but when no one answered I ventured down a set of steps and called out, "Hello, is anyone home?"

A woman opened the door. As soon as I introduced myself and

explained why I was there, she was so overjoyed she shouted to someone we couldn't yet see. She ran ahead of me back up the stairs, while calling out to a neighbour, "They're here! They're here! The Angel people are here!"

Wearing only socks on her feet, she ran out through the snow to the car and began thanking us over and over again. She continued to thank us with each box we unpacked.

"We are just the delivery people," I gently explained. "These boxes are gifts from people all over the area." However, she could not contain her joy, and continued thanking us again and again.

At the second house there were young children, and after we introduced ourselves and explained why we were there, the children were sent upstairs and admonished not to peek. I knew then that what we were about to unload might very well be the total sum of their Christmas presents.

Jani carried in the teddy bears, the huge craft set and the two other toys, all of which had been specifically chosen by Angel Project volunteers for these children. The mother helped me with the heavier food boxes, and I knew this abundant supply would last a number of days.

Before we left we exchanged "Merry Christmas" greetings. Just before the door closed, the woman paused and looked directly at me, and with misty eyes she said, "Thank you so much."

When I climbed back in my car I fought back tears and a choked up feeling. A giant surge of emotion burst inside me as I pictured those children on Christmas morning opening the wonderful gifts chosen by strangers. I could see tummies filled with the holiday food we had delivered. All this because generous individuals opened their hearts and purse strings for people they did not know.

As for Jani and me? Well, we got to spend a very special day together being a part of something beautiful and unforgettable. And though we were the delivery people that day, I drove away feeling as though I was the one who had received the gift.

~Ellie Braun-Haley
Calgary, Alberta

Chapter

8

O Canada
The Wonders of
Winter

Lessons Learned

*Life is short. Break the rules, forgive quickly, kiss quickly,
love truly, and never regret anything that once made you smile.*

~Author Unknown

Super Bear

Christmas is a necessity. There has to be at least one day of the year to remind us that we're here for something else besides ourselves.
~Eric Sevareid

I attended university away from home and always looked forward to coming home to Halifax for the holidays. One Christmas, my mother, a store manager in a local shopping mall, was asked if she knew anyone who might be interested in some part-time work and extra money over the holiday season. Within a few hours of arriving home, I had a job.

I was hired to work as "Super Bear," sort of a superhero sidekick to Santa. Basically, it was my job to wander the mall during Santa's visiting hours and send children Santa's way. Being only nineteen years old, and a cynical university student, I thought I was well aware of just how commercial Christmas had become. But not even my jaded ears were prepared for the onslaught of "I wants" that faced poor Santa daily.

Santa was quite good about not promising anything. In fact, when one five-year-old girl appeared with a five-page typed list, Santa asked her how she would feel if he brought all those toys to the children next door and then had nothing left by the time he got to her house. In no uncertain terms, she told him exactly what she thought.

Every night when I got home, I thought about what had

happened to children, to society. Had everyone, right down to five-year-olds, become so involved in "stuff" that "stuff" had become what we valued? Was getting oodles of gifts under the tree all that mattered? What were parents teaching their children? What happened to "good will toward men" and all those kind, neighbourly thoughts in the English Christmas Carols I loved so much?

As Christmas Eve approached, I began to look forward to the end of the job. Besides losing five to seven pounds a day in fluids and earning some much needed pocket money, I was not enjoying myself. On the second to last day of work, I was on one of my patrols around the mall. I spotted a young boy, perhaps six or seven, and tried to point the way to Santa's workshop. He came up to me and said that he and his mother were just leaving and that he didn't have time to go see Santa. He asked if I could tell Santa what he wanted for Christmas. I nodded my head and bent down on one knee. He looked up at me and said, "Super Bear, will you please tell Santa that all I want for Christmas is a cure for my little sister's leukaemia?"

I was glad that Super Bear didn't talk, for at that moment, I began to cry. Here was a little boy, who like most his age, probably had several items he could have wished for—for himself. But all he wanted was that one thing, that one intangible thing. I looked at his mother, gave her a hug, whispered to her that I would see what I could do, and waved goodbye as they left the mall. Then I went to my mother's store, took off my bear head, and cried for half an hour.

That little boy and his mother restored my faith in people, and reminded me that some people do know what the holiday season is all about. I don't know whatever happened to that little boy and his sister, but I like to think their house was the first stop on Santa's rounds.

~Heather J. Stewart
Dartmouth, Nova Scotia

Christmas Cookies

It isn't the size of the gift that matters, but the size of the heart that gives it.
~*Quoted in* The Angels' Little Instruction Book
by Eileen Elias Freeman, 1994

I t was 1955. My dad made $47 a week as a watchmaker, and Mom took in mending for a local dry cleaning shop in order to make ends meet. Our small wartime house on Fifth Street was clean and organized, but sparsely furnished. Our blue living room rug was secondhand; a pathway of jute backing marked the flow of family traffic from the front door, through the living room and into the kitchen. We had very little, but lacked for nothing as Mom could make, grow or create whatever we needed to sustain us. My brother, Alan, and I, never knew that we were poor.

Just before the Christmas holidays, Miss Campbell, my grade two teacher, suggested we have a party. She brought a real tree into the classroom, which we decorated with coloured paper and soda straw ornaments. She passed a box around which contained folded paper slips on which was printed each of our names. We had to buy a gift for the person whose name we drew, and we couldn't spend more than three dollars.

To me, Harvey Ferguson was the cutest boy in class. He was tall, had blond hair and freckles and got into trouble almost as often as I did. Being sent to the cloakroom at the back of the class was the "time out" of choice. Harvey and I spent a lot of time in the cloakroom.

When I talked him into peeing in the rubber boots I thought he was the funniest guy on the planet, even though he also peed in mine.

When I drew his name for the Christmas gift, I was thrilled. I couldn't believe my good luck and was determined to buy him the best gift ever. I ran home and begged my mom for the three dollars, but she refused.

"I can buy enough meat for several meals for three dollars," she said. She wasn't about to waste it on a school chum's Christmas gift. I begged and pleaded. I had imagined myself going down to Orek's Five and Dime and buying an airplane, or toy gun or something that wound up, but Mom said that all I could give him was something from home. She suggested cookies. I was devastated. Anybody could have cookies—Mom baked them all the time. Cookies were nothing special. I couldn't believe she would embarrass me like this—in front of Harvey and the whole class.

Mom made a special box and covered it with patterned Christmas paper and covered the lid with bright red foil. She lined the inside with tissue. Then she made sugar cookies. She cut the dough into three pieces and coloured two of them red and green. She then rolled the dough into ropes, which she cut into short lengths. She twisted the colours evenly to make candy cane shapes. She placed them on a baking sheet and sprinkled them with sugar before putting them into the oven. They smelled great, and they looked beautiful when they were cooked, but they were just cookies and I was still mortified by the thought of giving them to Harvey Ferguson.

On the day of the party we put our gifts under the tree. We sang carols and talked about the meaning and magic of Christmas, and then the time came. Ellen, the smartest kid in class was chosen to be "Santa" and she rose to the occasion with pride. She read each name aloud as she passed the gifts out to the class. We were to open them in unison. I stared at the small package on my desk without much interest. I was too busy feeling sorry for myself. I watched as Harvey received my mother's wrapped and ribboned box, and wished I could disappear into the floorboards. When the last gift had been presented Miss Campbell said "you can open them now!" and a mad rustling of paper began. I looked down at the present I'd been given. It was barrettes.

Harvey took his time. Other kids were holding up pencil crayons and cut-outs and plastic cars. Harvey opened the box my mom had wrapped, folded back the tissue paper and stared. "Cookies!" he said. I winced and shrank into my seat. "A whole box of homemade cookies—all for me?" He didn't know who had given them to him, but when I nodded, he looked at me and smiled. "My mom NEVER bakes cookies!" he cried… "This is the best gift EVER!"

He closed the box again and held it to his chest. He said he was going to take the cookies home and share them, and that he'd tell his family they came from me. I felt strange. It was hard to believe that his mom didn't bake cookies. We had homemade bread and cookies and pies and everything—all the time. I suddenly realized how lucky I was and how rich our lives were, even though we didn't have enough money to share—even at Christmas.

Harvey talked about those Christmas cookies again and again. Maybe he was hoping I'd bring him some more. I don't know. What I do know is—I'd given him something better than a store-bought toy, I'd given him something personal; something that had taken time to make. I'd given him a gift that, for different reasons, we both would always remember.

~Lynn Johnston
North Bay, Ontario

A Lesson in Gratitude

It doesn't matter what you did or where you were... it matters where you are and what you're doing. Get out there! Sing the song in your heart and NEVER let anyone shut you up!
~Steve Maraboli, Life, the Truth, and Being Free

I kicked at the icy mound with my boot, muttering angrily to myself. We'd gotten eleven inches of snow the night before, topping the twenty-three that had already fallen that week. I was fed up! I had prayed for an hour before falling asleep that we'd be housebound, that the ski trip my father planned wouldn't happen, but I was sadly disappointed. We were a Canadian family, and thirty-four inches was merely a "dusting" to us.

I hated winter with a passion. I despised the numbness and near-frostbite that permeated every limb and digit on my body. I detested trekking through drifts that reached my waist—and sometimes even my shoulders. I especially loathed the outdoor activities my parents insisted I participate in to get that "fresh air" they felt was beneficial to good health and well-being.

I was twelve years old, the only one of four children born to European immigrants on Canadian soil. My parents came here with my three brothers after the war, and settled in Montreal, Quebec. I never understood why they picked a place with such horrible extremes of weather when there were so many gentler climates in North America at their disposal. However, they did, and not only did they thoroughly enjoy each season to the max, they expected their children to embrace either below zero or thirty plus temperatures without complaint.

Over the years, my father had outfitted each of us with the proper winter gear for skating, skiing, tobogganing and bobsledding, not to mention the uncomfortable outerwear that accompanied those sports. On this particular day, he opted for skiing. Against my protests that I would rather curl up with my library book, he piled us into the car and headed for the slopes.

I sulked in the back seat, watching enviously as my mother waved us off. She had baking to do, and ignored my pleas to stay with her. Sitting scrunched between two of my brothers, I pouted and clutched my empty pickle jar in the event my usual carsickness decided to make an appearance.

It didn't. My last hope that losing my oatmeal breakfast might gain me a little sympathy vanished as the chairlifts came into view. Queasiness might have allowed me to sit in a warm chalet while Dad and my brothers tore down the hills, but that wasn't to be.

I stepped out of the car reluctantly. The cold air seemed to penetrate my bones in seconds as I pulled my equipment off the roof rack. I dragged my feet to get my tow ticket, and then headed to the T-bar to make my obligatory ten trips down the bunny hill. Then, and only then could I enter the heated lodge and buy my single permitted cup of hot chocolate, which I would nurse for as long as possible before I was forced to brave the elements again.

I finally completed my allotted runs, not daring to cheat. I knew my father would zero in on the lie like a hawk swoops on a field mouse. I made my way into the cabin, got my drink and curled up in a chair in front of a roaring fireplace. Sipping the bracing drink, I allowed the heat to seep into my chilled body.

About twenty minutes later my father came in, stomping his boots. He gave me that "get out there" glance I knew so well. Faking enthusiasm, I obeyed, and slunk past him back out into the bitter cold.

As I retrieved my gear, a little girl of about seven caught my eye.

Her parents hovered over her while she shuffled clumsily on skis. Her face beamed with delight as she stuck her tongue out to catch snow that was beginning to fall again in thick flakes. Every time she tasted one, she squealed with joy. She didn't even seem to feel the icy wind.

"Stupid kid!" I muttered, slamming my feet into the bindings. "Who the heck wants to eat snow?"

"She's not stupid," I heard a voice behind me proclaim. I whirled around to see a teenage boy glaring at me. "She's my little sister and she's blind. She also has leukemia. She just wants to enjoy one more winter before she dies."

Without another word he slapped his goggles into place and glided off to join the rest of his family, leaving me standing there in stunned, shamed silence.

For the next few minutes I stood there, mesmerized, watching those four people. I observed the brother's infinite patience as he coached his sister to glide several feet at a time on the flat base of the mountain. He grinned fondly when she cried out in glee, catching her the few times she almost slipped and fell.

I studied her little face and noticed its pallor. Unlike everyone else, her cheeks didn't display the heightened color that came from harsh kisses by an unrelenting wind. Her wobbliness was not caused by inexperience, but rather from not having the gift of sight or the stamina of good health. In the short time it took to move in five or six circles, it became evident from her panting that she was weakening and becoming tired from the exertion.

When she stumbled yet again I heard her father softly urge her to stop, but she refused, begging her brother for "just one more turn." He complied, taking her by her mittened hands and guiding her in an even bigger arc, while he sashayed backwards on his own skis.

Finally she had to admit she was spent. Her father picked her up, cradling her head tenderly against his shoulder. As the entire family came toward me, I saw that little girl crane her neck in exhaustion. She turned her face towards the sky to feel the sensation of frosty snow on her skin one more time before she closed her eyes and snuggled against her father in sleepy surrender. She was already in a soundless doze when they filed past me to enter the chalet. Her brother was the last to go by and our eyes met.

"I'm sorry," I whispered humbly.

To my surprise, he gave me a warm smile, yanked the toque off my head and ruffled my hair playfully.

"Feel the wind!" he told me. "You only live once." Then, tossing the hat into my hands, he hurried to join his family.

That afternoon, my father and brothers were stunned to see me test my skills on the intermediate hill. And for the rest of that year, I skied without urging or complaint, soaring down mountains and reveling in the good health that allowed me to do so.

Canadian winters can be incredibly brutal sometimes. Spring always arrives, however, replenishing the earth with lush greenery and warmth. Whenever I begin to feel resentment after long months of white and cold, I remember the little girl, long gone, who basked in the pure, simple delight of a snowflake melting on her tongue.

~Marya Morin
Saint-Lin-Laurentides, Quebec

Silent Lessons

The real voyage of discovery consists not in seeking new landscapes,
but in having new eyes.
~Marcel Proust

Every year, a few weeks before Christmas, I venture out into our back yard to string a few lights on our cherry tree, by then rendered naked by the onset of winter. The lights, which are visible from our kitchen table, have become a family Christmas tradition.

On this particular year, the air was cold but still and the stars shone brightly. A light skiff of snow lay on the ground. The quiet that one only finds on such evenings enveloped our neighbourhood. A tingle ran up my spine. I love being outside on such a night, with the cold nipping at exposed skin, and my breath visible in small clouds. Alone in the dark I worked slowly, not in a rush to go back inside the house again.

When I was a boy, it was on nights such as this that my father would flood our driveway to build an ice rink. For years I was too young to join him, so most of the time he worked alone. Often he would flood after a late shift at work, which often meant early in the morning. Even so, there were many nights when I silently watched him from my bedroom window. He would be outside—alone—for hours, slowly moving up and down the driveway, moving the hose in long sweeping motions to pour a thin layer of water as evenly as possible. The water froze almost immediately, and I noticed how carefully he had to step on the newly frozen surface so as not to fall.

I have no memory of my father actually skating on this rink, but he loved that we skated. In our family, three figure skaters and two hockey players skated thousands of hours and honed their skills on ice prepared tirelessly by their father.

As I grew older I began to join Dad on his late night ice-making duty. We seldom spoke. This was solemn work and the quiet of those dark cold nights was too special to disturb. The sounds of the water and the crackling noise it made as it reluctantly transformed into ice were all I remember hearing. When Dad did speak, it was to instruct. I was the oldest son, and I sensed on those nights that Dad had a great number of important things to teach me about life—things I would need to take on as my own responsibilities one day. Things like building an ice rink for my children. I was proud to think that my father believed I would one day be as skilled and capable as he.

As the years passed and I grew from young boy into young man, my perception of my father changed in many ways. I gradually grew to believe that, in fact, my father had little to teach me. While I was an honour student, he had never even attended high school. He was a small town policeman, a career he eventually settled into after starting and running a number of businesses that, while successful, always left him looking for something else. I was moving on a straight line into a career as teacher.

The things my father excelled at, like carpentry, car repair and handyman stuff, were of little interest to me. I was busy playing hockey and baseball, studying and writing. It seemed that in all of my chosen endeavours, my father was no longer my source of guidance and improvement. It occurred to me that he had become more of an observer than anything else. I wondered if maybe he was disappointed that he was able to contribute so little, or perhaps ecstatic that I had grown so far beyond him. We didn't even make an ice rink anymore.

It was many years later that I finally began to understand what my father had actually done for me, perhaps without even intending to. He stood alone in our driveway, holding a water hose in the cold for countless hours in order for me to become a better skater and hockey player than he had been able to. He worked endlessly in his shop on projects, always for someone else, frequently me. He volunteered to help out neighbours and friends at every opportunity. In spite of how narrowly I perceived his talents, he applied them in every way he could, for the benefit of others, especially for his family. When we needed a ride, he drove us. When I needed the car, he handed me the keys. When Ellen and I moved into our first home, he arrived with a new picnic table and a winter's supply of firewood. I have no recollection of a time when his needs ever came before mine.

And then, on this particular cold winter night, it struck me. On those long ago nights when my dad and I worked side by side flooding our driveway, he wasn't teaching me how to build an ice rink. He was teaching me how to be a good man. And despite there being many other men who have profoundly influenced my life, from teachers, to coaches to business mentors, none have put a permanent stamp on me like my father did by simply being the man he was.

My father died in October of 1987. But I never stop wanting to make him proud. I realize now that I was confused about him when I was a teen and young adult. But I had it right when I was a young boy—proudly standing on the cold ice on a dark night beside the man I would never stop admiring. It turns out he did have a lot to teach me. And every lasting lesson I learned was taught without the utterance of a single word.

The next day, the Christmas lights were on our cherry tree, but in the cold and without the proper tools, and without any real interest in "handyman" stuff, I hadn't managed to make them very symmetrical. I just kind of poked them up and onto the scrawny branches using a bunch of handles and hockey sticks held together with duct tape. My family thought the lights formed the shape of a question mark. Funny, while hanging them, I think I stumbled upon answers.

~William Bell
Newmarket, Ontario

78

The ABCs of Christmas

It is Christmas in the heart that puts Christmas in the air.
~W.T. Ellis

After fourteen years of marriage we agreed to divorce. Then came Christmas. For the sake of the children, we decided this first year they would spend Christmas Day with their dad's side of the family at the farm, far more exciting and normal than with just my parents and me. They would have the uncles and their wives, and Christmas commotion with the horses and the kittens to distract them and entertain.

For the children, it was a good plan. From my perspective as their mum... I felt lost. Empty. I had jumped into the void of divorce. How was I going to survive going back to my parents on my own? A failure. A statistic. I could not expect my friends to fill the gap. Filled with self-pity and brooding, I just couldn't get into the Christmas spirit. I must tough it out, I told myself. It was only a day.

My mother came up with an idea. She wanted to treat me to Christmas lunch at a well-known country restaurant. My thoughts raced. Wouldn't it be too obvious? Who dines out for Christmas dinner? People who didn't cook? Non-traditional types? People without kids? That was me. Not one to give up a good meal, I accepted.

Seeing my beautiful mother in her tailored, boiled wool Austrian jacket and matching skirt encouraged me to put on my Christmas sweater and dress up. It did make me feel a little better. We had something to do. Somewhere to go. A destination. That would occupy half the day, at least. My stepfather preferred to stay home, so Mum drove the two of us serenely through the snow, to the village, about a half an hour away.

Welcoming arms of snow-laced trees graced the main village street. Old-fashioned streetlamps were festooned with pine boughs and red ribbons. Boutique shops filled with antiques, art galleries, specialty bookstores and small cafés smiled gently, as we drove by. It was the kind of place where you expected to see a horse-drawn sleigh coming around the corner, with people snuggled under the warm blankets. I was beginning to feel better. Calmer. We drove through the town and arrived at the side street where the old white clapboard restaurant was situated, behind a small white picket fence. But here my bravado started to falter. I was there with my mother! On Christmas Day! How embarrassing! How pathetic at my age. Wouldn't it be obvious? My insecurities screamed inside my head.

"Come on darling," she encouraged, "this will be lovely. Chin up!"

I looked at the front door, decked in glorious fresh wreath with pinecones and tartan ribbons waving in the wind, daring me to be sad.

I told myself to breathe.

A doorman, in a velvet trimmed jacket and top hat, welcomed us into the foyer, treating us like long-established patrons. We followed him along the corridor to two enormous wooden carved doors, which he then opened with a flourish. Inside was a huge room filled with noisy families. There was laughing and the chinking of wine glasses. Kids spilled off the chairs and on to the richly patterned carpet, covered in toys and wrapping paper. A few people looked up and smiled. Most carried on with their hors d'oeuvres, happily ignoring me.

We were ushered to a table near the stone fireplace; the pine logs creating a welcoming warmth. Numerous real Christmas trees, decorated in silver and white, were positioned around the room. White linen tablecloths and pretty centerpieces added to the atmosphere of tradition and elegance. Focusing on the beauty of the room filled with happy families of all sizes, I knew I'd never forget this moment. We toasted to new beginnings.

"Thank you so much, Mum," I said, holding back the tears, knowing if I said more I would dissolve into a disgraceful mess.

"You are welcome, my darling," she said gently. "You will survive."

We carried on with the meal. The service was friendly. The food was exquisite. Savoury parsnip soup, perfectly cooked turkey with all the trimmings, and flaming Christmas pudding. Cocooned in the festive spirit of the room, I felt protected and loved. Privileged. Nourished and ready to face the New Year.

The love and support I felt from my mother that day has carried me forward into a new life filled with adventures and a new appreciation for the true meaning of Christmas. Over the years, my ex-husband and I have taken turns sharing the children at Christmas. I came to realize that being flexible was the best policy. And in those moments without the children, I remembered just how much I always wanted to be a mother. Having Christmas any day, as long as we were together, meant Christmas. Some years, I have asked single friends and their children to Christmas dinner, on Boxing Day. I call it "extend-a-Christmas," not being tethered to one day.

Since that Christmas, I have learned to do a number of things on my own: Walk into a movie theatre amongst crowds of couples and watch a movie; make new friends; enjoy my single friends. Pump gas even! And generally be comfortable on my own.

And then, just when I no longer needed anyone, along came Steve. My heart has been stretched and healed and stretched again. It now includes a new man whom I love, a pretty cool stepson and my own two beautiful, balanced adult children of whom I am very proud. Christmas has been condensed and simplified to the essentials: Appreciation, Beauty, Compassion. Love.

~Sue England
Aurora, Ontario

79

Christmas Spirit Regained

*Just as you have the ability to change your mind, you also have the ability
to change the state of your mind. Happiness and joy are states of mind to be
enjoyed any time you want.*

~Author Unknown

As a child I didn't really have fond memories of Christmas, so as an adult, Christmas became a time I just wanted to avoid. I particularly had trouble with all the Christmas music, which seems to be just about everywhere. I guess that was why I volunteered to work that Christmas Eve. The retail store where I worked in downtown Toronto was one of the few that didn't play Christmas music. But that year I was given the best gift ever—a stranger came along and rekindled my Christmas spirit.

It was the Christmas of 1992 and I was working at my sales job during the busiest season of the year. It's a time when customers become difficult to please, as tempers and patience seem to be lost in the crowds. Few people are nice to salespeople during this time and working in a store becomes a major challenge.

I was relieved that my shift was over and I could go home to avoid the rest of Christmas. I entered a subway car at the College Park subway station and found a single seat at the back of it, as far from others as possible. I just wanted to get home and be rid of my bad mood.

I hadn't notice which station we were in when the stranger with the homeless appearance and boisterous voice entered the subway car. When he started to chat with the other passengers, I purposefully turned my attention to something else. I wanted to make it clear I had no interest in talking to this guy. Then the train was delayed in the tunnel for ten minutes. As we sat there motionless, I was becoming more and more aggravated.

When the stranger started singing "Jingle Bells" I knew I'd had enough, but I was trapped. Then, slowly the other passengers joined in, and soon everyone sang with him. Then, to my shock, I found myself singing as well!

Well, with that guy leading, we sang every Christmas song I remembered from my childhood. When the train finally got going, we continued singing. As we stopped at other subway stations, passengers from other cars ran to join us. The thought of our car filling up with singing people while others were empty made me laugh. Never in my life had I witnessed so many strangers joining together like this to sing.

The subway train reached its last stop on the line and every one stopped to look around at each other. And then the boisterous voice of the stranger cried, "Merry Christmas" to each passenger as they left the train. As I ran to catch my bus, I could still hear people singing as they headed home for Christmas Eve.

Though none of us had ever met each other before that night, and never saw each other again, I felt we'd shared a special and unique bond of Christmas spirit. Since then I carry that spirit with me. I've never lost the spirit that I gained that Christmas Eve. I look forward to Christmas now, and when the music starts to play, I remember that special night.

You never know what you might learn from a stranger.

~Judith Smith
Peterborough, Ontario

The Christmas Dance

You may be only one person in this world, but to one person at one time, you are the world.
~Author Unknown

I have a particular fondness for grumpy old men. Perhaps because of this, they tend to be less grumpy around me.

In my work as a speech pathologist in a hospital, I cross paths with many such elderly gents. The one I remember the most is Harry. Harry was a fiercely independent soul and landed in the hospital after a stroke (thus, my involvement—he had speech deficits). Feisty and "difficult," Harry alienated many staff, yet he and I formed a close bond. Though he never said so, I think he found comfort in having someone try to communicate with him despite his poor speech.

Harry had a double whammy with his speech; he had grown up in Eastern Europe and never lost his thick accent, nor become fully fluent in English. He muddled along in speech therapy, using writing to communicate when the words just couldn't be understood. I never knew if it was the stroke or his age that gave him his stooped posture and shuffling gait.

He came into the hospital in November and was anxious to return home as soon as possible. As the end of December neared, he became more and more "crotchety" as his agitation and impatience grew. After numerous frustrating sessions, I finally found out why.

Though he'd kept it private before, Harry admitted he was married. His wife, Delores, now lived in a nursing home, and suffered from severe dementia.

They met later in life; he said he fell in love with her spirit and with her long white hair. She had been sick for more of their marriage than she had been well. Yet prior to coming into the hospital, Harry had visited his wife every day. Every single day, no matter what.

Naturally, Harry wanted to see Delores at Christmas. The medical team resisted—Harry continued to have cognitive deficits that would make it impossible for him to be discharged safely to live alone just then. I wondered what could be done. So, after much internal deliberation (and consultation with colleagues), I offered to take Harry to see his wife the week before Christmas. He was delighted, and the doctors agreed to allow him a two-hour pass for the visit.

The change was magical. I had never seen Harry look as happy as he did that day. He combed his wispy hair and pestered the nurses to help him shave. Though our two-hour time limit for the visit was brief, he insisted on stopping on the way to buy his wife a poinsettia. He told me she had always loved to have them around during the holidays, and he wanted her to see it and know she was loved.

Despite staff attempts at warmness, nursing homes during the holidays have a heavy air of loss and sadness. Delores's was no exception. We found her in the dining room sleeping in her chair with her white hair draped like a curtain across her face. She barely looked up at her husband as he tenderly woke her. Cafeteria noises tinkled in the background as he led her back to her room.

Once there, Harry fussed around and placed the poinsettia on his wife's bedside table. The air in the room was warm, yet the bare white walls and plain hospital style décor made it feel cold. An uneaten dinner sat on a tray on the small bedside table. Harry cut up the cold turkey and coaxed his wife to eat. While her face remained blank, she allowed him to feed her.

Then, he turned on the radio. The signal was weak but a CBC Christmas special drifted out, with Bing Crosby's "White Christmas" playing softly. When Delores heard the music she looked up and seemed to really see Harry for the first time since our arrival. She reached out to him shakily and touched his clean-shaven face. Harry closed his eyes for a brief moment as she traced her finger along his cheek. Then he took her hand and pulled her gently from the armchair, his unsteadiness magically quelled as he focused on his wife. They stood facing each other, not speaking. And then they danced. Her hands stayed gently on his face; his hands moved to her hips. A slow tender swaying dance. Delores's green eyes never left Harry's face, and she would occasionally hum through smiling lips. Harry glowed with love. I had never seen anyone, "crotchety" or not, express as pure a love.

It is a moment I will never forget, because that day I learned what it means "to love and cherish until death do us part." Most of us avoid thinking about what these words mean if our partner continues to live, but lives between the lines. Harry simply and generously lived this truth far past what many would consider necessary.

Though Delores spent the majority of her days lost within herself, Harry brought her out of herself in that Christmas dance. He loved her enough to invite those moments, savour them with her, and let the memory sustain him until the next time. I had often heard the term "unconditional love," but the day I watched Harry dancing with his wife, I finally knew what it meant.

~Crystal Johnson
Vancouver, British Columbia

81

The Wheels on the Bus

"Having adventures comes naturally to some people," said Anne serenely.
"You just have a gift for them or you haven't."
~Lucy Maude Montgomery, Anne of Avonlea

As a teacher, you learn very early in your career that every school has its own personality and idiosyncrasies, which are created not only by the students and staff, but also by the age, location and structure of the building. Maxwell Heights Public School's personality has to be the most memorable of my career.

This school was built on the edge of my hometown in Oshawa, Ontario. I say, "on the edge" because it was considered neither in the country, nor in the city, just a tiny four-room structure sitting on a hill looking down on the rest of the municipality. When I taught there, with the exception of three students who lived across the street, all of the children came to school by bus. They arrived together and left together every day.

Besides two classroom teachers, there was the vice principal, Doug, who also taught grade three, and a part-time janitor. I guess being such a small school didn't warrant any more staffing expenses, so we often found ourselves doing double-duty, or even doing jobs that defied description when necessary. For example, one day the boys managed to plug a toilet, which then overflowed and ran down the hall. Our part-time janitor had already left for the day, but luckily, my dad was a plumber, so I sprang into action and turned off the water. I just did what needed to be done.

Winter brought its own unique set of challenges to our little school. Sitting high on that hill made us a perfect target for high winds, drifting snow, icy roads, and little chance of seeing a snowplow until well after other city streets had been cleared.

One Friday morning in mid-January, the snow began falling lightly as I made my way to work. The children arrived right on time, bundled appropriately in snowsuits, mitts, hats, scarves, and boots. At morning recess they delighted in rolling huge snowballs with the perfect packing snow. The snow fell steadily and heavier. The milkman made his weekly delivery of milk and juice, the crates laden with a frothy topping of snow. "Looks like we're in for a good dumping," he growled as he gathered up the empty crates. "Roads are getting bad!"

By noon, the accumulation had grown by several inches, and the sky gave no sign of clearing up. Working tirelessly throughout the lunch hour, the children pushed the snowballs they had made during morning recess into shapes and formed forts. When the bell rang, they trudged into the school mired in snow that melted into puddles up and down the hall. With no janitor to mop up the mess, the water formed an obstacle course for the kids. They hopped and jumped along the corridor in a vain attempt to keep their socks dry.

Afternoon recess finally arrived, much to the delight of the kids, who were anxious to continue their building. The boys and girls packed fistfuls of snow into the openings between the huge snowballs to fortify their icy fortresses. The bell rang, and once again they dragged their snowy mess into the building. Wet hats and mitts were strewn along the old-fashioned radiators to dry before going home. The pungent scent of moist wool and damp, smelly feet permeated the air.

The snow fell harder than ever, and lights from distant houses and buildings looked like tiny stars twinkling through the white haze.

The last half of the afternoon marched on like a soldier and so did the winter storm. Shortly before three o'clock Doug arrived at my classroom door to report that the busses were running about half-an-hour late.

About forty-five minutes later I saw the ghostly outline of the yellow school bus making its way towards us. The children got their things together, bundled up for the ride home, plodded through the snow and climbed aboard. I stood watching as the bus pulled away.

And then it happened! The driver tried to turn out of the parking lot a bit too sharply, and the rear wheels got stuck near the edge of the ditch. He reversed back and forth several times hoping to rock his way free, but those back wheels just couldn't get a grip. The vice principal came out to see what was happening. After carefully assessing the situation, he decided the best idea was to call each parent asking them to come and pick up their child.

It was now well past four o'clock, and I knew my own two children would be at home waiting for me. I also knew that it would take hours for all the parents to arrive for their kids. There had to be a better option. The driver had already called dispatch and requested a tow truck, but in this weather, that could also take hours. My mind worked overtime. I remembered that once, when I was stuck and my wheels were spinning, I had used the rubber mats from my car to get some traction.

When I explained my idea to Doug, he looked at me with that look men give women when they say something foolish. "Our little, rubber, car mats are no match for the wheels on that bus," he joked sarcastically.

"Not those mats," I called over my shoulder as I waded through the snow in my stylish, high-heeled boots.

Leaning inside the school door I grabbed the huge, water-laden rubber carpet and tugged it out. "Get the other one!" I shouted to Doug. He reluctantly followed my lead. Together we jammed the heavy, commercial mats in front of the back wheels. The driver wasn't convinced, but he was willing to humour me. He started up the engine and slowly attempted to move forward. The wheels were almost there, but needed just a little more effort to make it. Without thinking how foolish I must have sounded, I yelled, "Push!" and leaped forward, heels and all, put my shoulder into that bus and shoved with all my might. I think Doug was so caught off guard that when I jumped forward, he did, too. It was just enough to help the wheels grab on, and that old bus moved out of the driveway onto the road. As it moved, Doug and I both lost our balance and fell face down into the slushy mess and were covered by the spray from the spinning tires. The children cheered and waved from the windows as the bus drove away. Doug took one look at me and burst into laughter.

"I don't believe it," he said, shaking his head. "You're crazier than I thought."

"Hey, desperate situations call for desperate measures. I wasn't going to stay here until eight o'clock tonight. Now let's get the carpets in, and get out of here!"

Working at Maxwell Heights had been a wonderful experience, but the following September I moved to a new school. When I was leaving, the staff and parents gave me a gift... a snow shovel!

Every once in a while, I'll meet a former student from that year, and they always say, "Remember the time you pushed the bus?"

~Penny Fedorczenko
Oshawa, Ontario

Northern Magic

They danced a cotillion in the sky; they were rose and silver shod;
It was not good for the eyes of man—'twas a sight for the eyes of God.
~Robert Service, from the Ballad of the Northern Lights

As we loaded our Volkswagen Beetle for our annual winter visit to our camp I wondered if it was worth the effort. Piling enough boots, jackets, bedding, and groceries into a miniscule car with three kids (ages eight, nine, and ten) and two dogs (a Lab and a Beagle) for a three-day stay was a monumental feat.

As my husband, Ron, fastened skis, poles, and snowshoes on the roof of the car, I looked at the kids, their faces bright with anticipation. Okay, just one more year.

Once we were packed and everyone was in place, wiggle room was non-existent. No one dared ask for a pit stop, not even the dogs. Their heads protruded from among the clothing, sleeping bags, and food. It was possibly the anticipation of the country freedom that kept them quiet.

We arrived at the camp to an orange-pink sunset slashed with purple brushstrokes above a snow-frosted forest of spruce and pines. As we huddled together on the doorstep, Ron quickly unlocked the door.

Bursting into the interior, we discovered the place felt colder than outdoors. While Ron ignited the oil space heater in the cabin's centre, the children and I scrambled to unload the overburdened car. The dogs, wild after their release, raced through the snowdrifts.

A half hour later, in the slowly warming room, we boiled wieners on a camp stove and softened half-frozen buns in the steam. As darkness fell, an oil lamp illuminated our sleeping bags spread out on the bunks. Outside, skis, poles, and snowshoes leaned ready against the wall beside a cooler that kept milk, eggs, meat, and butter from spoiling in a cabin not yet acquainted with refrigeration.

Traditionally, after we ate, we made a trek under the stars on snowshoes down to the river. However, on this particular night, Ron and the girls opted to try out their spanking new cross-country skis over the meadow. Since there were only three pairs, that left a disappointed eight-year-old Steve, the dogs and me for the river foray on snowshoes.

With a full moon at our backs, we started off. Our shadows stretched before us, elongated and mobile. The dogs cavorted in and out of the darkness of trees that snapped and crackled in the frost. An occasional mutter from Steve as we tramped along reaffirmed he still wasn't happy with our second choice excursion.

As we reached the bank above the river we paused, and then, suddenly... magic. Shy at first, then gradually sprouting higher and higher up among the stars in the night sky, the Northern Lights appeared. The Aurora Borealis. Undulating like mystic spirits gowned in green and white, they rose and rose, then doubled back on themselves to rise again. The heavens danced, alive with their essence.

I glanced down at Steve. He stared at the sky, spellbound.

In the Far North, people say they've heard the Northern Lights speak in the whistling voice of migratory birds. Auroras, they claim, are sent to buoy up people's spirits during the long winter when the sun doesn't shine.

Apparently they had the same effect on my son.

"Wow!" he breathed, delighted astonishment erasing all traces of discontent.

When the mystic dance finally began to recede, we turned and headed back to the camp. The enchanted lights of the winter night would fade from the sky but never from my memory or that of the entranced boy by my side. A magical moment in the moonlight that would live forever in our hearts, one we could never have experienced if we hadn't made that annual winter trek to the camp.

~Gail MacMillan
Bathurst, New Brunswick

Chapter
9

O Canada
The Wonders of
Winter

Traditions and Celebrations

*Canada may be cold between November and March
but that doesn't mean we Canadians stay indoors.*

~Jane McLean

83

The Real Santa

Our hearts grow tender with childhood memories and love of kindred,
and we are better throughout the year for having, in spirit,
become a child again at Christmas-time.
~Laura Ingalls Wilder

"My turn, Daddy, my turn!" I begged from way down on the icy sidewalk. From where I stood, all I could see were scratchy wool coats and buttons, and people stretching above me for what seemed like miles.

"Okay, Schnookums," said Dad, as he lifted my little sister down off his shoulders. Then, suddenly I was airborne as he picked me up, and with a pretend groan swung me up and dropped me down onto his shoulders. My dad was six feet tall, so now from this enormous height above everyone else I could see everything!

"Here he comes!" I squealed with glee, pointing up the street. "There's Santa now—here he comes!"

For over a hundred years the Toronto Santa Claus Parade has taken place on a bone-chilling cold Saturday in mid-November, always damp, and usually with drizzle or snow flurries. Started in 1905 by Eaton's department store with just a single float, the parade has grown to include over twenty-five floats, twenty-four bands, 1,700 participants, and now stretches over five kilometers. One of the biggest annual productions in North America, the Toronto Santa Claus Parade is the oldest annual parade in the world.

Of course at age six I knew none of this. All I knew was that Christmas was on its way, we were at the Santa Claus Parade, my feet and hands and everything else were freezing cold from standing on the hard sidewalk, and Santa was coming down Yonge Street in his huge sleigh straight from the North Pole.

Mum picked up my little sister Ruthie so she could see, and finally the giant float on which he rode was directly alongside us. We were giddy with excitement. Santa's wonderful, giant, red sleigh was pulled by eight reindeer prancing along with the music and the bands, and there was Santa himself! An enormous man in his red suit and white beard—larger than life—he was standing in his sleigh and waving to the crowds, and calling to us in a huge voice; "HO HO HO! MER-RY CHRISTMAS BOYS AND GIRLS! HO HO HO!"

It was absolutely thrilling!

Once it passed us, the parade would take Santa to the big Eaton's department store where he would remain for the next few weeks right up until Christmas. Sometime before that Mum would bring us back downtown to see him. We would sit on his knee and tell him what we wanted for Christmas, and have our pictures taken.

I could hardly wait!

• • •

At some point we stopped going to the Santa Claus Parade. After all, it was really just for kids. Christmas became about other things... and as a working adult much of the magic of Christmas was replaced with juggling the chores and stress of the season.

After graduating with a degree in fashion design, my first career was as a photographic fashion stylist; I worked with photographers and models and produced fashion pages for various different catalogue and retail clients like Simpsons, Sears, The Bay, and of course, Eaton's. My first summer in the catalogue studio was a real eye-opener. Most people can simply not imagine the pace and excitement of a big catalogue house in the full production of busy season. In order for those beautiful Christmas gift books to arrive at your door in

November, all those photographs have to be taken months before. So in a catalogue studio, every year, Christmas comes in July.

That July we were doing a Christmas shoot for Eaton's. Our client had arranged for Santa to come to the studio for the photo session. He would arrive incognito, of course, and would need time to change into his red suit. Once he entered the men's dressing room, we were instructed, he would need it to himself for a full hour. That dressing room was a busy place, but once he went in the door would be locked, and no one else would be allowed to enter until he emerged.

The set was ready with an elegant traditional fireplace and a wing chair. Last-minute touches were being applied to a gorgeous tree. The photographer and his assistant were checking the lighting. Several children were dressed and ready in the studio; a lovely little six-year-old girl with blond curls in a velvet Christmas dress stood waiting quietly with her mother.

Then the door opened, and Santa stepped out of that dressing room — and I gasped. Everyone gasped. An enormous man in his red suit and white beard — larger than life — he was standing right there in front of us, and as he entered the studio he greeted everyone present by saying in a voice I remembered very clearly, "HO HO HO! MER-RY CHRISTMAS BOYS AND GIRLS! HO HO HO!"

He then bent down and spoke to the little blond girl in the velvet dress — whose eyes were now as big as saucers, and whose mouth had simply fallen open and refused to close.

The chills went up and down my spine. My hair stood on end. Goosebumps rose everywhere, and my eyes prickled with tears.

I'm sure my eyes were as big as saucers too. I felt just like that little six-year-old girl. I BECAME that little six-year-old-girl.

Because it was HIM — it really was SANTA. And not just any Santa — this was the real Santa — the one I'd seen years ago in the huge sleigh pulled by eight dancing reindeer, coming down Yonge Street in the Parade. I know because I recognized him — and his voice, and because he told me.

Somehow, Eaton's once again had managed to transport the real Santa down from the North Pole for this special event. And

I was transported too… back to my childhood, and the magic of Christmas.

The photo shoot went off like thousands of others I would be part of over the next twenty years, but nothing ever came close to that first summer Christmas, when the real Santa came back to Toronto in July.

That day I realized that Santa Claus may be just for kids, but there is a six-year-old-child inside of each of us just waiting to emerge and remind us of the magic of Christmas.

I also learned there really IS a Santa Claus.

I know. Because I've met him.

~Janet Matthews
Aurora, Ontario

84

Penguins and Polar Bears

A lot of funny stuff happens in Canada!
~Samantha Bee

In the Vancouver area, as in a number of other areas, where cold air and colder water are a natural part of winter, a New Year's Day tradition has emerged that baffles even the most open-minded logician. It's called The Polar Bear Swim. Swim is actually a misnomer, because no one is really in the water long enough to swim; however people do don bathing attire and occasionally more bizarre costumes, and plunge into English Bay for a few microseconds. Then they return to dry land and celebrate their survival with a quick shot of something warming that they may have been drinking the night before as well.

As a keen observer of questionable human behaviour, I am drawn to understanding this odd phenomenon. My initial thoughts about the impetus behind this strange tradition center on the excessive use of alcohol the night before which, we can agree, is an even more established tradition. There are many theories. The first simply postulates that those who participate are still in advanced stages of inebriation and therefore do not have any clue as to what they are doing. They just attach themselves to some screaming herd of equally inebriated persons, and en masse head in a random direction, which ends up at the low tide mark of the local beach. However, evidence does not support this, for if it were true, we would expect to see other random herds of drunken people doing equally stupid things like cramming into busses naked or riding the baggage carousels at the airport. We don't see those, or at least not often, so clearly the New Year's dip is not a random drunken event, especially since we see it repeated reliably each and every year.

Another possible explanation is cold water as counter-irritant therapy to a severe hangover. However, this does not make a lot of sense either. I liken this to sitting on a soldering iron to distract from the pain of a toothache. In the most severe cases of post partying pain, attempting suicide by drowning might seem plausible but if one's mood were that low, one would not likely wear a Spandex Grinch costume to one's demise.

There could, perhaps, be a more spiritual explanation. The New Year symbolizes a new beginning, re-birth, starting over etc. This could provide a plausible explanation, with the ocean being the metaphoric baptismal font—a celebration of life. The fact that a number of emergency vehicles, with resuscitation equipment, are present might cloud that theory. However, it might also be supported by the fact that most men's private parts have already begun to shrink down toward neonatal proportions just by thinking of the cold water ahead.

All of this questioning and considering has now led me here, on the beach in my neighbourhood of Port Moody, where a smaller clone of the English Bay event is being celebrated. It is called the Penguin Plunge. Against my better judgment I am here with my *Nightmare Before Christmas* T-shirt, and my red Santa booties.

The ratio of observers to participants hovers around 6,000 to one, indicating once again, that jumping into freezing water is a questionable pastime enjoyed by only a special few, and that voyeuristic sadism is a very popular form of entertainment. We are relegated to a roped off area of the beach while the observers are stationed high above where they can't be splashed by any errant drops. The semi-naked shivering people around me are attired in Christmassy water themes.

There are only two emergency vehicles here. This disturbs me very much. I think that there should be a hell of a lot more. I am also deeply concerned that if someone should expire, they may face the eternal humiliation of meeting St. Peter while half naked, wearing felt reindeer antlers and a *Little Mermaid* life-ring.

The countdown takes place. I nervously turn and look at my wife Barbara, who is there with our dog Rebus, just in case some family emergency arises that would sadly take me away from this. She smiles and waves her gloved hand back at me in encouragement. Rebus is next to her in his doggy hoody and matching booties. He looks at me oddly—oh God, maybe he is unwell, maybe I need to rush him to the vet right now....

The run begins and I pray to St. Darrell, the patron saint of silly buggers. I need his help like last year in Pamplona. He must protect me. I hit the water screaming with all the others. One million stinging needles shatter my body and I feel death trying to snatch me—and then the water hits my knees and it is much worse... and then I am frigid, and iced and glacially frozen but I am not cold.

No—I am, in fact, very cool!

~Stefano Mazzega
Coquitlam, British Columbia

Rice Pudding Winterlude Triathlon

Runners just do it — they run for the finish line even if someone else has reached it first.
~Author Unknown

O ur Ottawa winter tradition began four years ago with an e-mail I sent to the members of our informal Saturday morning runners group. Most of the nine of us are in our mid-sixties, with three in their late fifties.

Hello Friends:

This morning Kristin and I had another brilliant idea: We're going to do our own version of the Winterlude Triathlon on Saturday February 5th. Like the "real" Winterlude Triathlon, ours will also involve an 8k skate from Dows Lake to Pretoria Bridge and back, a 5k ski through the Arboretum and a 5k run.

The gimmick is that we're doing ours just after the real one which starts at 8 a.m. (We're just too speedy for those hundreds of flashing blades in the mass start, so we're giving them an hour to head out ahead of us :-).) Once they're done with the ski tracks set in the Arboretum, we'll use them by ourselves, and then run by ourselves when the others are finished. So we get all the benefits and excitement, with none of the stress. It will be a collegial activity, which we're doing together. Anyone want to join us?

Louise

Although we thought we'd ask, Kristin and I truly figured we'd just be in this together, two sixty-plus latecomers to athletic pursuit with more enthusiasm than talent. However, by mid-January that year we had at least six fellow triathletes on board to share the experience, including Anna, who had actually done the real Winterlude Triathlon many times, but appreciated our low-key approach.

The "real" Winterlude Triathlon is one of the oldest of Ottawa's Winterlude Festival activities, combining skating on the Rideau Canal, cross-country skiing in the nearby Arboretum and running along Queen Elizabeth Drive—when the weather co-operates. Standard distances of the February event are an 8k mass start skate, a 5k ski and a 5k run. However, in reality it varies depending on too much or too little snow, or rain. There have been ski/run/ski, skate/run/ski, run/ski, just a run, and various skate, ski and run course configurations. We vowed to do whatever the "real" one did.

With others now on board, Kristin and I felt a responsibility for them in our "Rice Pudding Runners" group. The name "Rice Pudding" was born after my friend Lynn and I ended a two-hour-long snowy run with a bowl of rice pudding at a local restaurant. It tasted so good we thought we should share the experience. The next time we invited other running women to join us, and long after we'd stopped eating rice pudding, the name stuck and we kept meeting. That is until Hazel, one of our members, decided she didn't like rice pudding, and we then became "The Antiques of Steel!"

Kristin and I spent days on the Rice Pudding Winterlude Triathlon logistics, setting up our start time, organizing clothing and equipment, and questioning our sanity in creating the activity in the first place. Unlike the real Winterlude Triathlon, we parked in the Dows Lake parking lot and used our cars as the transition zone for the skate/ski/run.

Some of the fit and fast athletes in the official Winterlude Triathlon actually skate to their 8 a.m. start with their skis and backpacks over their shoulders! We, on the other hand, had so much stuff packed into the car we couldn't even walk with it all, let alone balance with it on skates!

It was a happy exercise in camaraderie and support as we glided cautiously from skate to ski to run. We paired up frequently, and each of us always had company, whether we were fastest or slowest in each activity.

After that first Rice Pudding Winterlude Triathlon, we drank wine at Mexicali Rosa's while overlooking Dows Lake Skateway, wore the Rice Pudding Medals Kristin had engraved for us at a Vanier trophy shop, and toasted our plan to repeat the event the following year when several of us turned sixty-five.

As four of our group now approach age sixty-seven, we've done three of our own Winterlude Triathlons, are planning our fourth, and are looking forward to many more!

~Louise Rachlis
Ottawa, Ontario

86

Decoding Groundhog Day

The trouble with weather forecasting is that it's right too often
for us to ignore it and wrong too often for us to rely on it.
~Patrick Young

After removing my toque, gloves, scarf and parka, I rubbed my hands together, trying to get the circulation going. "I really, really, really hate winter," I said, my fingers tingling as they began to warm up.

Susan, my best friend and an avid cross-country skier, sat across from me in the restaurant. "You are such a wuss," she said. "It's barely minus ten."

I groaned. "That's at least twenty degrees too cold for me." The waiter placed a cup of coffee in front of me and I wrapped my hands around it. "Besides, it's not my fault my hands are always cold. If I lived somewhere warm..."

"...you'd be complaining about the heat," Susan finished. "It's already February. Tomorrow is Groundhog Day and winter is practically over."

"Right. Like some rodent knows more about the weather than we do. If it weren't for reporters trying to take his picture, he'd still be fast asleep in his den."

I took a sip of coffee, savouring the heat flowing into my body. "Now there's a job I'd like. Sleep through the worst of winter, wake up for ten minutes, and then go back to sleep for another month or two."

Susan drank half her coffee before speaking. "Considering how much you hate winter, maybe you were a groundhog in a previous life. Or a bear."

I shivered. "With my luck, it was probably a polar bear."

After breakfast we went for our traditional Sunday morning walk. Too cold to snow that day, what had already fallen on the ground crunched under our feet. With the sun shining, it truly was a beautiful winter day. Not that I would have admitted it to Susan. An hour later, cheeks red with cold, we headed back to my house for something warm to drink.

After unwinding, unzipping and pulling off layers of clothes again, I thought back to our earlier discussion. "Susan, have you ever wondered how many groundhogs are forecasting weather tomorrow across Canada? Is there some kind of Groundhog Weather Network? What happens if one of them says early spring, and the other says long winter? Do they just flip a coin—heads it's spring, tails it's winter?"

Susan shrugged. "I thought you didn't care about groundhogs."

"Well, it is almost a national holiday. Just because I don't think they can predict weather, doesn't mean I'm not curious," I said. "I'm going to check."

Two minutes later we were sitting in my office in front of my computer. A quick Google search brought up pages of sources. I scanned the titles and clicked on one, then another and another.

"I was right about the provinces each having their own ground-hog weather forecasters," I said. "Wiarton Willie may be Ontario's most famous prognosticating rodent, but he has a bunch of cousins spread across Canada."

I counted them as I read out their names. "There's Nova Scotia's Schubenacadie Sam, Alberta's Balzac Billy and Manitoba's Winnipeg Willow, the only female. If you're feeling bilingual, there's even Fred from Val-d'Espoir in Gaspésie."

"See," Susan said, "with all those groundhogs, at least one of them has to be right."

I clicked on a couple more articles, skimming their contents. "Aha," I said triumphantly, "Willie and his kin are more lover boy than meteorologist. Our furry weatherman couldn't care less about whether he sees his shadow. He's channeling his hormones. The little guy just wants to get lucky."

I paused to read a bit more. "If it weren't for the publicity and the urging of his handlers, Willie wouldn't be interrupting his annual hibernation for a chance at some nooky until the middle or end of March. If he waited, then his score—meteorologically speaking—would be much higher. He'd probably find more female groundhogs, too."

"So what is his score?" Susan asked, peering at the computer screen.

"Not good," I responded. "Groundhogs have a worse record of predicting the weather than Environment Canada. Willie and his cousins are right only thirty-seven percent of the time. In any other country, they'd have been fired years ago. Here, we take their pictures and splash them across the front page of the newspaper."

Susan shook her head. "You really know how to take the joy out of winter, don't you?

At my grin, she continued. "I guess that means you're not going to be checking out what Wiarton Willie has to say tomorrow?"

"That's exactly what it means," I said. "I'm going to be curled up in bed under a flannel sheet and two polar fleece blankets, wearing my favourite turquoise toque."

"A toque?" Susan interrupted. "You wear a toque to bed?"

"You bet I do. I turn down the thermostat at night to save energy and it gets really cold. The toque is my modern equivalent of a night-cap. Unlike Willie, I don't have a fur coat, but I do have a big orange tabby cat or two nestled beside me to help keep me warm." I paused. "Now that's how to spend a Canadian winter."

I lied. The next morning I did, in fact, get up and check the news to see what Willie had to say. Like millions of other Canadians, I decided that if waiting for a groundhog to declare an early spring gives us even a thin ray of sunshine in the middle of a cold, dark winter, so be it.

Willie predicted an early spring. Environment Canada disagreed.

Since I wasn't teaching that day, I went back to bed, complete with toque and a couple of cats. This human groundhog knew we'd have at least another six weeks of winter. Remembering the year I wore turtlenecks into June, I shivered and snuggled deeper under the blankets.

Goodnight Willie and sweet dreams. See you in a month or so.

~Harriet Cooper
Toronto, Ontario

87

A Christmas with *Nutcracker*

To dance is to be out of yourself. Larger, more beautiful, more powerful.
This is power, it is glory on earth and it is yours for the taking.
~Agnes de Mille

I t is the magic of Christmas that made it my favorite holiday as a child, and I still love to see the faces of all the children when they light up with joy during the holiday season. My family has strong traditions that have been passed down through generations. Preparation would always start with decorating the Christmas tree, which my sister and I always made sure was set up well in advance. We each had our own little wooden boxes full of Christmas ornaments delicately wrapped in tissue paper from the year before. Christmas music had to be on at all times; my sister and I loved it to the point of obsession. An almost life-like nutcracker was positioned in the foyer of our home to greet guests, and we also had white Christmas lights on the outside of the house and up the banisters.

Christmas Eve was so special I could hardly contain myself. We always attended midnight mass, but first came the delicious oyster stew, a recipe from my father's side delicately made by my mother. After dinner my sister and I would dress up in pretty little dresses that usually matched. I think getting ready for mass was my mom's favorite part, as I think she thought of us as sort of her Barbie dolls.

Our Christmas day was totally relaxed and all about family: on the phone to relatives, sharing stories and eating together. Growing up in Winnipeg truly tests your capacity to face the frigid cold winter nights, but the cold didn't seem as bad around Christmastime when we were surrounded by family and friends.

I moved away from home at the age of ten when I was accepted into Canada's Royal Winnipeg Ballet School Professional Division. Even at that age, I knew it was a privilege and honour to be accepted to one of the most prestigious ballet schools in the world. We were overjoyed by the news that my sister was also accepted.

Every day we worked hard. We never saw the sun. Occasionally, I would pass a company member in the hall and this would make my day brighter. A smile and a simple hello was all it took to keep me going. I remember one time when prima ballerina Evelyn Hart stopped me in the hallway and asked how my classes were going. She gave me a couple of hints and a smile I will never forget. I had an adrenaline rush for weeks!

Each year the RWB prepares for the famous ballet, *Nutcracker*, a Christmas tradition for many ballet companies. The coveted roles are Clara, the Snow Queen, and of course, the Sugar Plum Fairy. When the company went into the theatre for the last stage of rehearsal we students were invited to watch a preview. This was the perfect night out for a young artist in love with Christmas—live orchestration, beautiful costumes, and incredible dancing.

While our holiday traditions at home didn't include *Nutcracker*, it has now become a huge part of my own Christmas traditions. Now, as the Principal dancer with the RWB, I have adrenaline rushes when it's me out on the stage performing the role of Clara for all the young aspiring artists.

I've been a member of the company for ten years now. We have company members from across the globe—Japan, Russia, China, and Brazil—and I'm honoured to be part of such a diversified culture of people, especially during the holidays. I have learned many different traditions while working with this wonderful and dedicated group of people. We share stories, food, music and so much more.

Christmas will forever be my favorite holiday and hold that extremely special place in my heart. I will continue to pass on the beloved family traditions from my own childhood and I look forward to creating new ones with a family of my own some day!

~Amanda Green
Winnipeg, Manitoba

88

Calling All Swans!

Stratford is so swan-crazy, it once had an official Honorary Keeper of the Swans, the only person in North America to hold such a title.
~Mike Fuhrmann, The Canadian Press

Canadians have many traditions, customs, and holidays that welcome in the seasons, especially winter. I think perhaps one of the most delightful of these occurs in a town called Stratford, Ontario. My son Benjamin and I happened to come across it quite by accident.

This quaint and delightful town has been a favourite haunt of my family's for years and not just because of its beauty. Stratford has the Stratford Shakespeare Festival which has been claimed by many, including famous actors, to be the best in North America. For Benjamin, a professional pianist, and my daughter Miriam, an actress, Stratford is their home away from home. There is comfort in those theatres like no other place I know and during the festival season we spend almost as much time in Stratford as we do in our own town, Amherstburg.

Actors and musicians from all over the world work onstage for the festival and they gladly chat with fellow performers, i.e. my two kids, about the craft of performing and anything pertaining to theatre and the stage.

On one very chilly and frosty day, Benjamin and I had decided to go to Stratford to do some early Christmas shopping. We had just bought a picnic lunch at Pazzo's restaurant.

"You should eat lunch by the river," said the waitress. "They are trying to gather the swans to bring them in for the winter. It's fun to watch all these city workers running after the birds—kind of like a game of tag, only the swans always win. I wish I wasn't working."

"That must be impossible to do," said Ben. "And there are so many of them."

"Nah, maybe thirty," replied the girl.

We quickly headed for the Avon River. Sure enough, City workers could be seen coaxing huge swans to get into the back of their truck. Some went willingly but others squawked and hissed and ran around the truck.

"Come on, sweetheart," we heard one worker say. "You know it's that time of year and you'll be warm and—OW!"

I laughed when the swan snapped at the man's feet and began chasing him.

"Hey, Mom," said Ben. "It's that man who always feeds the swans."

I looked to where he pointed. "Oh, I see him," I exclaimed and waved at the gentleman.

We had met several times before on our visits.

He smiled when he saw me. "They're playing around with these poor men," he said with a chuckle. "Patience is required."

He turned back to the swans that had already gathered around him and tossed out some food, then made a trail to the truck.

Some of the swans followed him into the truck. They looked positively regal—well as regal as a bird can look while waddling—as they climbed into the truck.

"Did you get them all?" Ben asked one of the exhausted workers.

"No, only about half," he said. "It'll take us a few more days to get them all. Are you enjoying yourselves?"

"Absolutely," I said. "What an awesome way to start winter."

"If you enjoyed this day you'll have to come back in the spring for the Swan Parade when they return to the river," he said. "That's a real celebration. These swans are special to our town. Some people think it's the actors who are the big draw here, but we all know it's the swans. They're royalty."

We watched the truck drive away and the swans looked back at us, or more specifically, glared at us.

"We're coming back in the spring, right?" said Ben.

"Wouldn't miss it," I said and laughed. One of the swans was waddling after the truck and squawking all the way.

Royalty indeed.

~Pamela Goldstein
Amherstburg, Ontario

Our Louis Riel Day

The difference between a hockey player and a football player or a baseball player, is this: Hockey guys play if they can breathe.
~Con Smythe

Two hockey teams battle for victory every year at our annual Louis Riel Day Classic. The players are a mixed bag of family, friends and neighbors. Some are local hockey greats, some are figure skaters with sticks, while others wear boots and aren't sure which team they're on. There are even a few who sit on lawn chairs. They sip hot chocolate and cheer for whichever team scores. Dogs on leashes bark as the players skate by them.

The Louis Riel Day Classic was my brother's brainchild. Back in 2008, parts of Canada were bestowed a statutory holiday on the third Monday of every February. It is a day to celebrate family. Manitoba calls it Louis Riel Day.

My brother proposed that we hold an outdoor hockey game on this day. We all agreed.

February here can be very cold. On February 18, 1966 the temperature set a record at -49 Fahrenheit (-45C). In 2012 our first annual Louis Riel Day Classic had temperatures soaring above zero. The ice melted and became slushy but we played anyway.

In 2013 the weather was cold, the ice good. That morning a text arrived on my phone—"Louis Riel Day postponed."

A look out the window quickly explained why. Blowing snow

and blizzard conditions were menacing. The rink would be covered by a few feet of snow and the brutally cold winds would be unbearable and would blow out any attempt to make a fire.

A few weeks later we made our way down to the rink at a place called Little Lake. I watched my sons and their friends head out with skates, lugging nets. It made me think of my own childhood memories at Little Lake: how I liked to skate on the edge, where the bullrush reeds poked through the ice, and how much fun it was to play Crack the Whip. My own children were creating their memories this day.

Once the fire crackled into flames and the skates were laced, it was game time! The rules were simple: no slap shots.

Apparently, pushing opposing players into snow banks was allowed.

The competition was fierce and teams played hard for victory. There was no prize, just a large rock presented to the winning team.

One very important person was missing from this day, someone who would have enjoyed it a hundred times more than any of us—my dad. He always encouraged us to "Seize the day," and reminded us that, "When the going gets tough—the tough get going." He proved these words when in the last throes of ALS he laced up his own skates at Little Lake and went for his last skate.

I like to think Dad is there watching the game in spirit. I see him in the faces of my brothers. I hear him in the words of my sister and I feel his love through my mother's presence. He is proud of us.

We will all hear the laughter, the cracking of sticks on ice, and the team cheers for many Louis Riel Days to come. And I will think of my dad and smile.

~Maureen Flynn
Selkirk, Manitoba

90

A Sweet End to Winter

A sap-run is the sweet good-by of winter. It is the fruit of the equal marriage
of the sun and frost.
~John Burroughs, Signs and Seasons

W inter seems to last forever in my small Ontario town.
But there's one thing that sparks everyone's appetite
for just one more winter day. Our town of Elmira
proudly hosts the "World's Largest Maple Syrup Festival" just at the
tip end of winter, while the snow still lies in heaps and frosting deco-
rates the trees.

When my family moved into town, we were unaware of the
magnitude of this event.

One morning at the end of that first winter we were rudely
awakened at 6:00 a.m. by clangs and bangs and tractors roaring past.
"What is all that racket?" we complained.

To see what all the noise was about, we dressed warmly and
headed downtown to find the area had been completely transformed
into an enormous fair that celebrated nothing but maple syrup.
Nearly 80,000 visitors were expected be ferried into town on hay
wagons throughout the day.

An absolute feast for the senses lay before us. Booths were set
up with delicacies like maple fritters, maple back bacon, maple burg-
ers, and maple candy. Giant jugs of sticky maple syrup were set out
everywhere, like ketchup, to be added as a condiment to coffee, hot

dogs, ice cream, fries, or just enjoyed on its own. The pet store even offered local maple syrup dog treats.

Just like Disneyland, it was impossible to sample everything in one day.

"The worse the weather, the more that people eat!" the grinning vendors declared, as snowflakes landed like icing on my maple donut.

We ate what we could, then carried a hot funnel cake back to our house, where we woke our three sleeping kids.

"You have got to go down there!" we said, as they devoured the sweet dough for breakfast.

Today visitors can enjoy all kinds of maple syrup festivities—there is the world's largest sap bucket for photo ops, crazy pancake flipping contests, maple taffy making demonstrations, horse and buggy tours of the sugar bush, and Flap Jack the pancake mascot to greet. Other events include farm animals, toy and antique shows, craft sales and log cutting contests. Everyone is selling something—from the farmers selling jugs of maple syrup ("liquid gold" they call it), to vendors of pussy willows and pickles on a stick and quilts, to street preachers, and even rides on a Mennonite horse and buggy.

For our family, this has become one of the most eagerly anticipated days of the year. My older son now spends the day dressed in medieval attire promoting local theatre, my daughter rides the hay wagons around town with friends, and this past year my younger son managed to spend $30 on maple sausage, pancakes and other treats before 8:30 in the morning.

The locals claim the Maple Syrup Festival is the last hurrah of winter—that spring just will not arrive until we've celebrated the event. This coming winter will be the 50th Maple Syrup Festival in Elmira. It has become a way to usher out winter with a grand feast, to delight in the sweet delectable gift from the trees just before they blossom into spring.

As you drive into town every day of the year, you are greeted with banners that read "Life is Sweeter in Elmira."

And as I pour maple syrup into my morning coffee, I couldn't agree more.

~Lori Zenker
Elmira, Ontario

91

The Swans of the Avon River

*It's not the longest parade in the world, but the swan celebration in
Stratford, Ont., may be one of the quirkiest.*
~Mike Fuhrmann, The Canadian Press

Spectators have come from all over Ontario and from as far away as Ohio, Ottawa and Chicago. They line the streets, and some have even climbed trees and perched themselves on branches, just to witness the exciting event! We haven't seen our swans since late last fall. As soon as the Avon River, which runs through the heart of our city, begins to freeze over in November, these beautiful ambassadors of Stratford are moved to their humble winter home beside the William Allman Arena, where they stay for the duration. But today—the first Sunday of April—that all comes to an end.

This is the magical date when we, the people of Stratford, watch our beloved swans return to the water. The excitement level goes up the moment we hear the first screel of the pipes from the Stratford Police Pipe and Drum Band, which adds a suitable royal pomp and tongue-in-cheek circumstance. Then, with the street lined with delighted spectators of every age, the doors to their winter home are opened, and twenty-eight very frisky white swans, black swans, and assorted geese are escorted back to the water by the pipes and drums. A fifteen minute march—err walk—err waddle… away—it's Stratford's famous Parade of Swans. There are no floats or speeches from politicians—just the simplicity of a small parade of our majestic swans heading back to the river.

Today there are upwards of 5,000 people here to watch this regal parade. Happy to be out of their brick winter quarters and anxious to get back to the water, the feathery herd offers their audience a charming entertainment as they make their way to the river. Following the pipes and drums, the swans make their way down Lakeside Drive before crossing the road, opening their wings, and joyously slipping into the waters of the Avon River.

It all started in 1918 when a former railway worker, J.C. Garden, gifted a pair of Mute swans to the city. Over the years other swans from different bloodlines have joined the flock, including descendants of Her Majesty, Queen Elizabeth's royal herd.

For almost fifty years the late Robert J. Miller was widely known as the "keeper of the swans." Bob truly loved his birds, and it was clear they loved him in return. He kept a protective eye on them, especially during the winter, and if one of them became sick or injured, he would nurse it back to health. During mating season he broke up battles between cobs (males), and monitored the nests. Bob's swans were featured in a 1999 documentary film *Swans on the Avon*. He later wrote a book, *The Swans of Stratford*. Both tell the story of Stratford's swans and their spring parade.

Our now famous "Swan Parade" was created by the late, former Mayor, Ted Blowes, "Mr. Stratford," who, along with the Civic Beautification and Environmental Awareness Committee, organized the first ever swan parade event.

"It's all about the swans," Ted would always say. "We keep it simple." So we've done exactly that, and keep it focused on the swans.

Over the years we have all come to the conclusion that the swan parade must be important to Canada celebrating the end of winter, because CBC and CTV national TV networks always show clips of it on their nightly newscast all across the country.

To Bob and Ted, from my family and many others, as well as future generations to come, thank you for this simple gift.

~Dan Mathieson
Mayor of Stratford, Ontario

Chapter

10

O Canada The Wonders of Winter

A Holiday to Remember

*Christmas waves a magic wand over this world,
and behold, everything is softer and more beautiful.*

~Norman Vincent Peale

92

The Year I Was Mrs. Claus

To give without any reward, or any notice, has a special quality of its own.
~Anne Morrow Lindbergh

It was the most fun job I ever had. At the time I was a college student raising my then nine-year-old son, Joshua, on my own. In fact, Joshua and I had been on our own since before he drew his first breath.

Single parenting came with both challenges and joys. All too often there was no money for the extras other families took for granted.

But somehow I always managed to make Christmas special for Joshua. In addition, I was able to buy a few presents for myself, usually things I was in need of, and open them Christmas morning. It prevented Joshua from wondering why Santa brought no presents for Mum.

The year he was nine I was in college and living on a student loan. It was tight. Christmas was less than three weeks away and I still hadn't managed to buy my son the few gifts he'd asked for. A church downtown was giving away toys and clothing to families in need. Swallowing my pride, I decided to go see what I could find.

I was ushered into a back room with a group of women of all ages. A long table held slim pickings, but I managed to find a couple of board games I thought Joshua might like. A middle-aged woman with stiff bluish hair approached me and asked how many children

I had. When I said, "one little boy," she bellowed, "One gift only for each child!"

Everyone looked at me as if I had been caught stealing. I was so embarrassed I put the games down and walked away with what pride I had left.

I didn't want to repeat that humiliating experience, but for Joshua's sake I began to consider swallowing my pride and perhaps visiting another church giving away toys.

One crisp snowy day, while walking downtown, a large poster of a fat, jolly Santa with an overflowing bag of toys in front of a fireplace caught my attention. On his knee was a smiling little girl with pretty golden curls whispering in his ear. A huge sign welcomed boys and girls to visit Santa at the department store for the next three Saturdays before Christmas.

An idea hit me. Rather than seeking church donations, I'd make Christmas for Joshua using my wits and imagination. The answer to my situation was staring me right in the face. Santa was coming to town, but what about Mrs. Claus? Why should she be left behind at the North Pole baking cookies, while Mr. Claus has all the fun listening to the giggled secrets of children?

Stepping into the store, I boldly asked a saleslady if the store manager was available. There was no turning back as I headed toward the manager's office and knocked on the door. I was expecting to see a middle-aged man wearing a starched white dress shirt and tie. Imagine my surprise when I found an attractive, young female manager sitting behind a desk.

Introducing myself, I pitched the idea of Mrs. Claus accompanying Mr. Claus to the mall. The words came with ease. I was in need of employment, trying to make Christmas for my little boy and was applying for a job as Mrs. Claus. The manager mulled over the idea, asked a few questions and hired me on the spot, more or less.

"You'll need to dress as Mrs. Claus if you want the job," she said. "We can try it for a day, and if it works out, you can come back the Saturdays leading up to Christmas."

I thanked her and left. I made a quick stop at a secondhand

clothing store and purchased a red top and a matching skirt. I stopped at a sewing shop and bought a huge roll of cotton and balls of white yarn. And I went home to put it together.

The next morning, I carefully packed a paper bag with my home-made costume, and raced downtown to the department store. After ducking into a changing room, I emerged dressed as Mrs. Claus.

"Come in," called the manager when I knocked on her door. Taking a deep breath I stepped into her office. "Good Morning, I'm Mrs. Claus." If she was taken by surprise, she didn't show it.

"You have the job," she said. "Tie your long hair into a bun, and be here Saturday morning by ten. You can pass out balloons to the children waiting to see Santa. You'll get paid before Christmas, like the rest of the staff."

"Sure, I can do that," I said casually, wanting to jump up and down with excitement.

I loved the job—it was so much fun. Joshua told all his friends that his mom was Mrs. Claus at the Mall. As the month wore on, my best friend, Liz, agreed to bring Joshua and her daughter, Katie, downtown to visit Santa on the last Saturday before Christmas.

The two kids were excited about seeing Santa and getting a treat. Liz jokingly told them to behave while they waited in the line-up because Mrs. Claus would be watching, and if they weren't good, she would put their names on the naughty list.

Katie and Joshua giggled when I offered them balloons. Joshua whispered in my ear that he had a wish list for Santa.

"What's on your wish list, Joshua?" I asked, worried about being able to fulfill his expectations.

"It's between Santa and me," he replied, holding the list tightly in his fist. Later I saw Joshua pass his list to Santa, while he pointed to Mrs. Claus who was talking with the waiting children. Old Santa winked at me and tucked Joshua's wish list in his pocket.

At the end of the last day, and after an endless line-up of children, it was quitting time for Mr. and Mrs. Claus. Before I left for home the store manager gave me a substantial paycheque—which included a very generous bonus. I was overjoyed, because now I could make Christmas for Joshua without having to resort to handouts.

Late on Christmas Eve, long after Joshua had gone to bed, there was a knock on my apartment door. "Who could this be calling so late?" I wondered. I opened the door a crack to take a peek.

"Ho, Ho, Ho," bellowed Santa Claus. "I can't stay long. It's my busiest night of the year," he said with a twinkle in his eye.

As I stood speechless at the door in a nightgown and housecoat, Santa dropped a bag of presents on the floor and then disappeared into the darkness of the night.

How did he know where I lived? Then it dawned on me that it had to be the items on the wish list Joshua had passed to Santa. Tomorrow morning, there would be even more gifts under the tree for Joshua. Boy, would he be surprised. Santa really came through for him.

But when I opened the bag, I found four beautifully wrapped presents ready to place under the tree. Tears welled in my eyes as I read the tags: To Stella, Love Santa.

~Stella Shepard
Morell, Prince Edward Island

93

Lucy's Gift

I am fond of pigs. Dogs look up to us. Cats look down on us. Pigs treat us as equals.
~Winston Churchill

L ucy, our "never meant to be eaten" pig, was due to farrow on Christmas Day and we had no suitable shelter prepared. Winters here on southern Vancouver Island are generally mild and wet. Our pigs, horses and steers, two of each, had four fenced and cross-fenced acres to roam, and adequate shelter from the rain. However, as it happened, this was a particularly harsh winter and Lucy was heavy with her first litter of piglets. She needed a birthing hut to keep her young warm and dry.

We were city dwellers originally. Buying this land on the Cowichan River and keeping chickens and other farm animals was part of my "back to the land" dream. I knew nothing about pigs, but quickly fell in love with Lucy when we bought her and another piglet from the farm auction. Lucy was special and was like a dog in many ways—often following us around the property as we checked the fence lines, sometimes carrying a big stick in her mouth, imitating our dogs who ran along as well. Her eyes were bright and intelligent, her snout tilting in such a way that she looked like she was grinning. She came when she was called, and I swear she understood when I talked to her.

But now it was mid December and time to build Lucy her shelter away from the dogs and other animals. We sectioned off part of the field closer to the river, and built a makeshift shed with a door-sized opening in the front and a roof sloping toward the back. I took her a bucket of hot mash for dinner and hay for her bedding, and waited while she sniffed and snorted around before leaving her to settle in.

Our first snow of the winter fell during the night and the next morning we discovered Lucy had spent her time re-modeling her new home. She had tossed out all the hay and the front of the shed was now lying on the ground. A small fir tree, roots and all, was pushed to the back of the structure, and snow was softly drifting across the floor. We nailed the front of her house back up that evening and left her for another night. Lucy knocked it down again and hauled in more fir and cedar branches and a couple of snowberry bushes. This went on for a few nights until we finally gave up. Obviously she knew what she wanted and there wasn't much point in arguing with a three hundred and fifty-pound pig.

Lucy continued to rearrange her house, letting me put the hay back in, but not on the cedar branches. I was reminded of my frenetic house cleaning and decorating in the days and hours before I had my babies.

Christmas day came and no piglets, but when I walked out to the shed on Boxing Day morning she was lying against the rear of the shelter in her bed of evergreen boughs with four piglets suckling on her teats. Cradling a mug of coffee in my hands, I gingerly lowered myself to the bale of hay by the open side of her shelter and quietly watched the miracle of birth unfold. Another piglet came out in a slippery rush, worked his way through the amniotic sac and found a teat. Lucy merely lifted her head for an instant.

With snow lightly swirling, I sat with Lucy most of the day, unconsciously matching my breathing with hers, sitting in a meditative state, remembering my own child-bearing, and marvelling at other births with thoughts of Bethlehem going through my mind. Occasionally I made forays to my house to get warm and lace my coffee with rum. Once, when I returned to the birthing hut, a piglet was lying deathly quiet, apart from the rest, still encased in his sac. Carefully, with a wary eye on Lucy and quietly reassuring her, I crawled in and gently pulled the caul from the animal's face, and then placed the now wriggling creature with the others. Lucy appeared exhausted and lay there in a stupor, breathing shallowly, eyes half closed, seemingly content with my presence.

We were both mothers, Lucy and I, having transcended the human/animal gap, sitting under the dark firs and towering black cottonwood trees, the river coursing nearby, snow drifting lazily down, muffling all sound and cocooning us in our birthing world.

Lucy had sixteen piglets that day and all survived. After a week she moved them across the pasture to a new home near the pond. She heaved around a couple of fallen trees and dug a den in the soft earth half under one of the logs. We had many more births on our little farm, but none of them held the magic of that Boxing Day. It was Lucy's gift of trust to me.

~Liz M. Forbes
Crofton, British Columbia

94

A Passage Through Time

The most incredible thing about miracles is that they happen.
~G.K. Chesteron

Approximately thirty-five years ago, my mother entrusted me with a family heirloom, a pine blanket-box. Due to its original grey milk-paint, chipped worn corners and lack of décor, I suspect it would not impress many. Yet, even as a small child, I was drawn to it and I suppose, its history.

Opening the lid time and time again I ran my small fingers over the names inscribed in pencil, the swirls of ornate lettering created by my ancestors who had traveled from England. I imagined them making their way as United Empire Loyalists into Upper Canada where they eventually settled at Stratford, which subsequently became my mother's hometown. From them, the box was passed down into her care and I'm certain it was my incessant interest that made her decision to pass this prize along to me instead of my brothers or sisters, an easy one.

As a married woman, I proudly presented the pine box, holding it amongst our most valued possessions. However it was not until the approach of my son's birthday that for me, its true purpose was revealed.

Jacob was born on Christmas Day... the best Christmas gift a mother could ever receive! As we approached his first birthday and of course Christmas, his natural inquisitiveness became evident as never before, as he was fascinated by the lights and glitter. Breaking with the past convention of an almost-to-the-ceiling tree, we decided to cut one down to a size that would fit on top of the pine box. After placing the tree in the stand we wrapped a tartan blanket around its base. Joyfully I hung the ornaments we had collected over the years and then methodically placed various bells around the bottom branches to serve as a warning jingle should Jacob's curiosity get the better of him.

Several years later, with his brother Bruce in the mix, our previous innovation had become a tradition. The trunk also served an additional duty. It harboured many of the treasures that were most dear to me: my wedding dress, the sleepers the boys came home from the hospital in, their baby shoes, special photos, and many of the other significant riches of our lives.

One year, while removing the ornaments after the holidays, I was shocked to discover that the tartan blanket at the base of the tree was damp. When I slowly peeled away the fabric it revealed that the tree stand had leaked. The top of the wooden box was discoloured and a large crack had formed on the lid.

I felt the beautiful trunk my mother had long ago so confidently placed in my care was now damaged and if that was not upsetting enough I still had to find out what treasures were ruined inside. My heart ached.

Earlier that same year I had experienced a different ache when I lost my mother-in-law. This very kind, gentle soul had finally succumbed to a weakened heart and quietly passed away.

When the extended family was packing up and removing articles from her home, my only request was for two of her china teacups and saucers. I wanted something, someday, far in the future, to pass along to my sons' brides... a gift of love from their nana.

I knelt in front of the damaged heirloom, took a deep breath and gently opened the lid. What I saw made me gasp. Sitting perilously, directly below the line of the crack were the two teacups and saucers now filled with yellowed water and pine needles. Miraculously, not one other item was wet; not one item was even remotely soiled, let alone ruined. All the water had dripped into those cups.

Stunned, I slumped back on my heels, my eyes filled with tears. I whispered a heartfelt thank you to my mother-in-law.

She was the one who protected our fortune, reinforcing in my heart that those who love us, whether physically with us or not, always surround us. This was her last Christmas gift to us.

As for the top of the box, oddly the crack, once dry, sealed as if never there. All that remains now is a slight blemish where some of the paint appears to have melted away, or as I choose to see it, a lovely reminder of this story. And as my mother and her mother and generations before her passed along this magnificent pine blanket box, so shall I, with the story of the tea cups added to its history, lovingly tucked inside.

~Nancy Koruna McIntosh
Niagara Falls, Ontario

95

Merry Christmas, Mum

A mom's hug lasts long after she lets go.
~Author Unknown

My parents were both actors. My father passed away only a few years ago at the age of ninety-one, but my mother died in 1973 at age fifty-three, when I was only seventeen years old.

The theatre was their particular sphere of influence. While not exactly stars, Hilary and Leslie Yeo were often recognized by knowledgeable theatregoers in both Canada and their native England. Even more to their delight, they reached the point where they were recognized by their peers as very accomplished and respected actors. The fact that they both possessed an energetic, devoted love of their craft (not to mention each other) had a great deal to do with their success.

In my mother's case there was also her undeniable physical and spiritual beauty, which friends, audiences and cameras alike found irresistible. Her effect on me was no less profound—I adored her.

As radio, television and film grew in popularity they both expanded their repertoire to include them. The television cameras were particularly fond of my mother and she appeared in several CBC shows—the *Festival Series* among the most popular in the 1960s. Dad found a great deal of TV and stage work as well, but had even more success as a Producer/Director in a new phenomenon called the *Industrial*.

I was an only child, and our small family was very close. They would often make sure they were both offered parts in the same production, and as much as possible, I would travel with them to various "seasons" at different theatres. When they did television, I would accompany them to the studio or the location whenever possible.

In the late 1960s Mum began to develop some inexplicable aches and pains. As time progressed, so did her pain. Then the doctors discovered the lump. A small thing, really. A little lump in her breast. It seemed those years of discomfort had been real after all.

The cancer that took her was not swift. It took two years to waste away one of the most beautiful and special people I'm ever likely to know. She died just after Christmas in 1973. I was a seventeen-year-old boy who adored his mother, and I did not deal with it well.

Her death altered my feelings and attitudes about many things. Predictably, Christmas was one of the things that was ruined for me. Dad and I each had to deal with some personal realities. He had lost his companion, lover and partner of over twenty years. I had lost my mother. Thankfully he and I had each other, and our warm loving relationship grew stronger with every passing year. But after Mum died, Christmas for me was never the same. In fact, it became a time of year when I really had to work at just staying level, let alone cheery. The reality was I wanted to skip the whole thing.

Ten years after Mum's death, the young woman I was living with was determined to alter my feelings about Christmas. But the harder she worked at making the house cheery and getting me into the spirit, the more I thought about Mum and how much I missed our family Christmases. I tried my best, but as usual, it was a very difficult time.

Fast forward to Christmas Eve. Not to be uncharitable, but thank goodness it was almost over. Val and I stayed up late wrapping gifts for family and friends and then it was time for bed.

I'm an early riser at the best of times, and as sleep was somewhat elusive this night, I was up even earlier than usual. I puttered around in the living room for a couple of hours—doing what, I don't remember. All I remember is that sometime around 6:30 or 7 a.m. I turned on the TV. And as I moved away, I heard something that stopped me in mid-turn. I hadn't heard that voice in over ten years. I hadn't seen a rerun, heard an audiotape—nothing. But in the early hours of this Christmas morning, the voice I was listening to was unmistakably that of my mother.

I quickly turned and saw an old black and white show appearing on the screen. It was unmistakably a Christmas winter scene. There was a barnyard where two men were standing, looking off to one side. And Mum's voice. The camera panned over to one side, revealing a door. As it opened, my mother stepped out.

I don't even remember sitting down, but I must have, because that's where Valerie found me, mesmerized, tears streaming down my face. She had never met my mother, but had seen photos. As soon as she looked over at the screen she knew. She sat down with me and together we watched my mother in something she had done at least ten years before she died. What made it even more incredible is that it wasn't a videotape. In those days television was live. The only way to record a live show was to actually film it off a television monitor. Rarely would the networks go to the trouble and expense of doing this. Apparently this was one of those rare occasions.

As much of an emotional shock as it was, I wouldn't have stopped it from happening if I could have. And I like to think that knowing how much I missed her, this was her little Christmas present to me. She was letting me know, that at this special time of year, and on this most difficult of days for me, she was with me, even as she always is.

One would think that having parents in that kind of business you would expect to see them on TV at some point. I constantly see my father's movies and series work on TV without warning. But I truly never even thought of the possibility of accidentally seeing Mum, and until that morning, in the ten years since her passing it hadn't happened even once.

It's been forty years now since her death, and I have yet to inadvertently come across another of her performances. But even if I do, it's unlikely to mean as much to me as that one special performance, on that Christmas morning in 1983.

~Jamie Yeo
Aurora, Ontario

96

Sugar Plum Fairies Danced in Her Head

It's the dream — if not a rite of passage — of every young female ballet student to dance the role of Clara in The Nutcracker.
~Karen Kain

When I think of Christmas I think of many things, but one of my fondest memories was seeing The National Ballet of Canada perform the *Nutcracker*.

So, it was a no brainer for me that I should take my own children to see that ballet, only this time it was in the city of Detroit, which is right across the river from Canada.

My daughter, Miriam, was four years old. When the curtain opened her eyes grew large. When the dolls that Drosselmeier had brought to the party began to dance she gasped with delight.

"They're real," she whispered in an awestruck voice. "Mommy, they're real!"

"Yes, honey. They're ballet dancers."

"I'm going to do that," she said with a conviction that was surprising for a four-year-old.

Miriam sat in her seat completely mesmerized. From that moment on all she ever talked about, dreamed about, breathed about was being one of the children in that show.

In truth she really wanted to be the Sugar Plum Fairy or Clara but she would settle for being one of the children.

Because we live so close to the U.S. and Canada border, a lot of kids took Arts lessons in both towns. This was so for Miriam when she turned seven. Her ballet instructor was the late Iacob Lascu who at the time was also the choreographer, director of the Nutcracker ballet for the Detroit Symphony.

My daughter was ecstatic when she auditioned in the fall and became one of those children.

Now, not only did she have ballet class on Tuesdays and Thursdays, she had rehearsals every Saturday and Sunday. They were long and hard but Miriam didn't care. I worried it would be too much but she refused to quit. She wanted to be on that stage. She would move heaven and earth for that chance. Neither my husband nor I had the heart to deny her this once-in-a-lifetime opportunity.

The warm autumn days soon turned into cold, bitter, winter days that darkened before five p.m. but Miriam insisted on going to rehearsals. She refused to miss any.

Rehearsal week at the Fox Theatre—twelve-hour days every day. The children were exhausted but so excited. Miriam was exhilarated.

The girls' hair had to be in ringlets for the show. Miriam's hair was thick and down to her waist. The rehearsal before opening night had ended late—ten p.m. I had to put in over 120 curlers in order to make those ringlets. Still Miriam didn't whine or cry. "Put more in the top, Mommy," she said. "It has to be poufy."

December 17th—opening night. After making sure she was dressed and ready to go on stage I joined my husband in the audience.

Curtain up—Miriam was radiant! If ever there was a child who was born to be on stage I was looking at one and she was my kid. This was not exactly the life I had planned for her.

Because Miriam was the shortest girl she had been put centre stage, right by Clara. Her little face even outshone Clara.

"I think we have a problem," said my husband. "Actors and dancers do not make a good living."

"We'll figure it out. Besides, she might lose interest."

"Are you kidding? Look at that face. I've never seen her so happy."

"Mommy did you see me?" cried Miriam. "Mr. Lascu says I was wonderful!"

"You were wonderful," I said and sniffled back my tears. "But are you really sure you want to do this all month? That's all of your Christmas holidays."

"Yes! This will be the best holiday ever!"

She flung her arms around my waist. "Thank you Mommy for letting me do this. I love it!"

Miriam went on to perform in the *Nutcracker* for three more years before Mr. Lascu retired. In all of that time she never once complained and her face became incandescent as soon as the curtain went up in every performance.

Miriam has since chosen not to pursue dancing as a career but has become an actress instead. However, every Christmas she and I sit together and watch the *Nutcracker* on TV. Over and over and over.

"Those were the best Christmases ever," Miriam says and she snuggles closer to me.

"Yes, they were," I reply.

~Pamela Goldstein
Amherstburg, Ontario

97

Our Blowtorch Christmas

There is no ideal Christmas; only the one Christmas you decide to make as a reflection of your values, desires, affections, traditions.
~Bill McKibben

Christmas dinner was in the oven and our electricity was about to fail. We stared out the window. In front of our house was a power pole with a black box near the top, and the black box was sending out a shower of sparks—pretty, like a small fireworks display.

"Better phone the power company," someone said.

"It's Christmas," someone else said.

"Will they even answer their phone?"

My husband made the call. "They'll send someone when they can," he reported, "but they have no idea when that might be."

I sighed. Dinner was supposed to be early for the sake of the kids. On the bright side, they had new toys to occupy them. There was Christmas music on the stereo. The lovely smell of roasting turkey was starting to fill the air. We adults drank our wine and ate our appetizers and watched the sparking black box in fascination.

Eventually, as we knew it would, the display of sparks fizzled. Then the lights and the music went out. That meant the furnace and the stove were out too. I felt panic. New at this Christmas-dinner giving game, I had prepared carefully, hoping not to appear too clumsy to my very competent mother-in-law.

Thank goodness we had a fireplace. We put more wood on the fire and made sure everybody had a sweater. We dug out lots of candles and set them up ready to light when darkness fell.

My vegetables and potatoes were scrubbed, peeled, cut up, sitting in a water bath, all ready, except that they were raw. Earlier I'd taken my homemade buns out of the freezer and put them in a brown paper bag ready to warm in the oven at the last minute. My cookbook said the turkey needed fifteen minutes roasting time to the pound, and that meant it needed at least another hour in the oven. Relishes and cranberries were lined up in their little dishes under plastic wrap; right now they seemed to be the only part of dinner we could eat. For one gloomy minute I contemplated ordering pizza.

My mother-in-law favoured improvisation. She had spotted the green salad and the tomato aspic, a tradition of my family, in the fridge. Why not, she suggested, dine on these, some cheese, and the buns? It would be everything we really needed.

So we had a plan. Just to check, I inserted the thermometer into the turkey and found it was actually already fully cooked! It seems that modern turkeys need far less roasting time than the old cook-book suggested. Things were really looking up.

Darkness was falling so we lit the candles all round the room. My husband carved the bird and we loaded our plates with the turkey and cranberries, the salad and aspic and pickles and buns. We barely missed the rest of the menu. Laughter and jokes replaced the music missing from the silent stereo.

In the slightly chilly air, nobody, even the kids, seemed very interested in the ice cream bombe I'd made. But thank heavens for seasonal excess. There were tins of Christmas cake and cookies and other good things ready to fill the dessert gap.

"Those look delicious," somebody said. "All that's missing is a good cup of coffee." There was, of course, no pot of coffee, no hot water, no prospects at all. An awkward silence followed the ill-timed comment.

Then my husband disappeared into the basement and returned with a shiny tool.

"What's that for, Uncle Don?" one of the kids asked, as he filled a pot with tap water.

"Watch and see," he told them.

He struck a match near the tool. We heard a whoosh sound, and blue flame poured out of the blowtorch. He trained it on the pot until eventually the water began to boil! He then poured the precious boiling water through a coffee filter, and waited while it dripped into a carafe. And we had rich, fresh coffee to finish our improvised Christmas feast.

It was around that time that two men from the power company knocked on the door. "This shouldn't take us too long," one of them said cheerfully. He breathed out a smell as he spoke. Mincemeat? Plum pudding? I realized then he'd been called away from his own Christmas celebration—to help us with ours. As we watched, these two heroes climbed the pole and started working on the black box.

While they worked, my husband's sister sat down at the piano. It was now getting dark and in the room lit only by candlelight we gathered around her and sang all the wonderful Christmas songs we'd lost when the stereo went silent.

And then the lights came on: the lights on the house, the lights on the plantings in the back yard, and most important of all, the lights on the Christmas tree. At the moment they came on, all of us, child and adult, gasped. This is what we had been missing. We felt, I think, the same wonder at the sudden and brilliant appearance of those lights as our ancestors who lived before electricity must have felt when, for a few shining minutes once a Christmas, they cautiously touched a match to the candles on their hand-cut spruce tree.

~Gail Neff Bell
Tsawwassen, British Columbia

98

Father Christmas

Family is not an important thing, it's everything.
~Michael J. Fox

A few years ago, I had to go out of town, and I was rummaging through our third-floor closets in search of my garment bag. In mid-rummage, I found an old cassette tape. When I picked it up it straggled from its tiny reel and lay in my hand like a clump of seaweed, brown and discouraged. The label read "XMAS 1968."

When the kids were little, we moved a lot, often many thousands of miles away from my parents, their grandparents. To banish those miles we sent tapes back and forth. "XMAS 1968" was one of them.

Suddenly hungry for history, I rewound it carefully, found an old tape player, and pushed play. Age had taken its toll; it hissed and moaned and squealed and crackled, my mother sounding now like a weary cello or a tipsy squirrel. Then all at once, after a moment of slow silence, I heard my father's voice, warm and true and real as a wound.

"Merry Christmas," my father said. "I wish I could be with you."

When I was small and I heard people say "Father Christmas," I thought they were talking about my dad. The two words just automatically went together. Each fulfilled, enhanced, and defined the other.

Father. Christmas. A permanent pair, yoked forever in my mind. Like movies and red liquorice. Father. Christmas.

In a way, this is surprising, for my father sprang from grave and frugal Scottish folk who viewed merriment as a crime against nature, tidings of comfort and joy with suspicion, and Christmas as something to be endured, like quinsy or sex or dry rot. Fortunately, he had married my mother, whose family was a little Irish, fond of laughter and theatrical generosity. He turned into a Christmas nut and just like the redeemed post-ghost Scrooge, he knew how to keep Christmas well.

In the good years the bounty was prodigal. I remember a doll's house whose small perfections enslaved me; a microscope, whose revelations introduced me to awe; a string of real pearls, which I still own and wear often, all the while thinking of my father; and books, and books, and books, always books.

In the bad years we still had a Christmas. I will never know to what lengths he sometimes went to in order to ensure we woke up to a gaudy tree, magnificently misshapen stockings, and that one gift—wrapped in red tissue paper with meticulous corners, the string as secure as his hand—we'd never known we wanted until we opened it. I do know he pawned all things pawnable, juggled debts like a vaudevillian, and sacrificed much—including, more than once, his pride—to give us Christmas.

Even in the worst years, and there were a few, he always found a special gift for my mother. A golden locket with a stone so throbbingly blue it seemed alive; kid gloves softer than air: a sterling silver compact engraved with her initials; silks and satins and midnight lace, just a little scandalous, to tell her again of his fierce and faithful love, while she murmured, "You shouldn't have," her face rosy with secrets.

But most of my father's gifts weren't wrapped up in tissue paper, nor were they found under the tree. Most of them are still around. When I look into myself I find his gift with words, the wit and the wonder of them, the way and the play of them. In me I find his joy and grief, his laughter, his scrupulosity, his knack for solitude, his continuing compassionate astonishment at his fellow humans, his reverence. And if I am at all wise or brave, if I am at all loving, it is because I looked at him and learned to be. I look at my sons and I see other gifts: his agility of mind and arduous curiosity are in one; his drive, his will and his steadfastness are in another; and his winsome buoyant innocence in the third.

My father spent his last Christmas in the hospital. We saw him on Christmas Eve, touched his hand, his cheek, kissed him. The surgery, against all odds, had gone well, and the doctors marvelled at his strength, shook unbelieving heads over his stubborn heart, smilingly promised a return home. Soon. It was a splendid gift for us, his strength, their promise. A week later, on New Year's Day, the great tunnels of his blood gave way, and in a minute he was suddenly shockingly, absurdly dead. The stubborn heart, that had loved us—me—so well, stopped.

My father gave us all he could for all of his years, and I wonder sometimes whether I ever said a proper thank you to him. Sometimes, when I am fanciful, I find myself hoping that what I have done with my life is a kind of thank you. And sometimes I even think my father hears it.

"I wish I could be with you," my dad said.

You are, Dad. You are. Always.

~Claire Mackay
Toronto, Ontario

99

The Memory Tree

When someone you love becomes a memory, the memory becomes a treasure.
~Author Unknown

I t's a quiet, moonlit night several weeks before Christmas. Diamonds sparkle on the new snow. I tighten my scarf around my neck and pull on my warm mitts. I'm standing outside the little Baptist church in South Brookfield where, as a child, I attended Sunday school and Worship Services. It's been over fifty years since I left my hometown in rural Nova Scotia, but I still get nostalgic when I return to my old church, nestled in the little alcove at the edge of the forest. There's something comforting about its familiarity. I suspect this comes more from my warm memories and the genuine welcome I receive from the people I meet each time I pass through its doors, rather than from the structure or its location.

I'm part of a group of thirty plus people who have gathered around a simple fir tree to pay tribute to our departed loved ones. Unlit Christmas lights poke their noses out through the prickly branches. At the end of the evening, this Memory Tree will be aglow with a rainbow of lights.

I look around and try to identify faces in the semi-darkness. I recognize some and see family resemblances in others. The pastor says a short prayer and reads a name—a petite, blond girl of four skips forward, giggling. She lights a bright yellow bulb in memory of her great-grandmother. My mind goes back to the times I attended birthday parties at her great-grandmother's house and ate homemade ice cream.

The next name is called and an elderly woman, with the help of a family friend, slowly makes her way to the tree. She lights a red bulb for her husband who died only a week ago. I remember them as a young couple driving to the corner store. She always drove—I guess she was more comfortable with him in the passenger's seat.

My aunt's name is called and I see her teen-aged grandson walk proudly to the tree. He lights an orange bulb in her memory. I recall the times I sat at her kitchen table and ate freshly baked sugar dough-nuts—the taste lingers with me!

Then I hear the names of my own mother and father. There's a lump in my throat—a tear slides down my cheek under cover of darkness. I walk to the tree and light my bulbs—one green and one yellow. Memories flood into my mind—good memories.

More names are called and the tree gradually comes alive with bright lights—red, green, blue, yellow, and orange. Many of the names called stir even more memories—my first schoolteacher, a schoolmate who died much too young, the old country doctor, and many more. I thank God for placing these people in my life and allowing them to help shape my destiny.

Afterwards, we go inside the church and enjoy tasty treats while three guitarists strum Christmas carols. There's a hug here, a touch to an elderly cheek over there, smiles and chuckles, happy fellowship. It's good to come home!

The memory tree has become a yearly custom in my home-town—one that I hope will continue for many years. I plan to add it to my family's Christmas traditions. What better way to celebrate Christmas than to recall loved ones who are no longer with us at Christmas time?

~Beverlee Wamboldt
Dartmouth, Nova Scotia

The Ultimate Gift

The pain of parting is nothing to the joy of meeting again.
~Charles Dickens

Another Christmas was approaching, and the dull ache of loss that was always with me began to increase. At the age of thirteen, my son, my only child, had died in a tragic accident. It had left my husband Tony and me with a sadness that was never far away and always amplified at this time of year. But this year, the Christmas of 2006—brought a kind of healing—a holiday miracle just waiting to be unwrapped.

It began in late November when I received a phone call from my cousin, Mary-Gail, our family genealogy expert.

"Gail," she said excitedly, "I have some wonderful news for you! I've just received some information that is simply astonishing! There is no other way to put this," she continued. "I believe you have a brother."

I listened quietly while she breathlessly recited all the details. Apparently my mother had given birth to a boy before I was born, and we had the same father. We were full siblings! She had his name, his address in Mississauga, and his phone number. But how had this happened? Why had he been adopted out? I had so many questions.

As a small child, each Christmas my wish list had comprised only one thing. "Can I please have an older brother?" Every year I would ask, and every year I was devastated when my special gift did not arrive. As I grew older and realized that my request for an older brother was genetically impossible, I still persisted in my quest for a sibling. Although I had a much older half-sister, I craved the companionship that only a brother could bring. I desperately wanted to put an end to the loneliness I experienced as an only child.

Still a little unbelieving, I was very anxious as I prepared to make this call. After fortifying myself with a healthy glass of wine, with trembling fingers I dialed his number. Listening to the phone ring at the other end, I could hardly contain my excitement. If this were really true, it would be the answer to my long awaited prayer and heart's desire.

A recorded message answered—a deep, pleasant male voice somewhat reminiscent of a radio announcer. Could this really be my brother? After leaving my name and number I hung up and, filled with anxious anticipation, sat down to wait.

The shrill ringing of the phone interrupted my thoughts. "Gail? This is Fred... I'm so excited to hear your voice." For the next three hours we got to know each other and exchanged family information. I learned he had a wife and two grown daughters. By the time I hung up I was convinced he was, in fact, my brother. We arranged to meet a few days later at his home, and I got off the phone in a kind of euphoric daze.

Meeting my brother for the first time could best be described as winning an emotional lottery. After the warmest greeting you can imagine, with my body shaking and my voice quivering, I called Fred my brother for the very first time. His wife, Janet, had prepared a lovely lunch, but I was far too excited to do it justice.

Almost immediately Janet noticed our similar characteristics and gestures. I could clearly see my brother's resemblance to our mother, both physically, and in his gentle caring nature. Fred told me he'd always been mystified by his life-long desire to be a pilot. He was amazed to learn that his half-sister and his father had both been pilots. His father had actually flown in the 1st World War with Billy Bishop.

Just before we parted, Fred said, "How would you and Tony like to spend Christmas with my family and me?"

With my world still reeling from the mindboggling events that were unfolding, I could only enthusiastically nod my head as I joyfully wrapped my arms around his waist.

Christmas Eve greeted us with just the right blend of falling snow. As I skipped up the path leading to his home I could barely contain my excitement. I could hardly comprehend that I was spending Christmas with my brother. With my *older* brother! Even after having repeated those words countless times, I was still overwhelmed by their significance.

At the door, Tony and I were warmly welcomed by my beaming big brother, a loving sister-in-law and two beautiful adult nieces. Suddenly, I was acutely aware of a sensation of family I'd not experienced since my parents' passing. I felt a tiny tear trickle down my check as I hungrily drank in the experience of the moment. At last, I was HOME!

To be home was just beautiful. Gathered around the living room we exchanged stories and pictures, and marvelled at the love that our parents had had for each other. It turned out that Fred's adoptive parents had provided him with a liberal amount of information about his background, and he was now able to share with me the part of our parents' story I never knew.

"Mother and Dad fell in love when she worked for him," he revealed. "But he was married to someone else and was simply unable to leave. When I was born," he continued, "Dad did care for us both and helped Mom out as much as he could. But it was 1938, and an unmarried woman with a child out of wedlock was simply not accepted. Mother's overbearing father insisted she could not keep her young son, and she gave in to that pressure. I was placed with my adoptive family when I was about six months old and, some time after that, Mother and Father went their separate ways."

"I know she loved me," he continued, "as she made me all kinds of knitted things, and came to visit me often before the adoption was final."

Through my tears I gently reassured him, "Our mother was a gentle, kind soul. Giving you up must have been the hardest decision she ever made."

"What's even more incredible," I continued, "is that several years later they met again by chance in Toronto. Dad was now a widower and free to marry. Mom was engaged to someone else, but immediately broke it off to be with Dad. After a short engagement they were married and, three years later, I was born. And it was the strangest thing," I shared. "When I was little, every Christmas I kept asking them for a big brother. It's almost like I knew...."

Gently Fred placed his hand in mine and said, "Gail, I always hoped that one day I would have a picture of my parents, but today you have given me so much more. It means the world to me to know they got married and loved each other enough to build a life together."

Christmas 2006 was a lot more than an exchange of gifts, a glass of wine and a wonderful meal. It was a priceless opportunity to embrace life in a way I never envisioned possible. I was able to hug my niece and thank her, for it was she who had made that initial call to my cousin.

I could feel the familiar cape of depression I had worn so close to my body since the devastating death of my son lifting. It turned out that in addition to being a loving wife and stepmother to three wonderful people, I was now a sister, an aunt and a sister-in-law to an incredible family.

My dad always said there was one special gift to treasure each Christmas. He called it the thrill of Christmas. I knew in my heart I would cherish the special thrill of this Christmas—my Christmas miracle—for the rest of my life.

~Gail Sellers
Aurora, Ontario

The Year the Animals Brought Christmas

The best remedy for those who are afraid, lonely or unhappy is to go outside, somewhere where they can be quiet, alone with the heavens and nature.
~Anne Frank

It was Christmas Eve of my fifty-eighth year. I lived by myself on a small farm in the hills above British Columbia's Fraser Valley. My mood was melancholy, for tomorrow would be my first Christmas morning without overflowing stockings, explosions of brightly wrapped packages, or the comforting laughter of excited family members. I was bereft of Christmas spirit despite the falling snow that transformed my land into the perfect Canadian Christmas card.

I was not completely alone, however, for I shared my space with four old rescue dogs, a cat, an abandoned alpaca, and a family of twelve potbellied pigs. The boar and very pregnant sow had been brought to me, a few months earlier, to be fostered after being seized in an animal cruelty case; their ten babies were born two weeks later.

As the snowfall finally eased to a few drifting flakes, I trekked out to the barn to check on the animals one last time, the dogs by my side. The snow was well over their heads, and our kindly neighbour had once again plowed the drive so we could move with some freedom if we stayed on the path. But of course, as dogs are wont to do, they bounded off into the deepest parts and surfaced with frosty, happy faces.

I stepped into the dark interior of my rustic, dilapidated barn. The snow reflected through the windows, casting a soft light over the old wood. The potbellied pigs were nestled deep in the straw; they raised their snouts high as I peered over the stall gate to check that all were warm and safe. I breathed in the scent of weathered timbers and fresh shavings, of wet dogs and healthy pigs, loving the feel of the barn and the silence of the night. I tucked a wool blanket over the oldest pig, and fed the youngsters a flake or two of hay, singing softly.

The oldest pig, Scotch, loved to be sung to. During his first weeks here, when he and his mate, Soda, were scared and unsure of themselves, I often sat in the stall with them at night, singing and humming and letting them get used to my scent and sound. I sang lullabies, children's songs, old campfire favourites. Scotch particularly liked "You Are My Sunshine." Whenever I sang it, he would softly grunt, lay his head on or near my lap, and roll over on his side to let me stroke his belly. It soothed both of us—me, a new foster mama to pigs, and Scotch, a finally safe piggy who was learning about the big world beyond a much-too-small and filthy wire cage.

And so, that Christmas Eve, I curled up in the straw beside him, my head on his back, and sang to him once more. He grunted and hummed along with me, and soon I felt another warm piggy body stretching out alongside my back—Whisper, one of the young piglets, had come to join us. Then I felt a nudge at my hand as another piglet let me know he, too, wanted contact.

Soon I was joined by another, and another, and another, until all the piggies were nestled around me, in straw and blankets, some touching me, each touching another. For a few moments in time, I was just one of the herd.

When they were all asleep, I slipped quietly from their stall, whispered good night, closed the big barn door and made my way across the pasture to the alpaca's stable. Martin was bedded down on his straw, well protected from the weather. In the dark of night, with only my small flashlight to provide a warm glow, I saw before me an image of a long-ago nativity scene: Martin, so like his camel kin who carried the three wise men to Bethlehem; the manger filled with soft hay, such as provided a crib for the child born long ago; and the snow sparkling like the brilliant star that shone in the East. I heard Martin softly acknowledge my presence with his low uhn-uhn-uhn, and smiled as I thought how those sounds would have filled the stable that first Christmas Eve.

I believe there is a reason why the animals figure so prominently in the Christmas story. Unconditional love, a sense of purpose, courage to go on, faith in tomorrow—lessons that the person called Jesus taught in his lifetime—are modeled for us best by the animals around us.

I whistled for the dogs and headed back to the house, back to the modern world of computers and microwaves, televisions and electric lights. Within me, I carried a sense of peace and reverence and awe, the Christmas spirit, found where Christmas first began—outdoors, in a crude and humble shelter, surrounded by the animals on a dark silent night.

~Jean F. Ballard
Crofton, British Columbia

Meet Our Contributors

Tanya Ambrose has retired from teaching grades seven and eight. She enjoys traveling, gardening, dancing, painting and writing. Although she has published some stories in Canadian literary magazines, her focus has switched to spending joyful time with two young granddaughters.

Jennifer E. Bailey's first published story, "A Son's Love," appeared in *Chicken Soup for the Canadian Soul*. She has been married to Roy for thirty-seven years and they have three children: Rijn, Jesse and Cassia (Joshua). She writes children's stories, songs and skits based on Biblical truths and edits university students' essays.

With a camera around her neck and a notebook in her backpack, recently retired **Barbara Baker** spends her free time racing up and down the Rocky Mountains to capture them. Her passion for writing is dedicated to finishing a YA novel, unless of course a bird flies by her window. E-mail her at bbaker.write@gmail.com.

Jean Ballard retired from teaching sociology at the University of the Fraser Valley, and enjoys writing and photography on Vancouver Island. She is a regular contributor to the *Chemainus Valley Courier* and volunteers with several animal rescue groups. She can be contacted via her blog at www.mylifewiththecritters.blogspot.com.

Ardy Barclay received her Bachelor of Arts degree from the University of Western Ontario. She started her teaching career in

1970, specializing in Special Education. Retired in 2007, Ardy enjoys winters in Florida as well as fishing, reading, and spending time with her granddaughters.

Gail Neff Bell is retired and a grandmother. She was formerly a teacher and a lawyer. She lives with her husband in Tsawwassen, BC, where she enjoys swimming, walking with stride poles, trying new recipes, and organizing community groups.

William Bell is a financial planner, and has authored two books, and numerous articles on business and the human condition. Bill is an avid photographer and golfer. Married to Ellen, they have three daughters—Leah, Deandra and Alexis—all of whom live in southern Ontario. E-mail him at billbell@bellfinancial.ca.

Susan Blakeney is a writer of fiction for children and young adults with several projects well underway. These include two historical novels and one work of speculative fiction—the story that awoke her passion for writing several years ago. E-mail her at susan@susanblakeney.com.

Marilyn C. Bodogh is a two-time World Curling Champion in 1986 and 1996. She loves to travel around the world with her husband Neil Dixon, taste fabulous wines, cook for family and friends and spend time with all of her grandchildren.

Dian Bowers is a child of the late forties and grew up in small-town Canada. She has lived in two countries, has had a fulfilling career and family life, and has travelled extensively. When she retired, she needed an outlet to document her life experiences, which writing has provided.

Ellie Braun-Haley started her writing career as a newspaper correspondent. Later she wrote books for adults who work with young children. Eventually her research took her to investigating miracles, a topic she thoroughly enjoyed! She has also written children's stories, true short stories and rhymes! She presents talks on miracles.

Kimberley Campbell resides in Lincoln, NB with her husband, two cats and two retired racing Greyhounds. She enjoys skating, walking and biking with her husband and hounds, as well as reading, writing and spending time with her three young nieces.

Judy Carter graduated from the University of Western Ontario and is a high school English teacher. She has previously published stories in *Chicken Soup for the Parent's Soul*. When she's not marking essays, Judy enjoys running, yoga, golf, playing guitar and doing a little creative writing. E-mail her at judycarter@bell.net.

Ian Charter has worked in the printing industry for close to thirty years in various positions including production, management and sales. He enjoys just about anything on the water and is a certified diver. E-mail him at icharter@rogers.com.

Cindy Clemens received her B.A. degree from the University of Windsor. She has had a diverse career but her most important title is that of Jacob and Jonathan's mom. Cindy and her husband live on a hobby farm in southwestern Ontario.

Harriet Cooper is a freelance writer and has published personal essays, humour and creative nonfiction in newspapers, newsletters, anthologies and magazines. She is a frequent contributor to the *Chicken Soup for the Soul* series. She writes about family, relationships, health, food, cats, writing and daily life. E-mail her at shewrites@live.ca.

Randall Crickmore is a retired teacher, inveterate traveller and sometimes writer now living in Niagara Falls, ON. He has published numerous articles in newspapers and magazines, written one novel and several books of children's verse.

Jo Darlington is a retired nurse-manager, married to her husband Steve for thirty-nine years, mother of four, grandmother of three, a life-long reader and writer, who lives in the country not far from Annie's Fish Pond.

Patricia A. Donahue is an award-winning novelist; her *Mighty Orion* series is set in northern New Brunswick. She is published academically and her short stories appear in anthologies. She is an R.N., with bachelor's and master's degrees from U.B.C. Patricia is a post-secondary instructor and therapist who likes hiking and sailing.

Lynn Dove is the author of the award-winning *Wounded Trilogy* and her popular blog, "Journey Thoughts." When she is not writing, she enjoys spending time with her family, and grandchildren. She has previously been published in *Chicken Soup for the Soul: Parenthood* and *Chicken Soup for the Soul: Devotional Stories for Wives*.

MaryLou Driedger is a retired teacher who works as a freelance journalist, a university advisor and art gallery tour guide. Her favorite role in life is being a grandmother.

David Eklund was born and has lived in Alberta all his life. The story of his father and his faithful dog Ring is well known in the Eklund family. They hope to share the story with animal lovers everywhere.

Sue England credits Clare Bolton (Aurora Cultural Centre) and Isobel Warren for inspiring her to resurrect her creative spirit. She is a member of Writers' Community of York Region, a Realtor with Royal LePage with her life partner Steve, and is writing a story for children.

Penny Fedorczenko is a retired teacher with a B.A. degree in sociology. She enjoys travel, writing, gardening, cooking, and spending time with family and friends. She is working on a fictional novel. This is her third story in the *Chicken Soup for the Soul* series. E-mail her at pfed@infinity.net.

Larry Fedoruk is a writer/broadcaster. His daily talk shows can be heard on 610CKTB in Niagara and on Newstalk1010 in Toronto. Larry covers a variety of social topics as well as news of the day. He was born and raised in Saskatchewan, but has called Ontario home for the last thirty years.

Maureen Flynn is a Canadian writer who enjoys time with family and friends. Her interests include golf, boxing and walking the family dog. Maureen writes for a local newspaper and is working on a series of fiction novels. The first, *Buckle My Shoe*, is soon to be released. E-mail her at grrrumpychick@hotmail.com.

Liz M. Forbes, a fifth-generation Canadian, was born in Victoria, BC, and now lives in the beautiful Cowichan Valley on Vancouver Island. She writes "stories from her life" and a column for a local paper. Liz is published in *Somebody's Child*, an adoption anthology by TouchWood Editions.

John Forrest is a retired educator who writes about the exceptional events and wonderful people in his life. He lives in Orillia, ON with his wife Carol, where they enjoy golf, travel and following the life adventures of their children Rob and Dana. E-mail him at johnforrest@rogers.com.

Hazel Fulford received a B.A. degree in English from Lakehead University in 1979, when she was fifty-seven. Since then she has published short stories, travel articles and nonfiction books. She enjoyed traveling, swimming, and secretarial work but is now retired from everything but writing. Hazel lives in Thunder Bay, ON.

Born in Tofield, Alberta, **Amanda Green** is a Principal dancer with Canada's Royal Winnipeg Ballet. She has appeared as Odette/Odile in *Swan Lake*, Princess Aurora in *The Sleeping Beauty* and Irene in Twyla

Tharp's *The Princess & The Goblin*. Green lives in Winnipeg with her husband, RWB Company dancer Eric Nipp.

Bev Sandell Greenberg taught for many years in adult ESL and literacy programs in British Columbia and Manitoba. A freelance reviewer and editor, Bev lives in Winnipeg, MB and is working on a novel about an immigrant family in crisis. E-mail her at bevgreen@mymts.net.

Ross Greenwood holds degrees from the University of Toronto. He is an educator, preacher, travel agent, career counsellor and a retired Royal Canadian Naval Reserve officer. His interests include writing, travel, gardening. Through experiencing many personal miracles, he knows there is a higher power! E-mail him at ross@rossgreenwood.com.

Astra Groskaufmanis is a mother of three living in Ottawa, ON. The zamboni fumes-inhaling years when all three of her kids played hockey inspired her to write her memoir, *Offside by a Mile*, that chronicles the frantic and hilarious moments and will resonate with hockey moms everywhere. Read her blog at www.thedustbunnychronicles.com.

Sarah Hodges is Head Coach of the University of Regina Cougar Women's Hockey Team. As a member of the Hockey Canada Coaching Pool, in 2010-11 she led the National U18 team to a silver medal at the World Championships in Stockholm. Sarah and her husband Chris live in Regina, SK with their daughter Annie.

Alison Karlene Hodgins is completing her first travel novel about her experiences in Australia. Born in Grande Prairie, AB, she has traveled to over twenty-five countries in her twenty-one years. Her hobbies include making hemp bracelets, learning foreign languages, and drinking really good coffee. You can follow her at aroundtheworldwithalison.wordpress.com.

Matty Hughes is twenty-eight years old and lives in Edmonton. He enjoys yachting, Golden Retrievers and espionage. E-mail him at thehughesician@gmail.com.

Crystal Johnson finds great joy in writing—it feeds her soul and acts as her creative outlet. She has worked as a Speech Language Pathologist in hospitals since 2008 and feels privileged to work with clients and learn with and from them. She has a supportive family who stand by her in her many and varied endeavours.

Lynn Johnston has been sharing the amusing, moving lives of the Patterson family with millions of readers since 1979 in her award-winning comic strip, *For Better or For Worse*. Nominated for a Pulitzer Prize, Lynn has received the Order of Canada and claims a star on Canada's Walk of Fame. Visit her at www.fborfw.com.

Carol Kavanagh longs to write the best poem ever, or the best short story ever, but feels this will be a lifetime endeavour. When she's not engaged in art, she cares for her mother and lives with her husband in Saskatoon, SK. This is her second short story publication.

Deborah Kinsinger, Ph.D., has been writing all her life. She has a private practice in Counseling Psychology in Ontario. Deborah uses the power of story in her work. The healing power of nature, and the precious moments of family life have long been an inspiration for her writing.

Gordon Kirkland has written eight books of humour. Six of these are collections of short stories, and three have received the Stephen Leacock Medal for Humour as runners up for the medal. The other two are novels. *The Plight Before Christmas* hit #1 on Amazon's Parenting and Family Humour Bestseller list.

Arlene Kochberg is a wife, mother and grandmother. She works with husband, Ian, a master printmaker who creates musical and spiritual works of fine art. Arlene handles the galleries, customers, books shows, frames the art, and still finds time to play violin in a string orchestra. Learn more at www.iankochberg.com.

Greg Lamothe is a career martial arts instructor with his own school that he operates out of Victoria, BC. He enjoys training, reading, writing and most of all, spending time with his wife and two children. E-mail him at greg.lamothe@hotmail.com.

Stephen Lautens is a lawyer and writer whose weekly column appears in the *Calgary Sun*. Stephen has completed one unpublished novel and is now working on his second unpublished novel. E-mail him at stephen@lautens.com.

Vincent Lecavalier is from Ile Bizard, QB. After fourteen years with the Tampa Bay Lightning, where he was Captain, he now plays with the Philadelphia Flyers. A member of Team Canada, he's played in both the World Cup and the Olympics. Vince has set multiple scoring records and won innumerable accolades and awards. He and his wife Caroline live in Tampa and New Jersey with their three children.

An award-winning author, playwright, filmmaker and journalist, **Mark Leiren-Young** won the 2009 Leacock Medal for Humour for his first memoir, *Never Shoot a Stampede Queen* (Heritage), which prompted him to write his second humourous memoir, *Free Magic Secrets Revealed* (Harbour). Learn more at www.leiren-young.com.

Jeanette Lynes grew up on a farm one hundred miles north of Toronto, ON. She is a novelist, poet, and writing teacher.

Dorothy MacAulay left us in the spring of 2008. She lived to write and entertain with her pleasant, upbeat stories and poems. She is missed dearly and it gives her family great pleasure knowing how proud she would be to appear in this wonderful book.

Zabe MacEachren has continued to follow her passion for nature-based education activities. She holds a PhD in what she jokes is "woodcraft lore" and coordinates the Outdoor and Experiential Education program at Queen's University. When she is not behind her office desk you can find her canoeing or snowshoeing.

Claire Mackay got her first job at ten years old at a public library. While hired to dust and put away books, she read them instead. Claire has three sons and five grandchildren, including twins. She was an editorial consultant for Houghton Mifflin, a feature columnist and a freelance writer.

A graduate of Queen's University, **Gail MacMillan** is the author of twenty-eight published books and several hundred magazine articles published both in North America and Europe. She lives in New Brunswick with her husband and two dogs. E-mail her at macgail@nbnet.nb.ca.

Carol Margaret received her B.Sc. degree from Mount Allison University in 1985 and her D.V.M. from the Atlantic Veterinary College in 1990. She lives in Ontario with her husband and four children. She enjoys gardening, writing, yoga and rowing. Carol is working on her first book.

David Martin's humor and political satire have appeared in many publications including *The New York Times*, the *Chicago Tribune* and *Smithsonian* magazine. His latest humor collection, *Screams & Whispers*, is available on Amazon.com. David lives in Ottawa, ON, with his wife Cheryl and their daughter Sarah.

Dan Mathieson, Mayor of his hometown, Stratford, since 2003, holds a Bachelor of Arts degree from the University of Guelph and a Master's of Public Administration from the University of Western Ontario. He enjoys golfing, travelling and spending time with his family and friends. E-mail him at mayorsoffice@city.stratford.on.ca.

Stefano Mazzega has been a forensic scientist with the RCM Police for almost thirty-four years. He is the General Manager of the forensic laboratory in Vancouver. He is nearing retirement and hoping to transition to a career in writing. Stefano writes humour and suspense.

Dennis McCloskey has a journalism degree from Ryerson University in Toronto. He is the author of the award-winning biography *My Favorite American*. This is his fourth story in the *Chicken Soup for the Soul* series. E-mail Dennis at dmcclos@rogers.com.

Nancy McIntosh works as a Food Bank Community & Development Coordinator. She's been a radio announcer, newspaper columnist, clothing and art designer and won numerous awards for corporate window displays, merchandising and advertising campaigns. She intends to focus on traveling, painting and illustrating children's books. E-mail her at nancymcintosh4@hotmail.com.

When not playing hockey with the Sharks, **Sandi McTavish** works in educational publishing and lives in Toronto, ON. She has a Bachelor of Arts degree with a major in English and a Master of Education.

Freelance writer **Chantal Meijer** lives in Terrace, BC with her husband Rick. They have four children and four grandchildren. Chantal's work has been widely published in magazines, newspapers and anthologies—including four *Chicken Soup for the Soul* editions. She is currently working on a memoir. E-mail her at meijer@telus. net.

Sharon Melnicer is a writer, artist and teacher in Winnipeg, MB. She has frequently aired the "Slice of Life" pieces that she pens on CBC Radio. A retired high-school English teacher and university instructor, she continues to teach life-story writing to adults and is a recognized artist who shows and sells throughout North America.

Paula Meyer received her Master of Education degree from the

University of Manitoba in 2011. A Vice-Principal in Winnipeg, she is a mother to three amazing women who have taught her so much about the importance of community. Paula enjoys travelling adventures and reading. E-mail her at pmeyer@mts.net.

Patricia Miller earned a B.A. degree in Social Sciences from UWO, and a Recreation diploma from Centennial College, before studying Creative Writing at Durham College. Patricia is a Coordinator and mom who enjoys snowboarding. In 2012, she wrote her first novel, *The Mausoleum Road Affair*. E-mail her at patriciamillerwriting@gmail.com.

Lisa Molinaro is a wife and mother of two busy boys. She is a bookworm, writer, blogger, teacher-by-trade and a yoga/Zumba/ boxing enthusiast.

Marya Morin is a freelance writer. Her stories and poems have appeared in publications such as *Woman's World* and Hallmark. Marya also penned a weekly humorous column for an online newsletter, and writes custom poetry on request. She lives in the country with her husband. E-mail her at Akushla514@hotmail.com.

Diane C. Nicholson is a professional photographer, photo artist (specializing in animals and nature) and writer. This is her sixth story published in the *Chicken Soup for the Soul* series. She lives in beautiful British Columbia with her menagerie and long-suffering husband. E-mail her at mail@twinheartphoto.com.

Sandra Pady is the founder of The Donkey Sanctuary of Canada, an animal rescue/animal welfare education charity (www. thedonkeysanctuary.ca). Although she retired in 2012, through her writing Sandra continues to encourage standards of positive care and respect for her equine friends.

Jacqueline Pearce spent four winters in Ontario seeking out the best skating ponds before finishing a Master of Environmental Studies degree at York University and returning to the west coast. She is the author of several novels for children, including *Flood Warning*, about the Fraser River flood of 1948.

Jon Peirce holds a Ph.D. in English from Dalhousie University and a master's degree in industrial relations from Queen's University. A retired union labour relations officer, he lives and writes in Dartmouth, NS, and teaches writing for the Nova Scotia Seniors' College.

Evelyn Pollock's career included teaching, educational politics, and human rights consulting. She retired to Horseshoe Valley to write and paint. She is active in local writers' groups and in the arts community. Since retiring, several of her short stories and a book of her art have been published. E-mail her at pollockconsulting@bellnet.ca.

Louise Rachlis is a freelance writer in Ottawa, ON, who spent twenty-five years at the *Ottawa Citizen* newspaper where she was the advertising features editor. She holds a Bachelor of Journalism degree from Carleton University and is a creative fiction writer, acrylic and watercolour painter, marathon runner and triathlete.

Lea Ellen Yarmill Reburn resides in beautiful central Ontario, and was born and raised locally. She is married, a dog lover, a caregiver to many, and loves to write true life experiences—some typical and some not! She has previously been published in several periodicals and newspapers. Guardian Angels Copyright ©2009 by Lea Ellen Yarmill Reburn, first published in *A Cup of Comfort for a Better World*, Copyright ©2010 by F+W Media, Inc. Reprinted with permission from the author and publisher. All Rights Reserved.

David Roberts is a retired lawyer. For twenty-nine years he was the editor of the *Advocate*, the legal magazine for British Columbia. David functions as an arbitrator and member of several administrative tribunals and keeps bees in his back garden, which he feels need less training than dogs, are not as arrogant as cats and... make honey.

Chris Robertson is an author and speaker who has been voted "Best Keynote Speaker." The diary of this first journey in history has been published in the book *To The Top Canada*. Order autographed copies of the book or get Chris as a speaker at your next meeting at www.chrisrobertson.ca.

Greg Ryan grew up in Toronto, ON. He attained a journalism degree from Ryerson in 1987. After a long career in network news writing for talent, he decided to try writing something else. Greg suspects he may be one of the only cello-playing boxer-golfers in the city.

Gail Sellers enjoys writing poetry and short stories. Her hobbies include swimming, reading, attending concerts, travelling and relaxing at the cottage. She loves animals, especially cats. She plans on writing inspirational children's stories, animal stories and poetry. E-mail her at gailsellers2011@gmail.com.

Stella Shepard is a journalist/photographer living on beautiful Prince Edward Island and married to Reg Phelan. Her son, Joshua, is daddy to seven-year-old Damian, who is a joy and a blessing. Stella's articles have been published in magazines, books and newspapers. She has just completed her first manuscript. E-mail Stella at rphelan@pei.sympatico.ca.

Leah Silverman grew up on a small Canadian farm, and has always loved animals and writing (in fact, she wrote this bio with one of her three cats on her lap). She lives in Texas with her beloved husband and son, though she misses Canada every day — even the winters.

Elizabeth Smayda has worked in the field of social services and health for twenty-three years. She co-authored a study involving eating disorders published in 2005 and was published in *Chicken Soup for the Soul: Finding My Faith*. Elizabeth enjoys her family, writing and work. E-mail her at brsmayda@shaw.ca.

Judith Smith lives in Peterborough, ON, where she received her PSW, and social services worker diploma. She is working with intellectual disabled adults, assisting them to live independently in their own home. She also has her own women's clothing consignment boutique called Back of the Closet Consignment Boutique.

Thomas Sullivan is the author of *So Much Time, So Little Change* (a collection of humorous essays from Wayman Publishing). He lives in Seattle and writes regularly for the site HumorOutcasts.com. Visit Thomas at www.thomassullivanhumor.com.

Heather Stewart grew up in Waverley, NS. She grew up with a love of learning, reading, and writing. After teaching for ten years in Thompson, MB, she returned home and now teaches at Brookhouse Elementary. Besides writing for her students, she enjoys cultural events and musical pursuits.

Deon Toban has been writing short stories and poems for the last fifteen years, as writing is one of her passions. When she's not writing, she enjoys her other passions such as cruising, reading and interior design. She is working on her first novel.

Shawna Troke-Leukert is a storyteller and an Infinite Possibilities Trainer. Shawna shares her stories in positive thinking workshops on the island of Newfoundland. She lives in the beautiful Codroy Valley with her husband Eric and Poodle Spud.

Mary Turner received her B.A. degree in English from the University of Manitoba. She is a mother and grandmother and lives in Victoria, BC. Mary has written for the *Winnipeg Free Press* and the *Victoria Times Colonist*. She also enjoys playing the violin and writing poetry.

With a long and distinguished career as a director-cinematographer, **Lloyd Walton's** films have won over 35 international, national and provincial awards. His films link history, culture and nature, as do his writings. Lloyd is also enjoying a successful career as a painter. His works can be viewed at Lloydwalton.ca.

Beverlee Wamboldt lives in Nova Scotia. She and her husband have traveled throughout Canada and the U.S. and visited the UK and Europe. She has two adult children and five grandchildren. She enjoys summer days at her cottage with her second "family" and a large group of lively hummingbirds.

Joanne Webster is a former teacher and life-long student from Orillia, ON. She is the proud mother of two teenage boys, and the happy wife of a kind and thoughtful man. Joanne enjoys pottery, piano lessons, singing in a choir, rug hooking, reading and writing stories.

Born in Sudbury, ON, **Martin Worthy** is a musician, singer, songwriter and composer. He has toured extensively across Canada with various groups including alt-rock band Joe Hall and the Continental Drift, folk duo Quarrington-Worthy and most recently, roots-blues band Porkbelly Futures. He lives and works in Toronto.

A video producer/director living near Toronto, ON, **Jamie Yeo** received his Bachelor of Applied Arts degree in Radio and Television Arts from Ryerson Polytechnical. A pioneer in multimedia development he began his early work in interactive laser videodisc. He lives with his partner Marilyn Cameron. E-mail him at jamieyeo@rogers.com.

Lori Zenker lives in Elmira, ON — home of the World's Largest Maple Syrup Festival. She enjoys maple syrup on her oatmeal and in coffee. She is a mom of three teenagers, who love maple syrup on everything from noodles to freshly fallen snow. E-mail her at lori@zenker.ca.

Meet Our Authors and Editor

Jack Canfield is the co-creator of the *Chicken Soup for the Soul* series, which *Time* magazine has called "the publishing phenomenon of the decade." Jack is also the coauthor of many other bestselling books.

Jack is the CEO of the Canfield Training Group in Santa Barbara, California, and founder of the Foundation for Self-Esteem in Culver City, California. He has conducted intensive personal and professional development seminars on the principles of success for more than a million people in 23 countries, has spoken to hundreds of thousands of people at more than 1,000 corporations, universities, professional conferences and conventions, and has been seen by millions more on national television shows.

Jack has received many awards and honors, including three honorary doctorates and a Guinness World Records Certificate for having seven books from the *Chicken Soup for the Soul* series appearing on the New York Times bestseller list on May 24, 1998.

You can reach Jack at www.jackcanfield.com.

Mark Victor Hansen is the co-founder of Chicken Soup for the Soul, along with Jack Canfield. He is a sought-after keynote speaker, bestselling author, and marketing maven. Mark's powerful messages of possibility, opportunity, and action have created powerful change in thousands of organizations and millions of individuals worldwide.

Mark is a prolific writer with many bestselling books in addition to the *Chicken Soup for the Soul* series. Mark has had a profound influence in the field of human potential through his library of audios, videos, and articles in the areas of big thinking, sales achievement, wealth building, publishing success, and personal and professional development. He is also the founder of the MEGA Seminar Series.

Mark has received numerous awards that honor his entrepreneurial spirit, philanthropic heart, and business acumen. He is a lifetime member of the Horatio Alger Association of Distinguished Americans.

You can reach Mark at www.markvictorhansen.com.

Amy Newmark has been Chicken Soup for the Soul's publisher, coauthor, and editor-in-chief for the last five years, after a 30-year career as a writer, speaker, financial analyst, and business executive in the worlds of finance and telecommunications. Amy is a *magna cum laude* graduate of Harvard College, where she majored in Portuguese, minored in French, and traveled extensively. She and her husband have four grown children.

After a long career writing books on telecommunications, voluminous financial reports, business plans, and corporate press releases, Chicken Soup for the Soul is a breath of fresh air for Amy. She has fallen in love with Chicken Soup for the Soul and its life-changing books, and really enjoys putting these books together for Chicken Soup for the Soul's wonderful readers. She has coauthored more than six dozen *Chicken Soup for the Soul* books and has edited another three dozen.

You can reach Amy with any questions or comments through webmaster@chickensoupforthesoul.com and you can follow her on Twitter @amynewmark or @chickensoupsoul.

Janet Matthews is a best-selling author, editor, inspirational speaker and spiritual mentor. As co-author of the Canadian bestseller, *Chicken Soup for the Canadian Soul*, since 2002 she has been inspiring audiences across Canada with her heartfelt journey of creating this unique Canadian book. With her stories, anecdotes and passionate delivery, Janet lights up a room. After spending the first twenty years of her professional life in Toronto's fast paced fashion-photography and advertising industry, in 1997 she became involved with producing *Chicken Soup for the Parent's Soul*. When Jack Canfield invited her to co-author *Chicken Soup for the Canadian Soul*, she jumped at the chance. When it was released in 2002 it shot right to the top of the bestseller lists all across Canada.

Since 2003 Janet has utilized her editorial expertise to help other authors bring their books of personal or spiritual growth to publication. Working with American co-author Daniel Keenan she completed a book-sized version of *The Navy's Baby*, an amazing story first appearing in *Chicken Soup for the Parent's Soul*. She has stories in seven *Chicken Soup for the Soul* books, and with *Chicken Soup for the Soul: O Canada The Wonders of Winter*, Janet is thrilled to once again be part of the Chicken Soup for the Soul family.

An eclectic individual with diverse interests and talents, Janet is a certified Love Yourself Heal Your Life workshop leader with training based on the philosophy of Louise Hay. She is a certified canoeing instructor, a couturier seamstress, passionate skater and cross country skier, and plays the violin.

Now living in Aurora, Ontario, Janet has been a guest on countless television and radio talk shows across Canada, and gives a very dynamic interview. She is generally available for guest speaking spots and interviews, and you may contact her through www.janetmatthews.ca or www.canadiansoul.com.

Pam Goldstein, editor of this book has been passionate about books and writing her entire life. After a twenty-year nursing career she became a host/producer of the award-winning *Boker Tov* radio show and continued for fifteen years. During that time she also produced another award-winning show, *Reach for the Stars*, and wrote ENG for local cable TV. Pam has also written three adult fiction manuscripts, one YA manuscript, and three plays. One of her plays *The Interview*, is opening November, 2013.

She has written several articles for newsletters and magazines and her latest one will be seen in Costa Rica's *Madre Natura* magazine come fall.

Pam's writing can also be read in over a dozen anthology books: *Bedpan Banter, Anthology: the Beauty of the Story* and of course many of the Chicken Soup for the Soul titles. Some of her favourites are *Chicken Soup for the Soul: Empty Nesters, Chicken Soup for the Soul: The Gift of Christmas, Chicken Soup for the Soul: O Canada,* and *Chicken Soup for the Soul: I Can't Believe My Dog Did That!* E-mail Pam at boker_tov2002@yahoo.ca.

Thank You

We owe huge thanks to all of our contributors. We know that you poured your hearts and souls into the stories that you shared with us, and ultimately with each other. As we read and edited these stories, we were truly amazed by your experiences. We appreciate your willingness to share these inspiring and encouraging stories with our readers. We could only publish a small percentage of the stories that were submitted, but we read every single one and even the ones that do not appear in the book had an influence on us and on the final manuscript.

We owe special thanks to Amherstburg, Ontario resident Pam Goldstein, a long-time Chicken Soup for the Soul contributor whose writing we have always admired. We enlisted her help with this collection because we wanted another editor from Canada to work with Janet Matthews, a long-time and accomplished Chicken Soup for the Soul coauthor, and a resident of Aurora, Ontario. Pam read all the stories that were submitted through our website and edited the entire manuscript before Janet and I set to work on it. Working with Janet was a real pleasure and we all learned a lot about Canada from her. Since my husband's grandmother was a Newfie, and he has dozens of cousins there, we hold a special place in our hearts for all things Canadian.

Janet's webmaster Tracy Bailey was a big help too. She reconfigured Janet's websites very quickly to announce Janet's involvement in this project. Latoya Dickenson, who showed up one day as a volunteer, offered to help Janet in any way she could and was a gift from heaven. Her assistance in contacting writers' groups across Canada was invaluable.

Our assistant publisher D'ette Corona oversaw this entire project, worked with Janet and Pam to put together the manuscript, and did her normal masterful job of working with the contributors to approve our edits and answer any questions they had. Our senior editor Barbara LoMonaco provided another set of eyes to proofread the manuscript, armed with a list of Canadian spellings so that we didn't by accident Americanize the book. Our editor Kristiana Pastir oversaw production and worked with our creative director and book producer, Brian Taylor at Pneuma Books, who designed the beautiful cover and interior for this book.

We also want to thank Mike Turnbull and the wonderful team at Simon & Schuster Canada, our distributors in your great land, for suggesting this book and helping us develop the concept.

~Amy Newmark

Improving Your Life Every Day

Real people sharing real stories—for twenty years. Now, Chicken Soup for the Soul has gone beyond the bookstore to become a world leader in life improvement. Through books, movies, DVDs, online resources and other partnerships, we bring hope, courage, inspiration and love to hundreds of millions of people around the world. Chicken Soup for the Soul's writers and readers belong to a one-of-a-kind global community, sharing advice, support, guidance, comfort, and knowledge.

Chicken Soup for the Soul stories have been translated into more than forty languages and can be found in more than one hundred countries. Every day, millions of people experience a Chicken Soup for the Soul story in a book, magazine, newspaper or online. As we share our life experiences through these stories, we offer hope, comfort and inspiration to one another. The stories travel from person to person, and from country to country, helping to improve lives everywhere.

Share with Us

We all have had Chicken Soup for the Soul moments in our lives. If you would like to share your story or poem with millions of people around the world, go to chickensoup.com and click on "Submit Your Story." You may be able to help another reader, and become a published author at the same time. Some of our past contributors have launched writing and speaking careers from the publication of their stories in our books!

Our submission volume has been increasing steadily—the quality and quantity of your submissions has been fabulous. We only accept story submissions via our website. They are no longer accepted via mail or fax.

To contact us regarding other matters, please send us an e-mail through webmaster@chickensoupforthesoul.com, or fax or write us at:

Chicken Soup for the Soul
P.O. Box 700
Cos Cob, CT 06807-0700
Fax: 203-861-7194

One more note from your friends at Chicken Soup for the Soul: Occasionally, we receive an unsolicited book manuscript from one of our readers, and we would like to respectfully inform you that we do not accept unsolicited manuscripts and we must discard the ones that appear.

www.chickensoup.com